*A Young Man's Benefit*
*The Independent Order of Odd Fellows and Sickness Insurance in the United States and Canada, 1860–1929*

In the past a family's chief cost of sickness was loss of the family head's earning, not expenses for health care. Since there were no government programs, sickness insurance provided by friendly societies, commercial insurers, and other institutions was important in partially replacing the wage earner's lost income. The Independent Order of Odd Fellows (IOOF) was the largest social society in Canada and the United States and also the largest provider of sickness insurance.

Using cliometric methods and records from six grand-lodge archives, *A Young Man's Benefit* rejects the conventional wisdom about friendly societies and sickness insurance, arguing that IOOF lodges were financially sound institutions, were more efficient than commercial insurers, and met a market demand headed by young men who lacked alternatives to market insurance, not older men who had above average risk of sickness disability.

George Emery and Herbert Emery show that many young men joined the Odd Fellows for sickness insurance and quit the society once self-insurance – savings – or family insurance – secondary incomes from older children – became feasible for them. The older men who valued the social benefits of membership and did not need the sick benefit gradually became a majority and dismantled the IOOF's insurance provisions.

GEORGE EMERY is associate professor of history, University of Western Ontario.

J.C. HERBERT EMERY is associate professor of economics, University of Calgary.

McGILL-QUEEN'S/ASSOCIATED MEDICAL SERVICES (HANNAH INSTITUTE) STUDIES IN THE HISTORY OF MEDICINE, HEALTH, AND SOCIETY
*Series Editors: S.O. Freedman and J.T.H. Connor*

Volumes in this series have financial support from Associated Medical Services, Inc., through the Hannah Institute for the History of Medicine program.

1 Home Medicine
The Newfoundland Experience
*John K. Crellin*

2 A Long Way from Home
The Tuberculosis Epidemic among the Inuit
*Pat Sandiford Grygier*

3 Labrador Odyssey
The Journal and Photographs of Eliot Curwen on the Second Voyage of Wilfred Grenfell, 1893
*Edited by Ronald Rompkey*

4 Architecture in the Family Way
Doctors, Houses, and Women, 1870–1900
*Annmarie Adams*

5 Local Hospitals in Ancien Regime France
Rationalization, Resistance, Renewal, 1530–1789
*Daniel Hickey*

6 Foisted upon the Government?
State Responsibilities, Family Obligations, and the Care of the Dependent Aged in Late Nineteenth-Century Ontario
*Edgar-André Montigny*

7 A Young Man's Benefit
The Independent Order of Odd Fellows and Sickness Insurance in the United States and Canada, 1860–1929
*George Emery and J.C. Herbert Emery*

# A Young Man's Benefit

*The Independent Order of Odd Fellows and Sickness Insurance in the United States and Canada, 1860–1929*

GEORGE EMERY

AND

J.C. HERBERT EMERY

McGill-Queen's University Press
Montreal & Kingston · London · Ithaca

ISBN 0-7735-1824-X

Legal deposit first quarter 1999
Bibliothèque nationale du Québec

Printed in Canada on acid-free paper

This book has been published with the help of a grant from the Humanities and Social Sciences Federation of Canada, using funds provided by the Social Sciences and Humanities Research Council of Canada, and from the J.B. Smallman Fund, Faculty of Social Science, University of Western Ontario.

McGill-Queen's University Press acknowledges the financial support of the Government of Canada through the Book Publishing Industry Development Program for its activities. We also acknowledge the support of the Canada Council for the Arts for our publishing program.

---

**Canadian Cataloguing in Publication Data**

Emery, George Neil, 1941–
A young man's benefit: The Independent Order of Odd Fellows and sickness insurance in the United States and Canada, 1860–1929
Includes bibliographical references and index.
ISBN 0-7735-1824-X
1. Independent Order of Odd Fellows – Canada – History. 2. Independent Order of Odd Fellows – United States – History. 3. Insurance, Fraternal – Canada – History. 4. Insurance, Fraternal – United States – History. 5. Insurance, Health – Canada – History. 6. Insurance, Health – United States – History. I. Emery, John Charles Herbert, 1965– II. Title.

HG9383.E44 1998 368.3'63'0061 C98-901218-2

---

This book was typeset by Typo Litho Composition Inc. in 10/12 Sabon.

*For Richard S. Alcorn*
*28 August 1943–25 October 1997*
*A Pioneer in Social Science History*

# Contents

# Tables

FIGURES AND MAPS

# Acknowledgments

Grand lodge officials of The Independent Order of Odd Fellows in six jurisdictions gave us access to their records, and shared with us their time, personal knowledge, and photocopy machines. Local officials of IOOF and Masonic lodges also gave us access to their records and time. For their assistance, we thank Denny Hubbard (British Columbia), Wesley Nelson (Alberta), Marvin Johnston (Saskatchewan), Lloyd Shelvey (Manitoba), Theodore T. Dusseau and Doris Kuhn (Michigan), and Don Wright and Bob Howard (Ontario); Bob Carr (Ingersoll, Samaritan Lodge, IOOF), Stewart Thurtell (Ingersoll, King Hiram, and St John's Masonic lodges), and Harvey Murray (Harrietsville, Hope Lodge, IOOF).

Our work has benefited from discussion of papers that one or both of us presented at the 1992, 1994, 1995, and 1997 conferences on Quantitative Methods in Canadian Economic History. These conferences have given us an exceptional, supportive scholarly culture for undertaking research in economic history.

We thank John Zucchi, Philip Cercone, Joan McGilvray, and the staff of McGill-Queen's University Press for seeing this project through to completion. We thank the Press and the Aid to Scholarly Publications program for arranging two anonymous expert readers for our manuscript. Their comments helped us to strengthen the work in several areas. We thank Diane Mew for her meticulous copy-editing. The book benefits greatly from her shrewd judgments about style and presentation.

As a father-and-son research team, we have enjoyed collaborating on this book and drawing on the insights of our two disciplines. The end product, we think, is more than the sum of our scholarly parts.

THE YOUNG MAN'S ACKNOWLEDGMENTS First and foremost, I thank Denny Hubbard who, as grand secretary of the grand lodge of British Columbia, gave me access to its head office records over a period of three years. Denny's cooperation made my doctoral thesis on the IOOFBC's sickness insurance arrangements possible.

I thank Angela Redish, Bob Allen, David Green, Ron Shearer, and Peter Ward for their patience, guidance, and support in the undertaking of my doctoral thesis at the University of British Columbia. I am forever indebted to Harry Paarsch for stimulating my interest in empirical economics and for what he taught me. Harry also provided friendship and support through my time at the University of British Columbia. Mary MacKinnon provided valuable comments, as the external examiner for my thesis, and later as a discussant for conference papers that I have presented. Alan Green has encouraged my work on the Odd Fellows since its inception, eight years ago. My colleagues in the Department of Economics at the University of Calgary have given my work their interest and support. Finally, I thank my wife, Carolyn, who has put up with this research longer than anyone else.

A SSHRCC doctoral fellowship supported some of my research for this book. Other financial support came from a University of Calgary short-term research grant.

THE OLD MAN'S ACKNOWLEDGMENTS As director of the Landon Project at the University of Western Ontario (1976–8), the late Dick Alcorn asked me to write a description of documentary sources that voluntary associations generated. I responded with archival research on the Odd Fellow and Masonic lodges in Ingersoll and accumulated a large box of notes and photocopies. Once the research paper had been written, the box ended up in a back corner of our attic. Twenty years later, against my advice, Herb made the British Columbia Odd Fellows his subject for doctoral research. On the completion of his thesis, he provoked me into engaging issues that his dissertation raised. Somewhere along the way, his work widened in scope and became our work. The box in the attic became important. Our work became my obsession.

Through Herb I have come to know a remarkable group of economic historians who are committed to each other, to the use of quantitative methods, the precise modelling of historical problems, and the advancement of knowledge in economic history.

I am grateful to my wife, Anne, for seeing me through this project. I thank Helen and Wilfred Ziegler for giving me a place to stay when I was doing archival research at the IOOF's Ontario grand lodge head office in Toronto.

Finally, I thank my university for an internal SSHRC grant to support archival research in IOOF grand lodge head offices at Litchfield, Michigan, Winnipeg, Calgary, and Vancouver.

Officers of Hope Lodge No. 69, Harrietsville, Ontario, about 1929. Six were farmers and one was a cheesemaker.

Herbert Thompson, grand master of the Grand Lodge of Michigan, 1913–14. In 1925, as sovereign grand sire, he led the campaign to abolish the sick benefit.

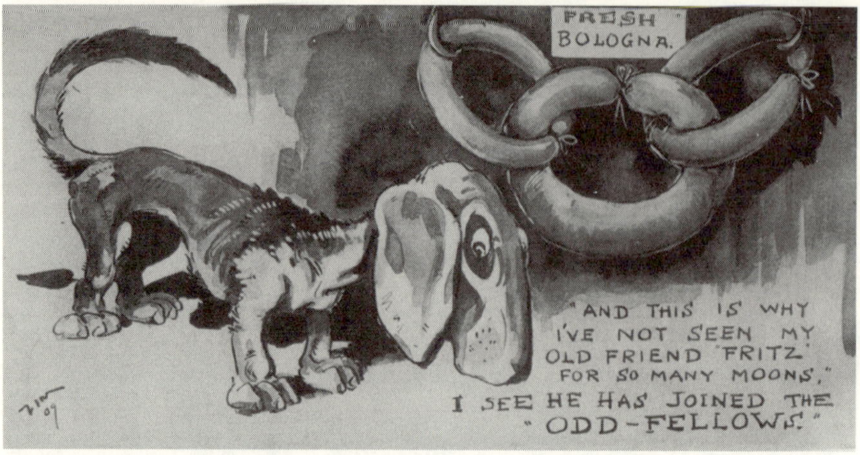


An Odd Fellow cartoon, 1909.

Grand Lodge of British Columbia sessions at Victoria, 1906.

Degree staff, Deborah Rebekah Lodge No. 13, Rossland, British Columbia, 1909.

Laying of cornerstone, IOOF Block, Victoria, British Columbia, 28 April 1879.

The Odd Fellow Building, Dawson City, Yukon, built in 1901 and still standing in 1964 when the lodge surrendered its charter.

# *A Young Man's Benefit*

# *Prologue*

Friendly societies were the major source of sickness insurance in the United States and Canada before the great depression of the 1930s. Historically the chief cost of sickness had been loss of the family head's earnings, and the friendly society's sick benefit provided a partial replacement for this lost income. The Independent Order of Odd Fellows (IOOF) was the largest of the friendly societies. In 1921, its peak year of membership, it had 16,268 lodges and 1,898,567 Odd Fellows in fifty-six state and provincial jurisdictions. Other large friendly societies in that year included the Knights of Pythias (908,000 members), the Loyal Order of Moose (558,000 members), the Fraternal Order of Eagles (500,000 members), the Improved Order of Red Men (500,000 members), and the Foresters of America (200,000 members).

Conditions have changed since the 1920s. The provision of health care for all family members, not loss of the family head's income, has become the chief cost of sickness. Government social programs and commercial group plans have become the principal sources of health insurance and disability insurance. Most friendly societies have discontinued their sick benefit and have lost members despite a rising population. In 1994 the IOOF had 115,000 members, down 93 per cent from 1921.

Our initial objective for writing this book was to discover when and why the IOOF ceased to be an important source of sickness insurance. A survey of the literature raised three possibilities: that the hard times of the 1930s ruined the lodges; that the IOOF's insurance provision collapsed because its financial practices were unsound; or that competition from commercial insurers and government social programs wrecked the friendly society sick benefit. Although each of these hypotheses had intuitive appeal, none survived the test of evidence. The decline of the sick benefit began in the 1890s, well before the 1930s depression. The IOOF's lodges were financially sound, and their financial practices were superior to those of commercial insurers. And finally, competition in the sickness insurance market was rising before the First World War but had stabilized by the 1920s.

If external pressure did not cause the decline of the IOOF's sick benefit, then Odd Fellows must have chosen to withdraw their sickness insurance provision. One influence was a rise in the opportunity cost of the sick benefit (a dollar spent for this purpose was a dollar forgone for other purposes whose attraction was increasing). Even so, the IOOF's growing indifference to the sick benefit was puzzling, given its aging trend in its membership. On the one hand, an Odd Fellow's risk of disability rose with age and became above average as he passed the age of forty. On the other hand, his lodge charged dues at a flat rate. Thus the longer he remained a member, the greater the value he received for his annual dues. Effectively, the dues of young members subsidized the sick claims of older members. If, however, the sick benefit was an *old man's benefit*, why did the IOOF's aging membership become less attached to it?

The explanation, we discovered in time, was that the sick benefit was a *young man's benefit*. Like older men, young men carried a risk of disability, albeit a lesser one. Yet unlike older men, they lacked alternatives to market insurance. At the start of their working lives, they had no older children to earn secondary incomes (family insurance). They also lacked savings to cover the disability risk (self-insurance). Thus men joined the Odd Fellows when they were young. Many then quit after a few years as alternatives to market insurance opened up to them. Other aging Odd Fellows continued in membership for social reasons but became less attached to the sick benefit. In this fashion, the sick benefit declined in the IOOF's priorities as the Odd Fellows aged.

## SCOPE OF THE STUDY

We have used the IOOF as a case study to explore questions about disability insurance in the United States and Canada. We consider issues such as trends for the insurance market; life-course influences on family purchases of market insurance; the viability of friendly societies in competition with commercial insurers; and social influences on insurance behaviours.

The primary period of study begins about 1860 and ends in 1929. Towards the end of the American Civil War, the American market for sickness insurance developed rapidly, the number of friendly societies proliferated, and the IOOF introduced its stipulated benefit system. By 1929, in contrast, the market for sickness insurance was stagnating, and the dismantling of the IOOF's sick benefit provisions was well advanced.

The book gives a social interpretation to disability insurance and the Odd Fellow sick benefit. On the one hand, cultural priorities and social change, not just material needs, created the market for insurance. On the other hand, friendly societies were multiple-function organizations that men joined for various reasons, not just for insurance.

The book's subject is the IOOF's sick benefit, not the IOOF in general. Nevertheless, its findings for insurance contribute to the literature on the social history of friendly societies. The insurance risk for sickness, for example, was the lost income of family breadwinners. The risk did not apply to the breadwinners' wives or their dependants, which helps to explain why friendly societies had all-male memberships. In contrast, all family members were at risk for burial, healthcare, or life insurance. Thus compared to friendly societies, life insurance fraternal orders and burial societies were more likely to have women members.

THE RELATIONSHIP TO EXISTING LITERATURE The British, American, and Australian literature offers useful information on the social history of fraternal orders, friendly societies, sickness insurance, health insurance, working-class insurance, and government programs for insurance risks (Gosden, 1961, 1973; Beveridge, 1942, 1948; Neave, 1991; Gilbert, 1966; Green and Cromwell, 1984; Johnson, 1985; Cumbler, 1979; Clawson, 1989; Thelen, 1986; Brody, 1980; Dumenil, 1984; Carnes, 1989; Starr, 1982; Naylor, 1986; Riley, 1997). Some recent studies provide stimulating challenges to the pro-welfare state assumptions that have dominated the literature (Gratton, 1996; Weaver, 1983; Green and Cromwell, 1984).

Nevertheless, this book seeks to advance the literature in several areas. It provides the first rigorous cliometric investigation of the business side of friendly societies in any English-language society. It is the first scholarly study of sickness insurance in the United States and Canada, and it is one of a few studies of Canadian fraternal societies from any viewpoint.[1] These empirical firsts underlie the book's substantive contributions. The book demonstrates, for example, that friendly society insurance provisions were more efficient than those of commercial insurers. The moral culture of friendly societies made their insurance provision more efficient, not less, and this efficiency contests the notion that pre-depression safety nets were fundamentally flawed.

At the same time, those safety nets were products of their times. At the turn of the century, sickness insurance was more important than health insurance and was a major candidate to become a compulsory government insurance program. However, sickness insurance was declining as a priority well before the advent of health insurance, the great depression, and the emergence of the welfare state.

## THE DOCUMENTARY SOURCES

The IOOF generated records at three levels of organization for its lodge and encampment branches. The lodge was the local unit of organization, and an encampment was a higher-degree auxiliary body at the local level. Men who had completed their four lodge degrees could apply for admission to an encampment and its three degrees of membership. A grand lodge and a grand encampment supervised the lodges and encampments in a particular state or province. The Sovereign Grand Lodge (SGL) in Baltimore presided over the grand lodges and grand encampments.

Our records are comprehensive for the SGL. They include the *Journal of Proceedings* for the SGL's annual meetings and the 1915, 1925, 1932, and 1943 editions of the IOOF's *Code of Laws*. The *Proceedings* for each year provides summary statistics for the fifty-six grand lodges.

We examined grand lodge records for six jurisdictions: British Columbia, Alberta, Saskatchewan, Manitoba, Ontario, and Michigan. We had requested permission to visit the SGL's reference library in Winston-Salem, North Carolina, as this library holds materials from grand bodies in all fifty-six jurisdictions. The sovereign grand secretary, however, discouraged us from coming. As he explained,

> The offices of the Sovereign Grand Lodge were moved from Baltimore to Winston-Salem in 1981. Since that time the necessary funds and labor to get the archives put into order have never been provided. We do have the estimate that it will take ten man years just to get it on the shelf and catalogued. And while much of the material was still in boxes the basement flooded with eight inches of water following a heavy rain and a blocked sewer next door. Needless to say much of the material was hauled out just to clean the basement ... Even the current material, when it is supplied by the Grand Body, is only taken to the basement in boxes and has not been put on the shelf. [We] just don't have the staff to put it in order.

In the circumstances, he advised us to write to the head offices of the grand lodges, and in only two out of eight requests for access were we unsuccessful. The grand lodge of Quebec, whose head office is the grand secretary's home, lacked the facilities to accommodate us. The grand secretary for the grand lodge of the Atlantic provinces wanted to help but could not, as a fire in 1990 had destroyed its head office and historical records.

All the grand lodge head office records include the *Proceedings* for annual meetings and constitutions for the grand lodge and its subordinate lodges. Beyond that, the records vary. The British Columbia and Michigan head offices, for example, hold good collections of bylaws for their lodges, while the Ontario head office has a superb collection of the semi-annual returns from its lodges and an IOOF directory for Toronto in 1911. The type of information in the records also varies. The semi-annual returns for Ontario lodges, for example, state the number of members who were in arrears for dues, whereas the form used in Manitoba and Michigan does not ask the question.

In our view, the six head office collections suffice to show developments at the grand lodge level. Once we had examined the records for British Columbia, Ontario, and Michigan, each additional collection furnished new detail but did not change the essentials of our developing story. Five of the six collections that we examined were for Canadian jurisdictions. American-Canadian national differences, however, mattered little for the issues that we were exploring.

Lodge records include minutes of lodge meetings, bylaws, membership registers, proposition books that report information about candidates for membership, and black books that list the names of expelled members. We visited the town of Ingersoll, Ontario, to examine a comprehensive set of records for the town's two IOOF lodges and encampment. We also examined records for two Masonic lodges in the town.

We travelled to Harrietsville, Ontario, to examine the records of the IOOF's lodge in that locality. The Regional Collection in the University of Western Ontario library holds the records of the IOOF's lodge at Point Edward, Ontario. The grand lodge head office in British Columbia holds the records of several lodges that have closed.

Other archival sources include annual reports of the insurance departments of the Dominion and Ontario governments; yearbook statistics for the United States and Canada; dictionaries of fraternal societies; statistics in *Almanacs* and the *Fraternal Monitor Statistics* (1909); published institutional histories from the study period; miscellaneous records of fraternal orders and lodges that are held in the University of Western Ontario library; records for industrial life insurance and group insurance in archives of the London Life Insurance Company; and city directories.

As one of the manuscript's expert readers observed, the data analysed shift frequently from location to location. The intent is to illustrate the process and variety of developments at different levels of the IOOF's organization (international, state, and local), with a view to grasping the whole. At the same time, we seek to examine developments in different places rather than in one, possibly unusual, region or locality. We use Ontario lodges to balance the selection from British Columbia. We use rural and small urban lodges to balance our evidence for Toronto and the large city case studies in the literature. For some of our issues, the information is scarce and varies by archive. By visiting several archives, one turns up idiosyncratic materials that help with an issue at hand.

When all is said and done, the book should open up rather than close off debate. It uses grand lodge records for just six of the IOOF's fifty-six grand lodge jurisdictions and local records for a small handful of the IOOF's sixteen thousand lodges. It investigates developments in one friendly society among the scores that helped to configure the American and Canadian social landscapes.

## THE ORGANIZATION OF THE BOOK

The book develops its argument in seven chapters. Chapter 1 provides basic background information. Its first section describes how the market for sickness insurance rose and stabilized in reaction to capitalist economic development. Its second section surveys the IOOF's institutional history: its growth over time and across space; and the development of its organizational hierarchy and auxiliary branches.

Chapter 2 examines the characteristics of Odd Fellows to determine the IOOF's market for insurance. It shows that Odd Fellows were adult white men, mostly Protestants in religion, and from upper-working-class and lower-middle-class backgrounds. The IOOF competed with insurers whose markets overlapped with its own.

Chapter 3 describes trends for the IOOF's benefit system between 1863 and 1931. It shows that friendly societies delivered sickness insurance with an efficiency that other insurers could not match. Despite this, the IOOF began to withdraw from the sickness insurance market during the 1890s. Its lodges faced rising costs because of an aging membership. In the main, they responded by cutting the benefit rather than raising the price of membership.

Chapter 4 rejects the hypothesis that unsound pricing practices caused the IOOF benefit system to collapse. Rising costs of the sick benefit were not financially ruinous. Net lodge profits predicted poorly which grand lodge jurisdictions were to abolish the sick benefit after 1925. Lodges in British Columbia had a negligible chance of bankruptcy from sick claims, even from unusually high claims in a given year.

Chapter 5 refutes the notion that competition from rival insurers drove the IOOF from the sickness insurance market. By the 1920s, as our evidence shows, competition from other sickness insurers was stable or declining. Indirect opportunity cost competition was another matter. Membership and the sick benefit each had an opportunity cost; that is, their popularity was weakening, while interest in competing attractions was rising.

Rising opportunity costs in the 1920s, however, cannot explain a decline of the sick benefit that dated from the 1890s. Nor do they resolve the most puzzling issue of the investigation: why did the IOOF's aging members begin to abolish the sick benefit when their collective exposure to the disability risk was rising?

Chapter 6 gives our solution to the puzzle. Young men purchased market insurance from the Odd Fellows when they lacked alternatives to market insurance. They later quit when other alternatives became available to them. Thus an Odd Fellow's chances of leaving his lodge increased the longer he was a member.

Chapter 7 discusses developments after 1929. It documents the continued decline of the sick benefit, the long-term stagnation of the market for sickness insurance, and the emergence of commercial group disability insurance as the chief source of supply. Group insurers prospered, however, by developing a new mass market more than through capture of a traditional market that friendly societies were abandoning. Conversely, rising opportunity costs and self-insurance, not group plans, did most of the damage to the IOOF's sick benefit.

## DEFINITIONS

*Sickness insurance* (or *disability insurance*) replaced part of the insured person's income lost due to a sickness or injury. Friendly societies provided an income replacement *benefit*. Commercial insurers provided an income replacement *indemnity*. In principle the insurance risk applied to any family member who had an income. The risk for market insurance, however, applied primarily to male breadwinners.

*Health insurance* covered expenses for health care services such as a physician's attendance, drug therapies, hospital diagnostic services, and hospitalization. The risk applied to whole families, including dependants, not just breadwinners. Market insurance for health care costs was unavailable until the 1930s.

*Adverse selection* refers to the probability that insurers will draw an adverse selection of customers. Unhealthy persons have greater incentive than healthy persons to purchase sickness insurance. To keep claims and costs manageable, the insurer must find ways to screen out poor risks, to avoid an adverse selection.

The *moral hazard* (malingering) alludes to the risk that a healthy person will claim to be disabled. The moral hazard is less of a problem for accident insurance than for sickness insurance. Disability from accident is definite as to time and cause, and external symptoms are usually self-evident. Disability from sickness, in contrast, is subjective and variable in definition; relatively minor complaints disable some people, while severe complaints fail to incapacitate others. The very possession of sickness insurance may increase a worker's willingness to consider himself disabled. Similarly, he may be more apt to consider himself disabled in periods of low unemployment, when his job is secure, than in periods of high unemployment.

*Risk diversification* refers to the pooling of the risks of individuals. The insurance claims in small groups may fluctuate from year to year. Thus the smaller the group, the greater the danger that high claims in one year could ruin the insurer. Conversely, the larger the insured group, the smoother the trend for sick claims. Thus a friendly society could diversify its risks by paying claims from a central fund rather than separate funds for each of its lodges. Alternatively, the society could adopt a scheme of reinsurance, whereby each lodge is partly liable for claims that the other lodges incurred.

*Market insurance* refers to the purchase of insurance from an institutional provider. *Commercial* insurers sell policies for profit. During the study years, casualty insurance companies were the chief source of sickness and accident insurance for individuals. In contrast, life insurance companies pioneered the development of group disability insurance. *Cooperative* insurers sell insurance on a non-profit basis. During the study years, the cooperative group included friendly societies, fraternal orders, labour unions, and company-sponsored mutual benefit associations.

*Self-insurance* alludes to the use of savings to cover the risk. The resources for self-insurance tend to change with age. A male family head, for example, might accumulate savings during his younger adult years and then draw upon savings during retirement.

*Family insurance* refers to the use of secondary incomes from two or more family members to cover the risk for any one member. During the study years, the resources for family insurance tended to change with the family head's age and the family's life course. They were modest when the family had young children, increased when the children became old enough to earn secondary incomes, and decreased when the children left to found their own homes. Family insurance was a necessity for those with chronically low incomes. Such families could not manage on the income of the household head, so they got by with subsistence activities, barter, and secondary incomes (Bradbury, 1993). At best they saved in short bursts to spend, not over the long term to accumulate (Johnson, 1985). Market insurance or self-insurance was beyond their reach.

*Fraternal orders* were affiliated societies, or societies with branches. The branches were styled lodges in the IOOF, the Knights of Pythias, and the Freemasons. They were known by various names (tents, hives) in other orders. Fraternal orders emphasized benefits to their members rather than service to community. They used secret passwords, rituals, and benefits to attract, bond, and hold members and distinguish themselves from rival orders.

From an insurance perspective, fraternal orders divided into three groups. The Masonic Order and the Elks comprised the *no-benefit* group. Lodges in these orders aided their members on a discretionary basis. In contrast to other societies, however, they did not provide stipulated insurance benefits (stated, fixed amounts, available to members as a right and not as a charity).

The second group, the *friendly societies*, provided stipulated sick and funeral benefits to their members. As noted above, the IOOF, the Knights of Pythias, the Improved Order of Red Men, the Loyal Order of Moose, the Fraternal Order of Eagles, and the Foresters of America were the largest orders in this group.

The third group, the *life insurance orders*, provided stipulated life insurance, endowment, and annuity benefits to their members. The Maccabees, the Royal Arcanum, the Independent Order of Foresters, the Woodmen of the World, the Modern Woodmen of America, the Ancient Order of United Workmen, and the Catholic Order of Foresters were major orders in this group. In historical usage, the term "insurance" meant life insurance, but not sickness and funeral (burial) insurance. Thus the IOOF was a friendly society, not an insurance order.

The boundaries between the categories blur on close examination. Certain friendly societies, such as the Knights of Pythias and the Improved Order of Red Men, offered optional life insurance at extra cost through centrally-administered endowment branches. Certain insurance orders, such as the Independent Order of Foresters, offered optional sick and funeral benefits at extra cost through centrally administered sickness and funeral funds.

In other cases, the members of a society had privileged access to third-party insurance. The Canadian Odd Fellows Relief Association, for example, was entirely separate from the IOOF, but sold life policies exclusively to Odd Fellows. Neither Freemasons nor Elks made direct provision for insurance benefits. In 1927, however, the ten thousand Canadian Elks purchased renewable-term group life insurance from the Northern Life Insurance Company.[2] Similarly the Protective Association of Canada, in Granby, Quebec, sold sickness and accident insurance to Freemasons only.[3]

*Assessment insurance* refers to the classic method by which fraternal societies funded insurance claims. In essence the societies "passed the hat" to pay claims as they arose. For fraternal life insurance, the amount paid was the amount collected, to a maximum of the amount specified on the certificate (commonly $1,000 to $2,000). In contrast to commercial insurance, the assessment-method insurers could change the contract without the insured's consent. Also unlike commercial insurance, they kept no reserve fund to guarantee payment on the policies issued. As Kip (1953) observes, they had large amounts of insurance in force, with only a few dollars in the till.

Over time the insurance orders shifted from post-mortem "pass-the-hat" payments to pre-mortem premiums, based on the order's expected number of claims for a given year. Their commitment to the assessment principle ("keep the reserve in your pocket") also weakened. In 1910 the National Fraternal Congress prepared a model bill that required fraternal insurers to have a reserve fund. By 1911 thirteen states had enacted it.

The IOOF used assessments to supplement revenues from members' dues, joining fees, and investments. First, if a lodge's funds on hand became insufficient to meet overhead costs and benefit claims, the IOOF required it to levy a per-capita assessment on its members. Second, the IOOF permitted lodges to fund their funeral and widows' and orphans' benefits on the assessment method in lieu of including these in the price of membership. Third, the IOOF permitted grand lodges to levy per-capita taxes on the lodges to fund grand lodge homes for orphans and aged, indigent members. Finally, the IOOF levied per-capita taxes on the lodges to pay the overhead of the grand lodge and SGL head offices.[4]

*Industrial life insurance* was commercial burial insurance for low-income working-class families. It dated from 1874 in the United States (Carr, 1975). Industrial insurers issued policies for small amounts without a medical examination. The premiums were "a few cents a week," to be paid to neighbourhood collectors on their weekly rounds. Most industrial policies insured the lives of wives and children, in contrast to ordinary life policies, which were primarily on the lives of male breadwinners.

An *annuity* uses the proceeds of invested capital to pay a regular pension for life or a contracted number of years. The purchase of an annuity is a method of saving for old age.

*Endowment insurance* is a form of life insurance which pays the benefit to the insured person when he or she reaches a certain age. If the insured person dies before reaching the specified age, then the beneficiaries get the money.

*Group insurance* uses an employer's mass purchasing power to provide low-cost insurance without a medical examination. The insuring company makes the group plan contract with the employer, who issues certificates to individuals in the plan.

# 1 The Historical Market for Sickness Insurance and the Institutional History of the IOOF

This chapter provides background information in two stages. The first section discusses the market for sickness insurance during the years 1860–1929. This is followed by a description of the IOOF's institutional history and organizational structure.

## THE MARKET FOR SICKNESS INSURANCE

The market for sickness insurance arose from capitalist economic development during the nineteenth century. It originated in Great Britain and Western Europe and only reached the United States and Canada after a time lag. During the twentieth century, paradoxically, economic development caused the market for sickness insurance to stagnate. Other priorities came to the fore, and alternatives to market insurance were increasingly accessible.

THE EMERGENCE OF A MARKET FOR SICKNESS INSURANCE With nineteenth-century economic development, households became increasingly dependent on labour income. This left them vulnerable to loss of income when disability, unemployment, or death severed wage-earners from their work. At the same time, economic development strained traditional safety nets, such as networks of kin and neighbours. As the construction of railways knit isolated local economies into regional and national markets, men were increasingly on the move. As the scale of production increased, an impersonal wage relationship between employer and employee replaced the intimate tie between master and apprentice. Thus men were increasingly at risk of falling sick among strangers. Friendly societies pioneered the social response to this problem. Their national networks of lodges furnished sprawling proxy families that could help disabled members.

THE EXTENT OF SICKNESS DISABILITY Over time longevity rose and population aged. In the process, acute short-term illness became less common, and chronic long-term illness increased. The upshot was a rise in the crude morbidity rate – that is, weeks of disability per one thousand population. Effectively the longer duration of sick spells outweighed the decline in their number.

The trend for the crude morbidity rate, however, is misleading for individuals. The crude rate rises because a larger percentage of the population moved into the older age categories that had above-average risk of chronic illness. Only age-specific rates could establish whether morbidity at different ages was rising. Comparative cohort rates, for example, could show whether persons at ages forty to forty-nine were sicker in 1890 than in 1870.

We lack information about age-specific trends for the nineteenth century. One scholar uses British friendly society sick claim statistics for the purpose (Riley, 1987, 1989, 1990, 1991, 1997; Alter and Riley, 1989). However, members who were behind in their dues were ineligible for the sick benefit (see chapter 3), which makes his data unreliable. A drop in the percentage of brothers who made sick claims could mean a rise in membership arrears rather than a drop in morbidity. Unfortunately, the records do not report statistics for paid-up members, which would be required to make this calculation.

In any case, the breadwinner's risk of disability was substantial during the early twentieth century. Five state commissions and two morbidity surveys by the United States Public Health Service documented the risk for American households during the years 1917–36 (Epstein, 1933; Millis, 1937; Britton, 1940). In a survey of Illinois workers for 1919, 20 per cent were disabled for more than a week, which meant on average a loss of 14 per cent of their annual income. The burden of disability fell unevenly on the families affected. A third of them lost just 5 per cent of their income, while 8 per cent lost between 50 and 100 per cent.

The burden also fell most heavily on low-income families. In the Public Health Service's national survey for 1935–6, the morbidity rate was 176 per thousand population for families with less than $1,000 annual income. This compared to 156 per thousand for families in the $1,000–$1,500 range and 146 per thousand for families in the next four income groups. The excess illness of the low-income families, moreover, was in the productive ages between sixteen and sixty-four (Britton, 1940).

SOURCES OF INSURANCE Depending on its circumstances, a family could cover the disability risk with market insurance, family insurance (secondary incomes from other family members), or self insurance (savings). Market insurance became available from commercial insurers, friendly societies, life insurance fraternal orders, labour unions, and company-sponsored mutual benefit societies.

Market insurance from all sources covered a minority of the population. Only 30 per cent of Illinois wage-earners had market insurance for the disability risk in 1919 (Millis, 1937). In some cases, the worker used savings or family insurance to cover the risk. Most of the poor workers could not afford market insurance, despite having above-average risk of disability. By 1929 workmen's compensation programs marked the limit of government's provisions for disability insurance. Although most American states and Canadian provinces had these programs, their coverage missed much of the labour force. What is more important, workplace accidents were a minor cause of disability.[1]

Typically a sickness insurance benefit or indemnity equalled part of the wages of a worker with average wages. The principle of partial income replacement kept down the cost of the insurance and answered the insurer's concern that full income replacement might act as a disincentive to return to work. Lodges of friendly societies provided for a flat-rate benefit. In contrast, commercial group plans commonly scaled the amount of the indemnity to the employee's income level or position in the company. Similarly, union benefits for men in highly paid railway trades and commercial indemnities for middle-class clients were available in variable amounts up to full income replacement, at a cost beyond the reach of most workers (James, 1947: 262–6; Rubinow, 1913: ch. 18).

SOCIAL INFLUENCES ON THE MARKET FOR SICKNESS INSURANCE Social attitudes permeated the market at every turn. Friendly societies, for example, responded to a widespread stigma attached to recipients of charity. The secrecy of lodge affairs allowed a distressed brother to receive help without public humiliation (Burley, 1994: 69–71). What is more important, the lodge's stipulated sick and funeral benefits were available to members as a right, not as a charity.

The class structure also influenced market behaviour. In Britain, for example, clerks and artisans had similar incomes but spent differently. Artisans tended to buy sickness insurance *with fellowship* by joining friendly societies. In contrast, clerks were more likely to buy insurance *without fellowship* from centralized bureaucratic organizations such as the Hearts of Oak (Johnson, 1985).

Working-class families were conscious of the stigma attached to a pauper's grave and gave sickness insurance less priority than burial insurance for one or more family members. As Johnson explains, "funerals were public events, and the ways they were conducted reflected on the status and esteem of the family. Sickness, on the other hand, was private suffering and medical attention was a private benefit" (Johnson, 1985: 86).

Thus for social reasons, working men regarded membership in a friendly society as additional to the purchase of burial insurance from a burial society or industrial life company. In this regard, the friendly society funeral benefit was a minor source of burial insurance. It covered the member's funeral cost, but not the funeral costs for other family members. In contrast, burial societies and industrial life companies would sell policies to cover the risk for any family member, not just the male breadwinner. To illustrate the historical importance of burial insurance on the lives of dependants, we drew a random sample from 18,742 industrial life contracts issued by the London Life Insurance Company in Canada during the years 1887–90. Children under fourteen years of age accounted for 44 per cent of the sample contracts, females (all ages) for 49 per cent, and adult men (over twenty years of age) for just 21 per cent.[2]

Because of the priority placed on burial insurance, friendly societies found their market among the better-paid workers. Such men could afford the price of membership in addition to purchasing burial insurance for other family members. They also had status incentives to join a friendly society. By joining a lodge and participating in fraternal processions, these working men showed their peers that they could afford the dues, were above the poverty line, and were respectable (Johnson, 1985).

For social as well as economic reasons, the demand for market insurance for sickness came chiefly from family breadwinners and aspiring breadwinners.[3] To make this point, we class families into three types. The first, the *multiple-income family*, relied on income from two or more family members (the "family economy" strategy). The second, the *breadwinner family*, relied exclusively on the income of its male family head to make ends meet and amass savings. The third, the *post-breadwinner family*, obtained its primary income from the male family head, but also secondary incomes from adolescent children, until they left to establish their own households. However, the jobs of older children expressed family choice, not necessity. The older sons with jobs were breadwinners in training.

Families had a strong preference for the breadwinner model during the study years. By attaining breadwinner status, the family head signalled to contemporaries that he and his family were respectable. Conversely, a family's reliance on secondary incomes from the wife or children signalled that the family head earned too little to make ends meet (Bradbury, 1993; Burley, 1994). In this context, unlike breadwinners, few multiple-income families could afford market insurance for sickness.

Clearly males in post-breadwinner families could afford to buy market insurance for sickness. As aspiring breadwinners, moreover, older sons were likely to do so. We have two incompatible hypotheses for male heads of post-breadwinner families. According to the first, the *old man's model*, these heads acquired above-average risk of disability as they passed the age of forty. At the same time, market insurance became available to them at a subsidized price. Consequently, their demand for market insurance rose, regardless of whether their older children earned secondary incomes. According to the second, the *young man's model*, the incomes from older children allowed them to use family insurance or self-insurance to cover the sickness risk. Consequently, their attachment to market insurance was decreasing. Each hypothesis has intuitive appeal. Chapter 6 investigates which of them makes better sense of the evidence.

THE DISABILITY INSURANCE MARKET DURING THE TWENTIETH CENTURY As the findings from several state commissions and national health surveys showed, the cost to families of income lost due to sickness remained substantial into the 1930s. Given the rising trend for the crude morbidity rate, those costs may have been rising.

Purchases of market insurance appear to have increased steadily during the first two decades of the twentieth century. Then they stagnated during the 1920s, despite the introduction of commercial group disability insurance during the decade. In constant-dollar per capita terms, the amount of premiums received by Canadian insurers rose by 48 per cent during the decade 1920–9, a respectable rate of increase. The statistics for the much larger American market, however, fell by 1 per cent during the same years.[4] Chapters 6 and 7 discuss the causes of market stagnation during the 1920s.

Market stagnation, however, did not kill the IOOF's sick benefit. The decline of its benefit dated from the 1890s, well before the market stagnation of the 1920s (see chapter 3). Conversely, the benefit persisted into the 1950s in many jurisdictions (see chapter 7). Simply put, the IOOF's sick benefit deteriorated in a long-term process that transcended the market conditions of any one decade.

## THE IOOF'S INSTITUTIONAL HISTORY

Friendly societies originated in the industrial towns of Britain and came to North America with British emigrants. In 1819 the largest British society, the IOOF Manchester Unity (IOOFMU), chartered a lodge in Baltimore, Maryland. By 1825 it had chartered nine lodges, four state grand lodges, and a national body, the grand lodge of the United States. During these early years, the Odd Fellows were mainly "English and Scotch operatives and tavern-keepers – plain, honest, uneducated, unpretending men, who were better fitted to follow the lead of capable rulers than to govern and guide" (Stillson, 1897: 234).

Even so, the grand lodge of the United States asserted its sovereignty for American affairs in 1833 and ten years later separated from the IOOFMU to head a separate American organization. "The separation," Moffrey reported, "arose over a question of ceremonial. While the English branch was bent on simplifying the initiations and various degrees, the American brethren felt that the ceremonies should be elaborated" (Moffrey, 1910: 33–4).

Between 1850 and 1929 the IOOF followed the spread of white settlement. It had thirty state and provincial grand lodges in 1850, thirty-nine in 1860, forty-two in 1870, forty-eight in 1880, and fifty-three in 1890. With the addition of Oklahoma (1893), Alberta (1905), and Saskatchewan (1907), the order had grand bodies for all American states and Canadian provinces.[5]

The IOOF entered Canada in 1843, when the grand lodge of New York chartered a lodge in Montreal. Although the grand lodge of the United States chartered a grand lodge for British North America in 1844, the Canadian body fell apart within three years. In 1855 the order returned to Canada and chartered grand lodges for Canada West (Ontario) and the Lower (Maritime) Provinces. The grand lodge of the United States chartered grand lodges in British Columbia in 1874, Quebec in 1878, and Manitoba in 1883. In 1878 the Canadian delegates capped a six-year campaign to rename the Grand Lodge of the United States the Sovereign Grand Lodge. In 1880 the SGL met for the first time in Canada, in Toronto. In 1890 the SGL elected Dr Clarence T. Campbell of London, Ontario, to the post of grand sire, the first Canadian to fill the IOOF's highest office.

THE IOOF'S ORGANIZATION The IOOF had four branches: lodge, encampment, patriarchs militant, and Rebekah. In each branch, the IOOF organized local bodies (lodges, encampments) into state and provincial grand bodies (grand lodges, grand encampments). The grand bodies, in turn, fell under the IOOF's supreme authority, the SGL. Only grand lodges and grand encampments had representatives at the SGL. The IOOF required, however, that the representatives hold the patriarchs militant and Rebekah degrees.

The SGL and its subordinate grand bodies came together at their respective annual meetings. At each level, representatives from the subordinate bodies were the voting members. The presiding official, elected for a one- or two-year term, was the grand sire in the SGL, the grand master in a grand lodge, and the grand patriarch in a grand encampment. The presiding official did not vote, except to break a tie. Other non-voting members included elected and appointed officers and past grands (past presiding officers for the body concerned).

*The Lodge Branch* This branch consisted of local lodges and state (or provincial) grand lodges. Its members were the Odd Fellows, who held up to four degrees of membership (including the initiation degree). The presiding officer for a lodge was the noble grand, whom the members elected for a six-month or annual term. To stand for election to this post, the lodge member had to have served as vice-noble grand and one lesser post. When his term of office ended, the noble grand became a past grand and qualified to represent the lodge at the annual meeting of the grand lodge. Depending on the size of its membership, a lodge elected from one to three representatives.

A grand lodge elected two grand representatives to the SGL if it had one thousand members in good standing; otherwise it sent one. To be eligible for election, a candidate had to be a past grand (of a lodge or encampment) and a member in good standing of a subordinate lodge, a Rebekah lodge, and an encampment. The grand representatives for the Ontario grand lodge were invariably past grand masters, not just past grands.

*The Encampment Branch* This branch consisted of local encampments and state (or provincial) grand encampments. An encampment was a higher-degree lodge for Odd Fellows who held the four lodge degrees. Its members, known as patriarchs, held up to three higher degrees of membership in the IOOF. The chief patriarch was the presiding officer for an encampment. The grand patriarch was the presiding officer for a grand encampment. Like a grand lodge, a grand encampment elected one or two grand representatives, depending on whether it had one thousand members.

The encampment branch was an American innovation that dated from 1827, before American Odd Fellows had broken from their British parent. Compared to the subordinate degrees, the rituals for the three patriarchal degrees offered more opportunity to display dramatic skill. In 1841 the SGL gave representation to grand encampments on the same basis as grand lodges. In 1845 the encampment branch introduced a sick benefit. The SGL made this benefit mandatory in 1881 and subject to its minimum benefit law in 1891. During the years 1857–74, the encampment branch survived several attempts to merge it with the lodge branch (Stillson, 1897: 560–70).

*The Patriarchs Militant* In 1882 the SGL recognized a uniformed degree for patriarchs in street processions who wished to wear a "very specific costume, to wit: chapeaux, crooks, swords, and belts and military paraphernalia." In 1884 the uniformed degree developed into a patriarchs militant branch. Holders of the degree, known as chevaliers, organized themselves into an army of cantons, grand cantons, battalions, regiments, brigades, and army corps.

*The Rebekah Branch* This branch became primarily a women's auxiliary branch, though it had male members. In 1851 the SGL introduced the degree of Rebekah as an honorary (or side) degree for Odd Fellows and their wives. In 1868 it authorized the organization of Rebekah lodges, each headed by a noble grand. Thereafter it gradually broadened the Rebekah membership requirements to include any unmarried white woman over eighteen years of age.

During the early years, only Rebekah men could serve as Rebekah lodge officers. In time, however, much of the management of Rebekah affairs was "surrendered to the ladies" (Ross, 1890: 472), and by 1890 women could serve as lodge officers. By 1915 all officers of a Rebekah Assembly had to be women. Meanwhile the proportion of women in the Rebekah lodges rose from 57 to 73 per cent during the years 1895–1929.

In 1884 the SGL permitted grand lodges to allow Rebekah lodges to organize into state bodies, headed by a president. The state bodies were known as Rebekah Conventions until 1894 and then as Rebekah Assemblies. In jurisdictions with an Assembly, the Rebekah lodges answered to the Assembly rather than to the all-male subordinate lodges of their respective localities. The Assembly, however, answered to the all-male grand lodge. By the 1920s, most of the assemblies had affiliated with an Association of Rebekah assemblies, headed by a president. The association could make recommendations to the SGL, but had no legislative powers. Thus assemblies in the Association remained answerable to their respective all-male grand lodges.

The Rebekah lodges provided their members with mutual aid, but not stipulated benefits. Their stated objectives expressed a nurturing role: "to aid in the establishment and maintenance of Homes for aged and indigent Odd Fellows and their wives ... and Homes for the care, education, and support of orphans of deceased Odd Fellows and deceased sisters of the Rebekah degree"; "to cultivate and extend the social and fraternal relations of life among lodges and families of Odd Fellows" (*Code*, 1915).

*Passwords, Representation, and Regalia* An Odd Fellow had to know a password to gain admission to a lodge or encampment meeting within a given jurisdiction. The grand body changed the password at regular intervals and communicated each new password to its subordinate bodies, who withheld the word from a member whose dues were in arrears. A grand body could withhold the password from a lodge or encampment that had failed to submit its required reports, returns, and per-capita taxes and assessments. It also could suspend a recalcitrant subordinate body's right to send representatives to the grand body's annual meeting. In extreme cases, it could recall or suspend the subordinate body's charter. Grand bodies faced the same discipline. In 1934, for example, the SGL "arrested" the charter of the grand lodge of Tennessee.

Regalia and jewels identified a member's rank and rights of membership at Odd Fellow gatherings. The lodge member's collar, for example, was plain white for the initiatory degree, white trimmed with pink for the first (friendship) degree, white trimmed with blue for the second (brotherly love) degree, and white trimmed with purple for the third (truth) degree. The noble grand's collar was scarlet trimmed with white and silver, that of a past grand scarlet trimmed with white and gold. The encampment member's collar was plain black for the first (patriarchal) degree, black trimmed with yellow for the second (golden-rule) degree, and purple trimmed with yellow lace for the third (royal-purple) degree. A collar of purple velvet marked a grand officer or past grand officer. Past grand sires and past grand representatives each wore a distinctive medal.

In its totality, the IOOF's organization resembled that of the Freemasons. Like the Odd Fellows, the Masons had lodges, higher-degree lodges (like encampments), and a woman's auxiliary branch (Daughters of the Eastern Star). The IOOF's organization differed, however, from that of other friendly societies. The Knights of Pythias, for example, had nothing comparable to the encampment branch, declined to recognize a female auxiliary branch, and offered an optional endowment degree for Knights who wished to have an annuity benefit.

PROGRESS OF THE ORDER Table 1.1 reports statistics for lodges and encampments, the two IOOF branches that had a sick benefit. Be-

Table 1.1
IOOF Lodges and Encampments in the United States and Canada, 1850–1930

| | *Lodge Branch* | | | *Encampment Branch* | | |
|---|---|---|---|---|---|---|
| | *Members (000s)* | *Lodges* | *Grand lodges* | *Members (000s)* | *Encampments* | *Grand encampments* |
| 1850 | 175 | 2,354 | 31 | 20 | 499 | 27 |
| 1860 | 174 | 3,547 | 39 | 24 | 671 | 39 |
| 1870 | 299 | 3,767 | 41 | 56 | 1,059 | 41 |
| 1880 | 456 | 7,147 | 48 | 80 | 1,857 | 40 |
| 1890 | 611 | 8,744 | 53 | 115 | 2,295 | 50 |
| 1900 | 861 | 11,912 | 54 | 142 | 2,589 | 54 |
| 1910 | 1,524 | 17,069 | 56 | 218 | 3,645 | 54 |
| 1920 | 1,863 | 16,451 | 56 | 311 | 3,447 | 56 |
| 1930 | 1,425 | 13,766 | 56 | 268 | 3,217 | 56 |

*Source*: The data are from SGL, *Proceedings*, 1850–1930. Unless indicated otherwise, all other tables are generated from information in primary sources.

tween 14 and 19 per cent of lodge brothers were members of encampments during the years 1850–1930. A stable 2 per cent of lodge brothers held the patriarchs militant degree, and between 14 and 18 per cent the Rebekah degree.

The IOOF's membership showed a rising trend through to 1921, a flat trend to 1924, and then a declining trend. In 1921, the IOOF's peak year for membership, it had twice the membership of the Knights of Pythias, the second largest friendly society. In 1921 it had seven times the membership of the Maccabees, the largest of the life insurance fraternal orders that offered an optional sick benefit. In 1915 the Freemasons had become the sole fraternal order to surpass the Odd Fellows in membership. The Freemasons, however, did not offer insurance benefits.

ODD FELLOW ORGANIZATION AND THE SICK BENEFIT During the years 1863–91 the IOOF entrenched the stipulated sick benefit in its constitution. The SGL made the stipulated benefit compulsory for lodges and encampments, prohibited non-beneficial membership, and specified a minimum amount for the benefit. It also empowered grand bodies to add requirements, such as a higher minimum benefit than the SGL required.

Once in place, the constitutional provisions for sick benefit were hard to dismantle. First, the SGL's *Code of Laws* required that a written proposal of the amendment be entered in the SGL's journal and laid over until the next annual meeting. The one-year delay gave grand bodies the chance to discuss the proposed change and instruct their grand representatives on whether to support it. Second, the passage of the amendment required a two-thirds majority of the votes cast.

As a member moved up the IOOF's organizational tree (from lodges to grand bodies to the SGL), the character of the Odd Fellows changed. At the local level, lodge members commonly fell behind in their dues and were suspended within a few years of their initiations. About 80 per cent of them held the lodge degrees only. In contrast, representatives at grand lodges were paid-up members and past grands of lodges. Similarly, representatives at the SGL were past grands and members in good standing of their lodge, encampment, and Rebekah lodge.

Compared to the membership at large, in other words, the men who decided the fate of the sick benefit were older, more active in the auxiliary branches of the order, more involved in the social side of Oddfellowship, and more committed to the IOOF. Although the character of the decision-makers affected the sick benefit, the nature of their influence is unclear. As older men, were they deeply attached to the benefit because of their above-average risk of disability and the subsidized price of the benefit for older men? Or were they weakly attached because the alternatives of self insurance or family insurance were open to them? Whatever their views, the decision-makers differed from other members in their manner of expressing dissatisfaction. They were less likely to quit the IOOF than they were to try to change it.

IOOF LODGES AS MULTIPLE-FUNCTION ORGANIZATIONS In IOOF lodges the sick benefit complemented or competed with other priorities (Dumenil, 1984; Brody, 1980; Carnes, 1989; Charles, 1993; Clawson, 1989; Rotundo, 1989; Burley, 1984; Tucker, 1990). They also offered a funeral benefit and, less commonly, widows' and orphans' benefits, discretionary aid to members in distress, and access to IOOF homes for widows and orphans of members and aged indigent members. In an era of high mobility, networks of lodges helped men to locate employment, business contacts, and sources of credit. Finally, lodges provided their members with social benefits such as respectability, fellowship, intimacy with other men, entertainment, and ritual that bolstered male confidence.

In the circumstances, motives unrelated to insurance influenced decisions to join, stay in, or quit the order. A new arrival, for example, might join the local lodge to make business contacts and then quit once he felt at home.[6] Peer pressure was decisive in the case of Harvey Campbell, a knitting-mill worker in Carleton Place, Ontario. In 1931, on his twenty-first birthday, his foreman and two co-workers approached him with the suggestion that he would make a good Odd Fellow. Campbell found it hard to disagree.[7] In other cases, the pressure came from Odd Fellow fathers who treated initiation into membership as a rite of passage for their sons. In 1936, for example, one Wilbur Davis joined the lodge in Harrietsville, Ontario, when his stepfather, a local farmer, brought him to a lodge meeting on the occasion of his eighteenth birthday.[8]

The IOOF's membership entered a long-term declining trend during the mid-1920s. Here again, several non-insurance influences were at work. For example, the fraternal lodge meeting faced competition from new forms of entertainment (radio, cinema, automobile travel). The development of instalment buying and consumerism undermined fraternal culture and working-class institutional life. The easier ways of meeting the opposite sex sapped the appeal of all-male social activities and the fraternal ritual of lodge meetings. The rising popularity of luncheon club organizations (Kiwanis, Lions, Kinsmen) expressed a popular shift to a community-service orientation, as opposed to the fraternal tradition of services to members. The luncheon clubs also exemplified a popular shift to class-specific organizations, at the expense of fraternal orders, which had a cross-class appeal. With the waning popularity of lodge meetings, lodge night became less useful as an occasion for making business contacts. Finally, no doubt some left because they had lost their jobs, or their income had slipped, and they could not afford the dues.

To summarize, IOOF lodges were multiple-function organizations. After 1890, moreover, the sick benefit was a declining priority in the bundle of benefits that came with lodge membership. In the circumstances, Odd Fellows had many possible motives for joining, remaining in the order, or leaving. Clearly they did not make these decisions solely on the basis of insurance considerations. This makes it tricky to isolate the sick benefit as an attraction or disincentive for membership. We deal with this problem in chapters 3 and 6. In the meantime, chapter 2 turns to a crucial preliminary issue: who were the Odd Fellows?

# 2 The Men Who Were Odd Fellows: The IOOF's Market for Insurance, 1863–1925

The Odd Fellows were the IOOF's clients for sickness insurance. The SGL's *Code of Laws* required each lodge to include a stipulated sick benefit in its price of membership. It allowed a non-beneficial class of membership, but only for veteran Odd Fellows who were over fifty years of age. Thus all but a handful of Odd Fellows were beneficial members.

This chapter describes the IOOF's market for sickness insurance. The evidence shows that the IOOF's clients were adult white men, most of them Anglo-Protestants. They came from all social classes, but predominantly from the ranks of better-paid workers and lower middle-class men. They had above-average health and had satisfied the IOOF's moral requirements for joiners. A larger percentage came from small urban places rather than large cities and rural places.

## RACE

The SGL's *Code of Laws* restricted membership to men of "pure white blood." "The day the word 'white' is stricken from our constitution," the IOOF's official historian exclaimed in 1897, "the star of Odd Fellowship will begin to descend. It will go down, to sink behind the dark waves of disgrace, to rise no more forever."[1]

The race requirement surfaced in New York in 1842, when the IOOF refused to issue a lodge charter to a group of freed coloured men (Brooks, 1902: 12–13). The SGL barred Indians from membership in 1847, half-breeds in 1849, and quarter-breeds in 1900.[2] In 1857 it extended the bar to Chinese, in the process revoking highly restrictive terms of admission that it had granted Chinese in California in 1854. It judged that Syrians were white in 1906, but barred Japanese in 1889 and Arabs in 1911.

The development of a parallel institution for blacks acknowledged and reinforced the IOOF's colour bar. After they had been rejected in 1842, Negro men organized lodges of an English order, the Grand United Order of Odd Fellows. By 1907 the order had 270,000 Negro members in the United States and Canada (Stevens, 1907: 114, 119, 235–7). The black Odd Fellows were the largest fraternal order in three states (South Carolina, North Carolina, and the District of Columbia); in four other states (Mississippi, Virginia, Florida, and Louisiana), they outnumbered white Odd Fellows.[3]

Race requirements were widespread among fraternal orders in the United States and Canada. Other orders with a whites-only admission standard were the Knights of Pythias, Foresters of America, Maccabees, Modern Woodmen, Woodmen of the World, Elks, Improved Order of Red Men, and Freemasons. The Improved Order of Red Men excluded aboriginal Americans, even though its "ceremonies, nomenclature, and legends aim[ed] at conserving the[ir] history, customs, and virtues" (Preuss, 1924: 80). Conversely, black men developed parallel institutions for the Freemasons, Elks, Knights of Pythias, Foresters, and Modern Woodmen orders.[4]

Commercial insurers sold to non-whites, but charged them higher premiums. In 1893 the Equitable Life Insurance Company levied a surcharge for life policies on persons of "Negro blood." In 1927 the Manulife Insurance Company charged "oriental rates" to insure the lives of Asian clients.[5] In 1928 the London Life Insurance Company used its higher "female rates" for group disability contracts if Mexican, Japanese, or Chinese were more than 10 per cent of the insured group (*Gold Dust*, 1928: 53ff). Our evidence does not show whether commercial insurers had actuarial reasons for their higher premiums on sales to non-whites.

## RELIGION

The sole religious prerequisite for membership was "belief in a Supreme Being, the Creator and Preserver of the Universe." The requirement excluded atheists, but not Roman Catholics or Jews, although after 1880 few Roman Catholics or Jews joined. By default, the IOOF became a society of Protestants and a vehicle for expressing an Anglo-Protestant ethno-religious identity.

ROMAN CATHOLICS The literature differs about Roman Catholic participation in fraternal societies. According to Clawson, ethnic Catholics joined the societies after the American civil war, but withdrew from them after 1880 (Clawson, 1989, 131). On the one hand, the Roman Catholic Church became openly hostile to secret societies and created counter-institutions to meet the needs of church members.[6] On the other hand, the secret societies reacted to immigration from southern and eastern Europe with anti-Catholic nativism.

In contrast, other studies claim that Roman Catholics defied their priests and joined societies such as the Odd Fellows and Knights of Pythias. According to Cumbler, fraternal lodges in Lynn, Massachusetts, were part of a network of working-class institutions that knit Roman Catholics into the city's class-conscious, working-class community (Cumbler, 1979, 48). According to Thelen, fraternal lodges in industrializing Missouri helped to integrate Roman Catholics into parochial community societies that were resisting consequences of capitalist economic development. The fraternal emphasis on reciprocal bonds of obligation, for example, furnished opposition to competitive individualism in the larger society (Thelen, 1986: ch. 9).

The claims of Cumbler and Thelen are hard to appraise. Cumbler does offer circumstantial evidence that the church's opposition to secret societies did not settle matters. French Canadians in Fall River, Massachusetts, became staunch labour unionists after 1884, despite opposition from their priests. Neither author, however, reports information about the religious affiliations of the lodge members. Clawson relies on circumstantial evidence. From the church's perennial concern about secret societies, she infers that Roman Catholics were joining them before 1880 (Clawson, 1989, 130). She cites the suppression of German-language lodges in the Knights of Pythias during the 1890s for evidence that fraternal nativism helped to drive Roman Catholics out of secret societies. Her evidence does not show, however, whether the German Knights were Roman Catholics.

Developments in the Forester orders tend to support Clawson's interpretation. In 1879 Catholic members quit the Independent Order of Foresters (IOF) to form the Massachusetts Catholic Order of Foresters. They acted "in part because of the dominance of Roman Catholic influence among Massachusetts Foresters and a desire of those of the religious faith to place the control of the society in that State in the hands of their own religious faith." In a related development, disgruntled former members of the IOF founded the Catholic Order of Foresters in Chicago in 1883 (Stevens, 1907: 214–17). Another Forester order, the Foresters of America, had several "French courts" in Massachusetts until 1905, when it required the subordinate courts to conduct their affairs in English. In response, the French-language courts seceded to form *L'ordre des forestiers franco-américaines*.[7]

Given that Roman Catholics were quitting Forester orders, they were unlikely to be joining the Odd Fellows. In 1894, moreover, the Holy See in Rome prohibited Roman Catholics from joining the Odd Fellows, the Knights of Pythias, or the Sons of Temperance, under pain of excommunication.[8] "Any Catholic who joins such organizations," a church journal warned Lynn, Massachusetts, parishioners in 1903, "ceases to be a Catholic in communion with the Church. It means that at the hour of death unless a member of such society shall renounce such society ... he dies in his sins, an enemy to God and his Church" (Cumbler, 1979, 48).

Odd Fellows, for their part, expressed misgivings about the Roman Catholic Church. In 1912, for example, all but one of several Roman Catholic Polish immigrants who had joined an IOOF lodge in Michigan subsequently withdrew, on orders from their priest. The IOOF's grand master for Michigan responded that "any Roman Catholic may become an Odd Fellow ... [but no] Odd Fellow can remain a Catholic [unless the brother] decides that Odd Fellowship means more to him than his religion."[9] In another episode in Arkansas in 1914, the editor of the *Sovereign Odd Fellow* persisted in attacking the Roman Catholic Church as a political organization, despite the IOOF grand sire's attempt to silence him.[10]

Our Canadian evidence fits Clawson's argument that Roman Catholics and Odd Fellows no longer mixed. In 1921 the IOOF had forty-two members per thousand males in heavily Protestant Ontario, but only five per one thousand males in heavily Roman Catholic Quebec.[11] Similarly the number of Odd Fellows per thousand population in Ontario was well below average in francophone Roman Catholic localities (see Table 2.1).

Evidence from our lodge case studies also finds a striking absence of Roman Catholic participation. The membership registers for two lodges in Ingersoll included only one Roman Catholic from the town's 1881 and 1901 census populations. Similarly, the membership register for the lodge in nearby Harrietsville held no Roman Catholics from the 1881 and 1901 census populations for North Dorchester and South Dorchester townships.[12]

JEWS Jews were a small but rising proportion of the population in American and Canadian cities.[13] Judging by evidence for Toronto, they were unlikely to become Odd Fellows (Frager, 1992). Language, religion, ethnicity, class tensions, and working-class militancy kept Jewish men isolated from Toronto's Anglo-Protestant majority.[14] Jews lived in Jewish neighbourhoods near garment industries, their principal employers. They organized Jewish unions and Jewish friendly societies. In

Table 2.1
Odd Fellows per 1,000 Population in Ontario, Selected Communities, 1931

| *County* | *1931 Population* | *% Francophone* | *% Roman Catholic* | *Members per 1,000 population* |
|---|---|---|---|---|
| ONTARIO | 3,431,683 | .09 | .22 | 15 |
| Prescott | 24,596 | .79 | .85 | 0 |
| Russell | 18,487 | .79 | .82 | 4 |
| Glengarry | 18,666 | .49 | .68 | 0 |
| Nipissing | 41,207 | .47 | .63 | 8 |
| Sudbury | 58,251 | .41 | .61 | 7 |
| Cochrane | 58,033 | .39 | .59 | 7 |
| Stormont | 32,524 | .40 | .53 | 10 |
| ESSEX | 159,780 | .21 | .37 | 21 |
| Harrow | 989 | .07 | .11 | 163 |
| Essex | 1,954 | .05 | .08 | 149 |
| Kingsville | 2,174 | .04 | .08 | 109 |
| La Salle | 703 | .65 | .82 | 0 |
| Tecumseh | 2,129 | .75 | .88 | 0 |
| Belle River | 782 | .83 | .96 | 0 |

1921 Toronto had thirteen Jewish mutual-benefit societies with 1,994 members: fifty-seven members per one thousand Jewish population.[15]

Nevertheless, some Jews did join IOOF lodges. In Ottawa Archibald J. Freiman, a Jewish department store owner, was an Odd Fellow.[16] In Toronto the IOOF's Sunnyside Lodge No. 449, organized in 1914, had an all-Jewish membership.[17]

THE ODDFELLOWSHIP AS ETHNO-RELIGIOUS IDENTITY By the turn of the twentieth century, the Oddfellowship was acquiring an ethno-religious identity in the larger cities. Its members were part of a shrinking Anglo-Protestant majority in communities that were attracting large numbers of European immigrants. In 1910 Southeastern European ethnic groups made up 23 per cent of the population for the nineteen largest cities in the United States. These groups were largely Roman Catholic, Greek Orthodox, and Jewish in religion. Most of the immigrant men held unskilled, low-paying jobs and could not have afforded the IOOF's price of membership. Northwestern European ethnic groups, which included Catholics, also accounted for 23 per cent of the population in large cities.[18]

Like Canadian-born Catholics, immigrant men who could afford the IOOF's price of membership chose instead to join ethnic and Catholic societies. In 1911, for example, Ontario's insurance department licensed five Italian, one Ukrainian, one Lithuanian, thirteen Jewish, seven Canadian-francophone, and four Anglo-Irish Catholic societies for sickness insurance. At the same time, Anglo-Protestants became increasingly anti-foreigner, anti-Catholic, and anti-Jewish in reaction to large-scale immigration.[19] Some American Anglo-Protestants joined nativist fraternities such as the United American Mechanics and the Patriotic Order of Sons of America. It was in part to compete with the nativist orders, that the Knights of Pythias and the Foresters of America required their lodges to conduct their affairs in English.

Finally, class distinctions enhanced ethnic and religious differences between Odd Fellows and immigrants. By joining the Odd Fellows, young Anglo-Protestant men could assert superiority over the many foreigners who held low-paying, unskilled jobs and could not afford a friendly society's fees and dues. At the same time, they expressed cultural distance from the better-paid immigrant men who joined ethnic and Catholic societies.

## SOCIAL CLASS

The literature differs about the social class composition of Odd Fellow lodges. Most American studies view the lodges as cross-class institutions that helped to dampen class formation among urban workers. During the years 1845–85, for example, IOOF lodges in Albany, New York, were places where workers met non-workers (Greenberg, 1977). In contrast, British studies and a few American studies find that friendly societies were working-class institutions. In Britain, Johnson argues, membership in a friendly society became "the badge of the skilled worker" (Johnson, 1985: 55), but drew poorly from the "faceless, lower third" of the working-class population. A recent British study finds that friendly societies attracted rural wage labourers as well as urban working-class members. In the lodges of rural Yorkshire, agricultural labourers and farm servants were three-quarters of the members (Neave, 1991: 66–85).

Nineteenth-century official histories of the IOOF anticipate one or other of these interpretations. According to Ross, the IOOF retained the artisan flavour of its British parent order in 1890. American Odd Fellowship was "composed of the great middle, industrial classes almost exclusively" (Ross, 1890). In contrast, Stillson noted a change during the 1840s. During the 1830s, the order had been "composed, mainly, of English and Scotch operatives and tavern-keepers – plain, honest, uneducated, unpretending men, who were better fitted to follow the lead of capable rulers than to govern and guide." But by the 1840s, he argues, "the Order was finding its way into every department of business and employment. Every sphere of life was represented; men of every profession" (Stillson, 1897: 234).

Table 2.2 summarizes the published evidence on the occupational profiles of IOOF lodges.[20] The findings for the nine case studies support Stillson's judgment that the IOOF had a cross-class appeal. Even so, blue-collar men ranged from 35 to 80 per cent of lodge memberships. The social distance between the white-collar and blue-collar men, moreover, was small. The lodge brothers in Providence, Rhode Island, for example, were "shopkeepers, clerks, artisans, and other men from the lower middle class and the upper strata of the working class." Other members were wealthy older men who had joined when they were poor and young (Gilkeson, 1986).

Compared to Freemasons, the Odd Fellows drew more of their members from working-class men. The working-class percentage of their members was similar, however, to those in the Knights of Pythias, Improved Order of Red Men, the Ancient Order of United Workmen, the Maccabees, and Modern Woodmen of the World (Clawson, 1989: 95–108; Thelen, 1986: 165; Cumber, 1979: 50; Orr and McNall, 1996: 102). In all cases, the working-class percentage varied from one lodge to another, ranging from 23 to 83 per cent among seventeen lodges of the Knights of Pythias in Buffalo in 1891 and from 4 to 56 per cent among nine Masonic lodges in Providence, Boston, and Oakland.

The published evidence is useful but thin. Its broad categories of white collar and blue collar are crude for judgments about social class, and none of the case studies are for lodges in rural areas. Some authors lack basic knowledge about friendly societies, fraternal orders, and insurance.[21] With the exception of Clawson's work, the literature lacks information about the documentary sources. A lodge membership register, for example, reports a member's occupation on the day that he joined, but not for later years. Thus the register shows, over a period of time, the occupations of new members, not all members in a given year. In contrast, information in fraternal and city directories shows the occupations of all members at a given year.

To push the analysis further, we turned to evidence for lodges in Ontario and British Columbia. First, we traced men in a 1911 IOOF directory for Toronto to the 1911 city directory, which reported occupation. This gave us an occupational profile of Toronto Odd Fellows for that

Table 2.2
Blue-Collar Percentages of IOOF Lodge Memberships

| *Year* | *Locale* | *N of cases* | *% Blue collar* | *% Artisan* |
|---|---|---|---|---|
| late 19th c | Kansas, four towns (unnamed) | – | .47 | – |
| 1877 | Providence, R.I. | 107 | .46 | – |
| 1896 | Providence, R.I. | 99 | .42 | – |
| 1908 | Lynn, Mass., West Lynn Lodge | 229 | .75 | .57 |
| 1914 | Lynn, Mass., Kearsage Lodge | 261 | .80 | .65 |
| 1897 | Hannibal, Missouri, Lodge 41 | 36 | .45 | .39 |
| 1901 | Hannibal, Missouri, Lodge 26 | 38 | .68 | .42 |
| 1874 | Lexington, Missouri, Lodge 323 | 16 | .69 | .50 |
| 1881 | Lexington, Missouri, Lodge 6 | 31 | .35 | .25 |

year. Second, we analysed evidence from lodge membership registers and medical examiners' reports for lodges in seven small urban and rural communities. This evidence showed, over time, the occupations of new members.

THE EVIDENCE IN DIRECTORIES The *Official Membership Directory of the Independent Order of Oddfellows of Toronto for 1910–11* listed the names and street addresses for 4,624 members of twenty-seven lodges. All but 11 per cent were city residents. Through linkage to names in the *Toronto City Directory* for 1911, we obtained the occupations of 2,626 resident members.[22] For comparison, we drew a random sample of 386 men from the 147,210 names in the city directory.[23]

As Table 2.3 shows, the occupational profile of the linked Odd Fellows was broadly similar to that for men in the city directory sample. Wage workers and shopkeepers were the great majority in both groups. The linked Odd Fellows, however, had notably higher proportions of skilled labourers and shopkeepers, and a notably lower proportion of unskilled labourers. Artisans and shopkeepers, in other words, were the backbone of the Toronto lodges. They were the largest groups and the most fully represented.

Predictably, the occupational profiles of members varied among the lodges. Each lodge had its own territory in which to recruit members, and the economies of the areas varied. Most Odd Fellows in the rail-

Table 2.3
Toronto, 1911: Occupational Profiles for Odd Fellows and Men in the City Directory

| *City directory sample* | | | *Linked Odd Fellows* | | |
|---|---|---|---|---|---|
| *cases* | *%* | *Occupational category* | *cases* | *%* | *Difference* |
| 153 | .40 | Skilled labour | 1,253 | .48 | +.08 |
| 42 | .11 | Shopkeeper | 411 | .16 | +.05 |
| 70 | .18 | Clerk | 388 | .15 | −.03 |
| 26 | .07 | Professional | 233 | .09 | +.02 |
| 58 | .15 | Unskilled labourer | 136 | .05 | −.10 |
| 11 | .03 | Manufacturer | 98 | .04 | +.01 |
| 25 | .06 | Employee (Undesig.) | 96 | .04 | −.02 |
| 385 | 1.00 | | 2,615 | 1.01 | |
| 1 | | Unclassifiable | 11 | | |
| 386 | | | 2,626 | | |

Chi square = 76.451 DF=6 Significant at .01 level

way trades, for example, were in two lodges whose territories held the Grand Trunk Pacific and Canadian Northern railway yards (see Table 2.4). Employees of Eaton's department store were 11 per cent of the linked members in one lodge but were not represented in the linked members of several other lodges. A similar variety held for the occupations of carpenter, clerk, and salesman.

Sixty-seven physicians were members in the twenty-seven lodges (a mean of 2.5 per lodge). The high number arose from competition for the position of lodge physician, whose job was to certify the sickness of members who claimed benefits and assess the health of applicants for membership. Some lodges had agreements with their physicians by which the lodge physician attended sick members in exchange for an annual capitation payment.[24] This enabled physicians to use contacts with members and their families to build up their practices.

Some lodges counted prominent Torontonians among their members. The Reverend Isaac O. Stringer (Prospect Lodge No. 314) was the Anglican Bishop of Yukon. George R. Geary (Rosedale Lodge No. 357) was a lawyer and mayor of Toronto in 1910–11. Horatio C. Hocken (Broadview Lodge No. 394) was publisher of the Orange *Sentinel*, a past grand master of the Orange Lodge, and mayor in 1912–14.

Table 2.4
Toronto IOOF Lodges, 1911: the Percentages of Members in the Top Ten Occupations and Two Industrial Groups

| | *Percentage for all 27 lodges* | *Highest lodge percentage* | *Lowest lodge percentage* |
|---|---|---|---|
| Carpenter | .03 | .15 | .00 |
| Clerk | .05 | .13 | .00 |
| Employee | .04 | .13 | .00 |
| Traveller/salesman | .05 | .10 | .00 |
| Grocer | .03 | .09 | .00 |
| Machinist | .04 | .08 | .00 |
| Physician | .03 | .08 | .01 |
| Foreman | .03 | .06 | .00 |
| Painter | .02 | .05 | .00 |
| Barber | .02 | .04 | .00 |
| TOTAL (10 occupations) | .33 | .45 | .17 |
| Eaton's group | .03 | .11 | .00 |
| Railway worker group* | .07 | .16 | .00 |

* persons with railway occupations or reported railway employers

George B. Woods (Rosedale Lodge) was the founder and managing director of the Continental Life Insurance Company. George H. Gooderham (Rosedale Lodge) was a manufacturer, a capitalist, and a Conservative MLA from 1908 to 1916. Perhaps these men had joined the Odd Fellows before they had become prominent. If so, they were evidence of the IOOF's cross-class appeal and respectability since they kept up their memberships.

THE EVIDENCE IN LODGE MEMBERSHIP REGISTERS The registers report the occupations of joiners for seven small urban and rural communities in Ontario and British Columbia (see Table 2.5). If one includes farmers, ranchers, and fishermen in the blue-collar group, then blue-collar men ranged from 62 to 86 per cent of the new members.

Clearly the urban bias of scholarly case studies has missed the IOOF's appeal for farmers, fishermen, and ranchers. Farmers were a third of

Table 2.5
Occupations of Joiners for IOOF Lodges in Seven Communities

| | Ontario | | | |
|---|---|---|---|---|
| *Category* | *Ingersoll 1870–1929* | *Point Edward 1873–1929* | *Harrietsville 1873–1930* | *Total* |
| Farmer/fisherman | .08 | .06 | .73 | .20 |
| Labourer | .05 | .05 | .03 | .05 |
| Skilled labour | .49 | .68 | .10 | .43 |
| Clerical | .14 | .11 | .03 | .12 |
| Merchant/mfg. | .16 | .06 | .05 | .13 |
| PROFESSIONAL | .08 | .04 | .05 | .07 |
| N of cases: | 1,163 | 111 | 304 | 1,578 |
| Mean age: | 28 | 29 | 27 | |
| % blue collar | .62 | .79 | .86 | .68 |

| | British Columbia | | | | |
|---|---|---|---|---|---|
| *Category* | *Prince Rupert 1910–29* | *Cloverdale 1890–1929* | *Sandon 1897–97* | *Slocan 1902–29* | *Total* |
| Farmer/fisherman/ rancher | .04 | .31 | .03 | .08 | .15 |
| Labourer/deckhand | .03 | .10 | .06 | .19 | .09 |
| Skilled labour | .62 | .36 | .71 | .56 | .46 |
| Clerical | .14 | .06 | .03 | .09 | .09 |
| Merchant/mfg. | .10 | .07 | .10 | .01 | .06 |
| PROFESSIONAL | .07 | .10 | .06 | .08 | .08 |
| N of cases: | 147 | 178 | 29 | 90 | 444 |
| Mean age: | 32 | 29 | 31 | 31 | |
| % blue collar | .69 | .77 | .80 | .74 | .70 |

the Cloverdale's new members and two-thirds of those in Harrietsville (73 per cent with cheesemakers included). Like shopkeepers in urban lodges, farmers were self-employed but valued the sick benefit. During the years 1904–16, 75 per cent of the Harrietsville sick claimants had joined as farmers, although even though farmers represented only 65 per cent of the membership.[25]

Like ordinary labourers in urban communities, farm labourers were weakly represented in relation to population. According to 1901 census data, farm labourers were 16 per cent of the adult male population in the Harrietsville lodge's catchment area (North Dorchester Township), yet only five of the lodge's 304 joiners (2 per cent) reported farm labourer as their profession.[26]

This contrasts with the findings in Neave's British study. Farm labourers and farm servants were three-quarters of the lodge members in rural Yorkshire. However, such men were three-quarters of the local labour force. In Yorkshire agriculture, teams of waged labourers worked on large tenant-managed farms. In southwestern Ontario agriculture, in contrast, farmer-owners operated small farms and used family members for most of their labour needs.

Table 2.6 reports the occupational profiles of joiners by decades for Odd Fellows and patriarchs in the town of Ingersoll. During the years 1856–79 17 per cent of the recruits came from nearby farms and villages. As a consequence, Odd Fellows eventually organized lodges in several of the villages and the number of farmers and village residents who joined the town lodges declined. Due to change in the town's labour-force structure, clerks and machinists provided increasingly more of the new members after the 1890s.

Most of Ingersoll's 272 resident patriarchs had joined the encampment soon after completing their lodge degrees. The interval between joining their lodge and joining the encampment was up to one year in 59 per cent of the cases; two years for 13 per cent; three or four years for 9 per cent; and from five to twenty-four years for 19 per cent. By the 1920s, clerks were more likely than other new members to take the encampment degrees. Otherwise, the lodges and the encampment had similar occupational profiles for joiners.

As Table 2.7 shows, the occupations of joiners differed markedly between Ingersoll's IOOF lodges and one of its Masonic lodges (King Hiram No. 37). None of the Masonic joiners were ordinary labourers, and just 15 per cent of them were skilled labourers, compared to 54 per cent of the Odd Fellows. Within categories, the elitist profile of the Masons also showed through. In the professional group, the Masons had more lawyers and physicians and fewer teachers and photographers. In the shopkeeper/merchant/manufacturer group, they had more merchants and manufacturers and fewer shopkeepers.

IOOF-Masonic differences in joining costs contributed to the more elitist profile of the Freemasons. As Table 2.8 shows, the difference was

Table 2.6
The Occupational Distribution of IOOF Joiners in Ingersoll, Ontario

| | *Samaritan Lodge No. 35 and Oxford Lodge No. 77* | | | | | | |
|---|---|---|---|---|---|---|---|
| *Category* | *1870s* | *1880s* | *1890s* | *1900s* | *1910s* | *1920s* | *Total* |
| Farmer/cheesemaker | .10 | .12 | .10 | .05 | .03 | .03 | .08 |
| Labourer undesig. | .06 | .05 | .06 | .04 | .01 | .05 | .05 |
| Skilled labourer | .50 | .50 | .48 | .46 | .57 | .44 | .49 |
| Clerk/supervisor | .11 | .11 | .08 | .19 | .19 | .22 | .14 |
| Shopkeeper/mfg. | .16 | .15 | .16 | .16 | .11 | .20 | .16 |
| PROFESSIONAL | .06 | .08 | .11 | .10 | .09 | .06 | .08 |
| N of cases: | 364 | 197 | 116 | 200 | 129 | 157 | 1,163 |

| | *Unity Encampment No. 21* | | | | | | |
|---|---|---|---|---|---|---|---|
| *Category* | *1870s* | *1880s* | *1890s* | *1900s* | *1910s* | *1920s* | *Total* |
| Farmer/cheesemaker | .07 | .12 | .14 | .12 | .02 | .03 | .08 |
| Labourer undesig. | .13 | .05 | .08 | .04 | .04 | .03 | .07 |
| Skilled labourer | .40 | .55 | .42 | .45 | .51 | .37 | .45 |
| Clerk/supervisor | .21 | .07 | .14 | .18 | .22 | .43 | .20 |
| Shopkeeper/mfg. | .16 | .10 | .11 | .18 | .12 | .13 | .14 |
| PROFESSIONAL | .03 | .10 | .11 | .04 | .10 | .00 | .06 |
| N of cases: | 62 | 42 | 36 | 51 | 51 | 30 | 272 |

negligible before 1890. After that date, however, the real cost of joining dropped for the IOOF lodges and rose for the Masonic lodges. By 1901 the cost for the Masonic lodges was 2.3 times higher.[27]

Simply put, the Freemasons and Odd Fellows came to recruit from different strata of Ingersoll's male population. This finding accords with Thelen's evidence for Missouri and Cumbler's evidence for Lynn, Massachusetts. It also agrees with findings in Lynd and Merrell's classic study of Muncey, Indiana, in 1929. As Lynd and Merrell noted, Freemasons and Elks recruited "largely from the business classes" (cited in Gist, 1940: 44).

Table 2.7
The Occupations of Oddfellow and Masonic Joiners in Ingersoll, Ontario

| *Occupational category* | *1852–1905 Ingersoll Freemasons* % | *1870–1900 Ingersoll Oddfellows* % |
|---|---|---|
| Farmer | .22 | .11 |
| Ordinary labourer | .00 | .06 |
| Skilled labourer | .15 | .50 |
| Shopkeeper/merchant/mfg | .23 | .16 |
| Clerk/supervisor | .19 | .10 |
| PROFESSIONAL | .21 | .07 |
| N of cases | 274 | 677 |

## AGE

Odd Fellows joined their lodges as young men. Under the 1915 edition of the SGL's *Code of Laws*, the minimum age for membership was twenty-one, the legal age of majority in the United States and Canada. As Table 2.9 shows for Ontario during the years 1895–1914, two-thirds of the initiates joined in their twenties. The whole Ontario membership was young. Less than a quarter of it was over age forty-five.

The men who quit the Ontario lodges had been members on average for five to seven years. In 1895, for example, the initiates had a mean age of thirty and the ceased members had a mean age of thirty-five. The quitters were seven years older than the joiners in nine of the twenty years 1895–1914. They were six years older in eight years and five years older in three years.

Our information from lodge membership registers shows a five-year interval between joining and quitting (see Table 6.2). In four British Columbia lodges during the years 1891–1929, 258 quitters joined at the mean age of thirty and left their lodges at the mean age of thirty-five. The comparable statistics for 635 quitters in two Ontario lodges during the years 1856–1925 were twenty-six and thirty-two.

Over time the average age for members tended to rise. In 1907, for example, initiates in the Ontario lodges added 12 per cent to their membership for the previous year. Despite this all-time record intake, the average age of their members dropped by just 0.2 years. Between

Table 2.8
The First-Year Price of Membership in Ingersoll's Odd Fellow and Masonic Lodges

| | | *Joining Fees ($)* | | | | | |
|---|---|---|---|---|---|---|---|
| | *Year bylaws issued* | *Proposition & initiation* | *For three degrees* | *Total fees* | *Annual dues* | *Total first-year price* | *Ratio in constant dollars* |
| ODD FELLOW | | | | | | | |
| Oxford | 1890 | 5.00 | 6.00 | 11.00 | 6.00 | 17.00 | 1.3 |
| Samaritan | 1890 | 5.00 | 7.50 | 12.50 | 6.00 | 18.50 | 1.4 |
| Samaritan | 1902 | 5.00 | 6.00 | 11.00 | 6.00 | 17.00 | 1.0 |
| Samaritan | 1906 | 5.00 | 6.00 | 11.00 | 6.00 | 17.00 | 1.0 |
| FREEMASON | | | | | | | |
| King Hiram | 1873 | 20.00 | 0.00 | 20.00 | 3.00 | 23.00 | 1.4 |
| St John's | 1901 | 20.00 | 15.00 | 35.00 | 3.00 | 38.00 | 2.3 |
| St John's | 1911 | 25.00 | 15.00 | 40.00 | 3.00 | 43.00 | 2.3 |

*Note*: Ratio standard = Samaritan total cost for 1902 in constant dollars

1895 and 1914, their mean intake rate was 9 per cent. Despite this high rate, the average age for their members *rose* from 36.5 to 38.2.

The longer the lodge was in operation, the more likely it was to "fish out" its recruitment pool. Thus its intake of young men fell off, and the aging of its members accelerated. In 1899 the Ontario grand secretary demonstrated this by comparing the province's twenty-four "oldest" lodges with twenty-four "middle-aged" lodges for the previous eighteen years. For each year of comparison, the oldest lodges had a lower rate of initiations and a higher mean age for members.

The aging of the members accelerated in most IOOF jurisdictions during the 1920s. Until then, the IOOF had achieved high initiation rates and a rapid growth of membership. Its mean initiation rate for the years 1901–7 and 1919–20 had been 11 per cent. Once in the order, these large joiner cohorts had begun to age. Thus during the 1920s the IOOF needed high initiation rates to offset the aging of its cohorts from earlier years. Between 1920 and 1929, however, its initiation rate plummeted from 11 to 3 per cent.

In 1924 the SGL lowered its minimum age for joining to eighteen[28] in response to the decline in the IOOF's initiation rate and also to the contraction of its recruitment pool due to population aging. Between 1890

Table 2.9
Cumulative Percentage by Age for Members, Initiates, and Ceased Members in Ontario Lodges, 1895–1914

| *Age* | *Members* | *Initiates* | *Ceased members* |
|---|---|---|---|
| 21 | .01 | .13 | .01 |
| 25 | .12 | .40 | .10 |
| 30 | .31 | .65 | .33 |
| 35 | .49 | .80 | .57 |
| 40 | .64 | .91 | .66 |
| 45 | .76 | .96 | .87 |
| 50 | .85 | .99 | .94 |
| N | 650,414 | 66,984 | 29,970 |
| 1895 Membership | 22,095 | | |
| 1914 Membership | 53,655 | | |

*Note*: The membership total counts individuals more than once. The total for ceased members excludes members who died.

and 1930, for example, the median age of the American population rose from twenty-two to twenty-six (Weaver, 1983). In Canada during the same years, males under the age thirty-five fell from 72 to 64 per cent of the male population.

The IOOF's lower minimum age also matched the minimum age in rival orders, such as the Foresters of America, the Maccabees, and Independent Order of Foresters. By the early 1920s, moreover, membership in fraternal orders may have approached saturation levels. In the circumstances, the IOOF was casting its nets for younger fish; in 1923, the SGL authorized grand lodges to organize lodges of Junior Odd Fellows for white males in the age group fourteen to twenty-one.

## SEX

The IOOF admitted selected women to membership in non-beneficial auxiliary bodies, the Rebekah lodges, but barred them from membership in subordinate lodges and encampments. These arrangements arose partly from the centrality of the family breadwinners in the demand for sickness insurance. Actuarial considerations reinforced the IOOF's reluctance to offer the sick benefit to women. As a United States national health survey found for 1935–6, women had greater risk of sickness than men, at every age.[29] Social influences enhanced the moral hazard for female insurance risks. Due to family pressures, for example, an employed woman might claim to be sick in order to provide home care for a disabled child, spouse, or parent.

Finally, Odd Fellows idealized the male breadwinner and chose all-male fellowship for cultural reasons (Carnes, 1989; Burley, 1994; Laslett, 1992). Had they so wished, they could have offered the sick benefit to women clients who were breadwinners or earned wages. Commercial insurers allowed women employees to participate in group disability plans, albeit at a high price if they were 10 per cent or more of the insured group. Similarly, some life insurance fraternal orders provided an optional sick benefit for women members. A British friendly society, the Ancient Order of Foresters, permitted female courts in 1892 and allowed all-male courts to admit women as members in 1902 (Riley, 1997: 167). Similarly the IOOFMU recognized all-female lodges in 1899 and authorized mixed-sex lodges in 1902 (Moffrey, 1910: 118, 130, 142).

### HEALTH

Odd Fellows were healthier and lived longer than the general male population. This happened in part because the price of membership screened out low-paid workers who had the highest sickness risk (Britton, 1940). To minimize an adverse selection of risks, the SGL's *Code of Laws* barred from membership "any person who is totally deaf, dumb, or blind, or who is afflicted with any chronic, incurable disease, or who at the time of his admission was not in good health." Although not required to do so, most lodges elected a lodge physician whose duty was to ascertain the health of candidates for initiation. If the lodge also had a lodge practice agreement with the physician, then its capitation plan payment gave the physician an extra incentive to refuse applicants with poor health.

### MORALS

The SGL's *Code of Laws* gave lodges the duty of assessing the moral qualifications of applicants for membership. The ideology of Oddfellowship, as expressed through its degree rituals, stated the IOOF's formal moral goals. The Odd Fellow was to extend help to lodge brothers and their dependants who were in distress. His specific goals were to "visit the sick, relieve the distressed, bury the dead, and protect the widow and orphan."[30] Especially through service as lodge visitor or lodge watcher, he could improve himself by giving of his self. "Hand-to-hand, heart-to-heart" contact with distressed brothers was his path to moral uplift.

Conversely, the lodge was to screen out applicants for membership who came just for the insurance and so avoid the malingerers who submitted sick claims at the drop of a hat and shirked their duties as lodge visitors and lodge watchers. The ideal Odd Fellow might not submit a sick claim if he did not need the money or learned that his lodge's sick fund was low.

Odd Fellow morality also was about respectability. By joining his lodge and paying his joining fees and membership dues, the Odd Fellow showed his peers that he could afford the price of membership. By marching in processions in Odd Fellow regalia, he showed his community that neither he nor his family were headed for the pauper's grave (Johnson, 1985). Conversely, the lodge did not want men whose occupations undermined financial stability and respectability. In 1895 the SGL required lodges to reject applicants who were saloon-keepers, bartenders, or professional gamblers. In 1911 it directed them to reject hotel-keepers who were licensed to sell intoxicating liquors.

Like the churches of the day, an IOOF lodge censured its members for behaviour that was scandalous or harmful to a brother. In 1870 Samaritan Lodge No. 35 in Ingersoll expelled a brother for "leaving his wife in a sick and helpless condition and absconding with his servant maid under cover of night and suspicious circumstances and using dissimulation to several brethren of this lodge for the purpose of covering his scandalous conduct." In addition, the lodge published an account of the affair in Chicago and Detroit newspapers and communicated it to all IOOF lodges in Michigan and Illinois. In 1876 it expelled a brother who admitted to illicit intercourse with a sister of another Odd Fellow and leaving her pregnant. In 1877 it expelled a brother for having falsely passed himself off as a single man. In 1888 it expelled a brother for having absconded with another man's wife to live in Michigan.[31]

Odd Fellow practice, of course, sometimes differed from its ideological goals. One the one hand, ideology disdained the member who was out for himself. On the other hand, the sick benefit was a selling point in the recruitment of members. Had ideology rather than insurance been the Odd Fellow's prime motive for joining, long spells of membership should have been the order of the day. Each year during the period 1895–1929, however, the IOOF's lodges suspended 3 to 6 per cent of the membership. The suspended members, in turn, had been in their lodges on average for just five to seven years.

## THE IOOF IN URBAN AND RURAL PLACES

As Table 2.10 shows, the number of Odd Fellows per thousand population in Ontario was above average in small cities, towns, villages, and hamlets, and below average in large cities and rural places (a residual category). Given the Harrietsville lodge's attraction for farmers, the IOOF's apparent low popularity in rural communities was surprising. But this is in part a statistical illusion, since men in rural places without a lodge commonly joined lodges in nearby urban places. Thus an influx of non-resident members inflated the statistics for small-urban places and deflated the statistics for rural places.

What is more important, scattered rural populations were less accessible to lodges than concentrated urban populations; in 1921, 24 per cent of Ontario's hamlets lacked an IOOF lodge, compared to 6 per cent for all larger urban places. An extreme case, Haliburton County, had no incorporated urban places and no lodges for its small, scattered population (6,209 in 1921). One scholar makes this argument for American churches in the Old South during the years 1877–1906. The region was less churched than the American nation as a whole, Ayers argues, because it was more rural and its population was more scattered (Ayers, 1995). What was true of church-going also applied to IOOF lodges. In 1930, for example, the IOOF had eleven Odd Fellows per one thousand whites in the American national population. Its statistics for all twelve Old South states were below the national average.

In Ontario the IOOF's popularity statistics for large cities were always below average for the province, and they became increasingly more so over time. Between 1911 and 1931 the statistic for large cities fell from 88 to 60 per cent of the provincial figure. The contrast held, moreover, when Roman Catholics and non-whites are removed from the calculations. The statistics for small cities were above average for the province, but even, they followed a downward trend relative to the province as a whole (from 2.08 to 1.64).

The IOOF's below-average popularity in large cities arose partly from stiffer competition for its sick benefit. Compared to small urban places, cities also offered more social alternatives to lodge night. Finally, 46 per cent of the population of the nineteen largest American cities in 1910 were immigrants from continental Europe who tended to have below-average incomes and were largely Roman Catholic or Jewish. They had little prospect of becoming Odd Fellows.

## CONCLUSION

An IOOF lodge was an exclusive society, one that sorted people out, not an inclusive society that brought all people in a community to-

Table 2.10
Odd Fellows per 1,000 Population by Rural/Urban Category

| | | | *Percentage distribution for:* | |
|---|---|---|---|---|
| *Ontario* | *Members per 1,000 population* | *Ratio to prov. mean* | IOOF MEMBERS | *Ontario population* |
| 1911 | | | | |
| *Province* | 19 | 1.00 | | |
| Large cities (46,000–382,000) | 16 | 0.88 | .22 | .24 |
| Small cities (10,000+) | 39 | 2.08 | .17 | .08 |
| Towns (5,000–9,999) | 33 | 1.75 | .09 | .05 |
| Villages (2,500–4,999) | 42 | 2.23 | .13 | .06 |
| Hamlets (500–499) | 56 | 3.01 | .25 | .08 |
| Rural (residual) | 6 | 0.30 | .14 | .48 |
| TOTAL | | | 1.00 | .99 |
| 1921 | | | | |
| *Province* | 21 | 1.00 | | |
| Large cities (38,000–522,000) | 16 | 0.76 | .22 | .29 |
| Small cities (10,000+) | 39 | 1.82 | .22 | .12 |
| Towns (5,000–9,999) | 39 | 1.81 | .08 | .04 |
| Villages (2,500–4,999) | 51 | 2.37 | .14 | .06 |
| Hamlets (500–499) | 69 | 3.20 | .21 | .06 |
| Rural (residual) | 7 | 0.33 | .14 | .43 |
| TOTAL | | | 1.01 | 1.00 |
| 1931 | | | | |
| *Province* | 15 | 1.00 | | |
| Large cities (63,000–632,000) | 9 | 0.60 | .18 | .31 |
| Small cities (10,000+) | 25 | 1.64 | .23 | .14 |
| Towns (5,000–9,999) | 31 | 2.03 | .11 | .05 |
| Villages (2,500–4,999) | 41 | 2.68 | .13 | .05 |
| Hamlets (500–499) | 54 | 3.54 | .21 | .06 |
| Rural (residual) | 6 | 0.37 | .15 | .40 |
| TOTAL | | | 1.01 | 1.01 |

gether. It embraced adult white men from Anglo-Protestant backgrounds who had the incomes to become breadwinners and excluded non-whites, men with poor health, and men whose occupations or behaviour violated IOOF moral codes. It relegated women and minors to an auxiliary role. It had low appeal for Roman Catholics, Jews, and immigrants from continental-Europe. It was beyond the reach of men in low-income families.

The IOOF was a cross-class institution that brought together men from all major occupational groups. It was most popular among middle groups of the social hierarchy: skilled blue-collar workers, clerks, shopkeepers, and farmers. It had less attraction for men in low-paid occupations such as labourer and farm labourer. Wealthy men with well-paid white-collar jobs were a small group in the lodges, as they were in the larger population. Compared to Masonic lodges, such men were less common in IOOF lodges and lodges of other orders.

The Odd Fellows joined their lodges when they were young men. A large number of them quit their lodges after five to seven years. Over time, the lodges experienced an aging trend for membership which accelerated during the 1920s, when the IOOF made its sick benefit optional.

The Odd Fellows were men. For actuarial and cultural reasons, they barred women from their lodges and did not offer the sick benefit in their auxiliary branch for woman members. The Odd Fellows had above-average health and longevity. To varying degrees, they were upright men who prized respectability, selflessness, and self-improvement.

The Odd Fellows were a higher percentage of males in small urban places than in cities, which provided more competition in sickness insurance and more social alternatives to the lodge. In large American cities, a huge influx of Roman Catholic and Jewish immigrants from continental Europe also made recruiting difficult. Finally, Odd Fellows were a low proportion of the male population in rural places, primarily because the scattered rural populations were hard to reach.

# 3 The IOOF's Benefits System, 1863–1931

The IOOF made the stipulated sick benefit the cornerstone of its lodge-based program of benefits during the American civil war. Traditionally its lodges had aided sick members on a discretionary basis, according to need. In 1863, however, the SGL required that lodges provide in their bylaws for a fixed, stipulated amount. "The weekly benefit," the SGL declared, was "secured to members as a right and not as a charity." The "payment of a weekly benefit to sick members," moreover, was "a distinguishing characteristic of the Order and one of its fundamental principles."

In contrast, the sick benefit entered a long-term declining trend after 1891. In 1896 the SGL made the benefit optional for its encampment branch. In 1925 the SGL judged that the benefit "had outlived its usefulness" and made it optional for grand lodges. By 1929 half of the encampment branch and a third of the lodge branch were non-beneficial members.

## THE IOOF BENEFITS PROGRAM

THE IDEOLOGY OF THE PROGRAM "Friendship, love, and truth" was the motto of Oddfellowship, the "three-link fraternity." The motto found tangible expression in the "great duties" of the order, which were above all to "exercise over each other fraternal watch care, and moral discipline" (Grosh, 1871: 83).

An obvious goal of benefits was to bring relief to distressed brothers and their dependants. The point of Oddfellowship, however, was the moral benefit to the giver. In the larger society, men preoccupied themselves with the pursuit of wealth and interest in self. The Oddfellowship aimed to counter this social pathology. Through close personal contact with distressed brothers, Odd Fellows learned the joy of giving themselves. The gift of self, the *Odd Fellows' Amulet* stated in 1851, would make men "social and humane" (Bristol, 1851: 24). Through the gift of self, James Ridgley of Maryland, the sovereign grand secretary, exclaimed in 1873, Odd Fellows were "building up an improved civilization, in fact, a great moral empire" (Ross, 1890: 227). Conversely, in 1923 the grand sire, Lucian J. Eastin of Missouri, warned against the

danger of becoming a sort of corporate charity – an institution which is but little less soulless than the business corporation ... Associated effort, with enormous central power and almost imperceptible individual responsibility, is the outstanding contribution of the last century. The idea dominates the business world; is becoming popular with governments; and is being applied to religious work. But it is not the thought of Odd Fellowship. Our work was not designed to be a benefaction, but rather a service to each other. Our association is for instruction and not for the accumulation of a fund with which we may engage in a benevolent enterprise, with the fund as a capital. We seek to elevate and improve the character of men, to train them to be thoughtful towards each other, to watch and guard the interests of each other. In a word, to maintain toward each other a true fraternal relation. We cannot do this by merely giving money. Money is often the least of a brother's needs. We must give of ourselves, and to do this we must come into personal contact with the distress to be relieved.[1]

The importance of close contact between donor and donee made the lodge the key unit in the work of the order. "Each Lodge," *The Odd Fellows' Manual* stated in 1871, "is not only a Beneficial, or Mutual Aid Society, but also an Association for mental and moral improvement" (Grosh, 1871: 80–1). Conversely, grand sire Eastin cautioned in 1923:

The accumulation of a central fund has always been regarded as dangerous to the true interests of the Order; hence our law prohibits the payment of benefits by Grand Bodies. If such a fund existed out of which benefits or other relief could be paid, the members would be tempted to relax that individual effort so necessary to the accomplishment of our work and point to the fund. Under such an influence we should probably become a great financial institution and cease to be a fraternity. The directors or other managers would soon be awarding all relief while the individual members would refer all cases to them (SGL, *Proceedings*, 1923, 16).

Table 3.1
Types of Benefits Offered in Odd Fellow Lodges

1 *Stipulated sick benefit* (mandatory)
2 *Health-care benefits*
  i) Attentive benefits (mandatory)
  ii) Lodge contracts with physicians to provide members with medical attendance and medicines (optional)
3 *Stipulated Survivor's Benefits* (optional for lodges unless their grand lodge required one or more of them)
  i) Funeral benefit
  ii) Widows' benefit
  iii) Orphans' benefit (to orphans under twelve years of age)
  iv) Widower's benefit (payable to the member on the death of his spouse)
  v) Widows' and orphans' annuity benefit (dropped in 1906)
4 *Discretionary Assistance*
  i) To distressed brothers, widows, and orphans of deceased brothers, and indigent pensioners
  iii) Access to grand lodge homes for indigent, elderly members or orphans
5 *Indirect Benefit*
  Access to life and/or endowment insurance from organizations that sold exclusively to Odd Fellows

The members varied greatly, of course, in their support for the moral ideology. On average Odd Fellows quit their lodge within five years of joining. In many cases, this suggests a lack of ideological commitment. Moreover, men joined for various reasons; some joined for the insurance or to make business contacts, others to accommodate peer pressure or enjoy male fellowship and a chance to get out of the home. Even so, the IOOF's moral ideology, fellowship, degree ritual, passwords, and secret signs promoted the belief that lodge benefits were more than mere insurance. Contrary to conventional wisdom, this anti-materialist ideology strengthened the lodges as business operations: it helped lodge members to police the moral hazard for their benefits; it inspired them to do administrative work at no cost or nominal cost; it motivated them to recruit new clients; and it gave them resistance to the insurance products and blandishments of rival insurers.

THE RANGE OF BENEFITS THAT LODGES OFFERED The SGL's *Code of Laws* determined the benefits that a lodge could offer and which of them were mandatory (see Table 3.1). The *Code* required them to offer the sick benefit and the attentive benefit. A grand lodge could make other stipulated benefits mandatory. During the 1920s, for example, the grand lodges of British Columbia, Alberta, Manitoba, Ontario, and Michigan each had a mandatory funeral benefit. The grand lodges of Alberta and Ontario also had a mandatory widows' and orphans' benefit.[2]

To varying degrees, government regulated IOOF insurance activity. Under the Ontario Insurance Act, for example, an organization required a provincial licence to undertake insurance in the province.[3] A provision in the act allowed the grand lodge of Ontario to represent its subordinate lodges, thereby obviating the need for each lodge to become incorporated and licensed separately. The province registered the grand lodge as a friendly society until 1924 and then as a mutual benefit society. The licensing requirements for mutual benefit societies restricted the lodges to sick and funeral insurance, set their maximum weekly sick benefit at $12, and their maximum funeral benefit at $200.

Subject to SGL, grand lodge, and government requirements, each lodge selected the benefits that it would offer and their stipulated amounts. Similarly, the lodge alone was responsible for the benefit claims of its members. Simply put, the lodges ran the benefits program.

ARREARAGE AND SUSPENSIONS A member became ineligible for stipulated benefits if he fell behind in his dues. If he fell one year behind, his lodge could suspend him from membership or declare him ceased (dropped from membership). A member's unpaid dues continued to accumulate after suspension. Thus a suspended member had to pay the full, accumulated amount (or a maximum sum, if his grand lodge set one) to be reinstated.

Being in arrears was a major source of disqualification for benefits. As calculated from information in lodge returns, Odd Fellows in arrears rose from 19 to 33 per cent of the Ontario members between 1919 and 1929 (see Table 3.2). By our estimate, a third of the British Columbia members and half the Saskatchewan members were in arrears during the 1920s. For all fifty-six jurisdictions, men in arrears soared from 28 to 58 per cent between 1919 and 1929.

The lodges profited from these arrears. On the one hand, they reduced a lodge's liabilities; a lodge did not pay sick claims to members who were in arrears. Nor did it pay grand lodge capitation taxes for suspended members.[4] On the other hand, the lodge recovered some of its arrears. Most members in arrears paid their back dues before reaching the stage of suspension.[5] Further, some suspended members paid their arrears to become reinstated.[6]

THE RANGE OF BENEFITS OFFERED The mandatory stipulated sick benefit dated from 1863, when the SGL secured it for members. "The payment of a weekly benefit [was] a distinguishing characteristic of the Order and one of its fundamental principles" (SGL *Code of*

Table 3.2
Percentages of Members in Arrears for Dues, 1919–29

| | | *British Columbia* | | *Saskatchewan* | | *IOOF* |
|---|---|---|---|---|---|---|
| | *Ontario** | *Financial estimate* | *SNPD estimate* | *Financial estimate* | *SNPD estimate* | *SNPD estimate* |
| 1919 | .21 | – | .22 | – | .33 | .28 |
| 1920 | .23 | – | .31 | – | .41 | .36 |
| 1921 | .26 | – | .32 | – | .61 | .45 |
| 1922 | .26 | – | .36 | – | .67 | .47 |
| 1923 | .26 | – | .20 | – | .53 | .42 |
| 1924 | .28 | – | .26 | .53 | .51 | .46 |
| 1925 | .29 | – | .27 | .44 | .43 | .48 |
| 1926 | .31 | – | .17 | .53 | .42 | .47 |
| 1927 | .32 | .26 | .27 | .61 | .34 | .50 |
| 1928 | .32 | .27 | .36 | .52 | .46 | .54 |
| 1929 | .33 | .29 | .28 | .68 | .53 | .58 |

* The Ontario statistics are calculated from the semi-annual returns from the Ontario lodges. The financial estimate is calculated from reported totals for the amount of arrears. The SNPD estimate is calculated from reported totals for members who were suspended for non-payment of dues. It assumes that suspended members were 13 per cent of all members in arrears, the known proportion for Ontario.
Appendix B describes the evidence for Ontario and details for the two sets of estimates.

*Laws*, 1). In 1881 the SGL affirmed that subordinate lodges and encampments alike must pay "some benefits, however small" (Ross, 1890: 272). In 1891 the SGL enacted a minimum-benefit law, whereby the weekly benefit was to be "not less than $2 per week until the brother shall have received 52 weeks' benefits, and not less than $1 per week thereafter."

A member was entitled to attentive benefits even if he was behind in his dues. The SGL's *Code* required lodges to name visitors to call on sick brothers, inter deceased brothers with honour, and comfort widows and orphans of deceased brothers. If a disabled brother required continuous visitation, his lodge was to provide unpaid "watchers" for the purpose. Alternatively, his lodge could hire watchers or a nurse.

The *Code* also permitted lodges to elect a physician "whose duty it shall be to attend and render medical assistance to members" in return for payment from lodge funds. The 1931 bylaws of the IOOF lodge in Thamesford, Ontario, for example, provided "a physician whose duty it shall be to professionally attend each beneficial member ... if called upon to do so by the member or the lodge, and to supply necessary medicines ... For such service the physician shall be paid at the rate of $3.00 per annum for each member in good standing on the beneficial list."

The IOOF introduced the stipulated funeral benefit "to extend immediate aid to the family of the deceased brother." The beneficiaries could be "the widow, orphans under 21 years or dependent relatives of the deceased, or relatives upon whom the deceased was dependent at the time of his death." Where no eligible beneficiary existed, the lodge could apply the benefit to funeral expenses that relatives or a friend of the deceased brother incurred. Stipulated widows' and orphans' benefits, where offered, were in addition to the funeral benefit. Some lodges offered a widower's benefit, payable to the member on the death of his wife.

The small amounts of the funeral benefit, widows' and orphans' benefits, and the widower's benefit ($30 to $100) amounted to burial insurance. Thus these benefits were comparable to commercial industrial life policies on adult lives. As already noted, nearly half the industrial policies issued by the London Life Insurance Company during the years 1887–90 were on the lives of children. In contrast, IOOF benefits did not insure against burial costs for a member's children. This was a major gap but one that declined notably over time. In 1861 32 per cent of Canada's live-born infants died before age fifteen; in 1931 the proportion was 11 per cent.[7]

In 1877 both the Knights of Pythias and the Improved Order of Red Men made a centrally-managed endowment benefit available to members on an optional basis, and at extra cost. The amounts of the endowment benefit ($1,000 to $2,000) made it more than burial insurance and priced it for an upper working-class market. The SGL declined to match the initiatives of its friendly society competitors, in part because of its ideological stance against centrally managed funds. In 1877 it barred grand lodges and grand encampments from establishing funds for life insurance or endowment benefits, and in 1906 it declared that lodges could no longer "legally adopt and enforce" a widow's annuity benefit.

Odd Fellows in several jurisdictions, however, could purchase life, endowment, and accident policies from third-party insurers that sold exclusively to Odd Fellows. In 1890, for example, the grand lodge of Ontario recognized the Odd Fellow's Relief Association of Canada as its "auxiliary endowment benefit association."[8] In 1892 the SGL required all societies that sold insurance under the Odd Fellow name to obtain licences from the SGL and the grand lodges of states or provinces in which they did business. Thirteen of these societies duly applied for licences, but others ignored the requirement. Thus in 1898 the SGL cancelled all licences and denied all societies the right to sell insurance under the Odd Fellow name. In 1899, after vigorous lobbying by the Ontario grand lodge, the SGL made an exception for the Odd Fellow's Relief Association of Canada.

The stipulated benefit system evolved from discretionary benefits but never wholly replaced them. Many lodges did not offer some of the officially-sanctioned stipulated benefits. In some cases, the amount of the stipulated benefit fell short of the recipient's need. A brother who was "not sick, but merely infirm from old age" was not entitled to the sick benefit; however, a grand lodge could permit lodges pay the sick benefit to such members. In another area, Odd Fellows contributed to the education of orphans, half-orphans, and children whose parents could not support them. They also aimed to place orphans in families for adoption.[9]

The grand lodge home gradually assumed some of the lodges' obligations to orphans, widows of members, and aged, indigent Odd Fellows and Rebekahs. Lodges in Pennsylvania established the first home in 1872. In 1892 the SGL empowered grand lodges to levy a per capita tax on lodges for the "erection, equipment, support, and maintenance" of homes, and in 1911 it allowed them to tax Rebekah lodges for the support of homes. By 1929 the IOOF had sixty-three homes with 6,087 residents in forty-seven jurisdictions. Forty-four homes (70 per cent) dated from the years 1890–1916; nine homes (14 per cent) were established in the years 1919–26.[10]

ENCAMPMENT BENEFITS The encampments added flexibility to the IOOF's benefits system that lodges lacked on their own. Each lodge offered a sick or funeral benefit in one amount: the sum stipulated in its bylaws. Through membership in an encampment, however, an Odd Fellow obtained a second set of sick and funeral benefits, at a discount rate. On average in 1895, a member in an encampment added 69 per cent to his sick benefit and 45 per cent to his funeral benefit. In return, he paid 50 per cent more in annual dues.

The percentage of Odd Fellows who were patriarchs changed over time and varied from one jurisdiction to another. The number for all jurisdictions dropped from 17 to 14 per cent between 1895 and 1910 and recovered to 19 per cent by 1924. In 1895 it ranged from 10 per cent for the Maritime provinces to 27 per cent for Indiana. In 1924 it ranged from 7 per cent for Mississippi to 41 per cent for South Dakota.

ODD FELLOW CRITICISMS OF THE BENEFITS PROGRAM Neither stipulated nor discretionary benefits perfectly suited the IOOF's pragmatic and ideological goals.[11] On the one hand, discretionary aid was like charity. It went disproportionately to "those who are popular and who make their needs known" at the expense of "those who are not personally popular or who hesitate to disclose ... that they are in distress." Discretionary relief might be too niggardly in some lodges and too generous in others.

Stipulated benefits, on the other hand, resembled an insurance contract more than a moral contract. They drew men to the lodges for a selfish reason (to get insurance) rather than to develop character. They did not match actual needs, providing either too little or too much. From an actuarial perspective, the stipulated benefit contract was unsound, the revenue from dues being "greatly incommensurate with the financial obligations assumed." Finally, as an insurance activity, stipulated benefits exposed "the Order to intermeddling by civil authorities."

Opposition to stipulated benefits dated from their introduction. In 1865 the SGL voted to reject the creation of an honorary (non-beneficial) class of members, despite "strong opposition." In 1867 the grand sire, James P. Sanders of Yonkers, New York, recommended "the repeal of all the laws at present in existence with regard to weekly benefits, and that the matter be left wholly to the decision of our subordinate lodges." The SGL, however, dissented from the grand sire's opinions (*History*, 1879: 240, 311). By 1882 a growing number of grand lodges were fixing a minimum rate of benefits. Their reason for doing so was a fear that "lodges, if left unrestricted, would place their benefits at a mere nominal figure, and thus nullify the beneficial feature of the Order."[12] Similarly, as the Ontario grand lodge's committee on bylaws noted in 1887, many lodges showed "a disposition to load up the benefit clauses with disabilities and restrictions until they are rendered almost useless to the brothers whose necessities call for relief."[13]

In 1923 and 1925 the grand sire worried about the moral cost of IOOF homes.[14] On the one hand, from "a scientific, impersonal standpoint," institutional care for orphans and aged, indigent members was superior to what the individual lodges could furnish. On the other hand, the home had the disadvantages of a centrally-managed fund, which severed the personal relationship between donor and donee that existed at the lodge level.

A grand lodge capitation tax on lodge members was the chief source of revenue for the homes. Revenue from the tax, however, varied with membership size, which entered a declining trend in 1922. This development forced the grand lodges to consider raising their capitation rates for the tax. Alternatively, the lodges could aggressively recruit new members to replenish their numbers. Either way, the grand sire warned in 1923, the member became "needed for his financial contribution rather than for the character he brings to the Order."

## THE STIPULATED SICK BENEFIT

The sick benefit replaced part of the income that the member lost due to disability. The principle of partial income replacement was a standard feature of market insurance for the disability risk. It arose from the premise that the worker required the incentive of return to full income to remove himself from the sick list. Each lodge set the amount of its benefit, and once set, the amount was the same for all members.

Under the SGL's *Code of Laws*, a member was disabled for insurance purposes when "sickness, accident, or injury to his person" prevented him from "following any business, avocation, or employment whereby he may obtain a livelihood." The definition excluded men who were "able to attend to ordinary business though sick," even if the illness was terminal. It also distinguished between sickness and old age. It covered illness that was incidental to old age, but not old-age infirmity without illness.

To claim the benefit, the member had to notify his lodge of his disability within a week of its commencement. Where the member was a non-resident, the postmark of the receiving post office was the date of notice. The lodge could require medical or other evidence of the sickness, to be supplied at the claimant's expense, or require the claimant to submit to examination by the physician appointed by the lodge, at the lodge's expense.

Each lodge had a visiting committee of seven or more members. On receiving notice of a brother's illness, a member of the visiting committee was to visit the brother within twenty-four hours "to render him aid" and confirm his disability. Subsequently the chair of the committee was to make weekly reports on the brother until his disability ended. In the Harrietsville, Ontario, lodge, the end product was a completed sick benefit claim form, signed by the claimant, three members of the visiting committee, and the lodge physician.

The *Code* disqualified the member for benefits if he was in arrears for dues, as defined by his grand lodge constitution and lodge bylaws.[15] Disqualification also applied if the member's disability resulted from drunkenness or other immorality; if the member was not sick, but merely infirm due to advanced age; or if the member was unemployed or receiving public assistance.[16] Arrearage was by far the most important disqualification.

A grand lodge could add sick benefit requirements, subject to requirements in the *Code* and the SGL's approval of the changes. By the 1920s, for example, the Alberta, Manitoba, Michigan, and Ontario grand lodges barred their lodges from paying the benefit for the first week of sickness, but required them to pay the benefit for the second week. In contrast, the British Columbia grand lodge permitted its lodges to pay no benefits for the first week or first two weeks of sickness. The Alberta grand lodge set the minimum weekly benefit at $3 for the first six months, compared to the SGL requirement of $2. The grand lodges of Alberta and Saskatchewan set the maximum weekly benefit at 50 per cent of the member's yearly dues. The British Columbia maximum was $10 for six months, for each dollar of monthly dues; $7.50 for the next six months; and then $5 after one year. The Ontario maximum was 50 per cent of the "average yearly net receipts per member from dues and invested funds."

Each lodge set the amount of its benefit, subject to requirements of the SGL's *Code* and the grand lodge constitution and the grand lodge's approval of its bylaws. In Ontario 86 per cent of payments for the "relief of brothers" went to sick claims in 1929. The balance was for physicians' fees and the hire of nurses.

Assuming that sick claims in all jurisdictions received 86 per cent of the "relief of brothers" figure, we estimate that the mean amount of the IOOF weekly benefits in 1924 was $2.85 (86 per cent of $3.31). California and British Columbia had the highest mean amounts ($5.10 and $5.01), while the Maritime provinces and Vermont had the lowest mean amounts ($1.66 and $1.81).

Clearly some lodges ignored higher-level requirements. The mean amounts of the weekly benefit for the Maritime provinces and Vermont were below the $2 required under the SGL's minimum benefit law. In 1918 twenty Saskatchewan lodges paid a weekly benefit that exceeded their grand lodge's maximum amount. The grand lodge had no bylaws on file for twelve other lodges.[17]

## THE IOOF'S RESPONSE TO RISING-COST PRESSURES, 1860–1900

SGL statistics for 1901 illustrate the structure of the IOOF's balance sheet. The revenue from the 12,339 lodges less their expenses produced a profit of $1.77 per member. Members' dues furnished 56 per cent of the revenues; 19 per cent came from rents and investment income; 14 per cent came from joining fees (for the four degrees of membership); and 13 per cent came from other sources. On the expense side, the payment of benefits accounted for 68 per cent and 32 per cent went to overheads. The payment of sick claims was the major expense; in 1901 it consumed two-thirds of all benefit payments and 45 per cent of expenditures.

In this context, the IOOF experienced rising-cost pressures of the sick benefit. First, costs rose with age. The probability of a member making a sick claim increased as he aged and became above average when he passed through his forties. Second, lodges commonly charged a flat rate for dues, rather than scaling the rate by the member's age at joining, or increasing the amount as the member aged.

To keep costs down, a lodge needed many young members (under age forty-five) to balance the liabilities represented by the old members (over age forty-four). To discourage older men from joining, many lodges scaled the fee for the initiation degree by the applicant's age. Even so, the average age and amount of sick claims tended to increase over time. In many cases, the lodge's revenue from dues and joining fees eventually fell short of its expenses for benefits and overheads.

Apart from dues and joining fees, lodges had two other sources of revenue. The first was assessments on the members. Lodges could assess their members to pay funeral benefits, widows' and orphans' benefits, and expenses for official celebrations. In 1906 the SGL required lodges to assess their members if their funds on hand were insufficient "to meet current expenses and the accrued obligations for benefits due to their members." Frequent assessments, however, might encourage young members to quit and discourage young men from joining.

The second source of revenue came from rent and investments. Ideally a lodge accumulated savings during its early years of operation, when its members were young and sick claims were low. Then in later years, it had income from investments to help fund the rising claim rate of its aging members. IOOF reformers, however, regarded dues alone as a reliable source of revenue over the long term. Thus they urged lodges to raise the amount of their dues to a level that was sufficient to fund the costs of benefits and overhead.

Financial reforms in the IOOF's British parent, the IOOFMU, provided a model for the IOOF. During the 1840s, in response to rising costs, criticisms of its financial practices, and the threat of state regulation of friendly societies, the IOOFMU entered into "the dawn of actuarial science" (Moffrey, 1910). It required its lodges to furnish statistical information about their operations for the years 1846–8. Based on this information, the IOOFMU issued its "first authentic" experience tables for benefits in 1850. In 1853 it required its lodges to scale dues by the member's age at admission. In 1864 it required them to adopt "scientifically graduated tables of contributions and benefits" that actuaries had prepared from IOOFMU experience (a requirement widely flouted into the 1890s). In 1871 the IOOFMU issued the first of a series of actuarial valuations for its lodges, the first six of which reported net deficits. This appeared to show that the assets of the lodges were inadequate to cover their deferred liabilities (their expected claim rates through to the death of the last member). In contrast, the next two valuations (for 1899–1902 and 1904–7) reported a net surplus.

The IOOF's reformers made slower progress than their IOOFMU counterparts. In 1851 the SGL struck a special committee to investigate the financial stability of the lodges (Ross, 1890), and four years later the sovereign grand secretary produced an experience table for 66,071 members. Like the IOOFMU tables, it showed definitively that claim rates increased with members' ages. Although a hiatus of activity followed during the civil war and reconstruction period, annual reports on dues and benefits were a fixture at SGL meetings after 1873.

These efforts culminated in exhaustive reports by Dr Clarence Campbell of Ontario and Isaac A. Sheppard of Pennsylvania during the years 1880–2.[18] Using the IOOF's statistics from 1855 (66,071 members) and 1879–80 statistics for Delaware, Maine, and Connecticut (30,000 members), the two men demonstrated again how sickness increased with age. Additional tables, compiled from Pennsylvania experience, showed how the weeks of sick claims per member increased with the number of years the lodges had been in operation. The statistic for the longest-operating lodges was four times that for the most recently instituted lodges. For all lodges, the statistic for 1881 was up 50 per cent from that in 1873.

On the basis of the new experience tables, and the assumption that dues alone were reliable for revenue, Campbell constructed what became known as the "Campbell scale of dues and benefits." His objective was to have lodges scale their annual dues by the member's age at joining, in the fashion of the IOOFMU reform of 1853. His scale rates rose from $6 at age twenty-one to $17.80 at age sixty. These amounts, he believed, could fund a $4 weekly sick benefit and a $40 funeral benefit.

The Campbell-Sheppard report for 1882 urged the SGL to impose reform upon the lodges. First, lodges were to discontinue all stipulated benefits other than the sick and funeral benefits. The reformers were especially critical of the widowers' benefit (payable on the death of the member's wife) and the widows' annuity benefit, neither of which was subject to actuarial calculation. Second, lodges were to adopt the Campbell scale of dues or an $8 flat rate rather than the $6 rate then widely in use. Campbell and Sheppard based this on the expected sick claims of a member aged thirty-five, not twenty-one. The Campbell scale rates assumed a $4 weekly sick benefit and a $40 funeral benefit. If lodges chose higher amounts, they were to increase either their scaled or flat rate accordingly. As a guideline for lodges using a flat rate, their revenues per member from dues and investments were to be twice the amount of the weekly sick benefit and five times the amount of the funeral benefit.

The reforms were not implemented. The SGL endorsed the Campbell-Sheppard changes, but struck down the clause that made them obligatory. Although the "long, painstaking labors" of the SGL committee continued, the result, by 1885, was "nothing but the compilation of [more] statistics, which are studied by few" (Stillson, 1897, 165).

In 1898 the Ontario grand lodge required its lodges to adopt a sliding scale of dues (the Campbell scale or an alternative scale prepared by actuaries) for members initiated after 1 January 1899. Here Campbell's influence was evident. Now a past grand sire (1890–2), he was serving on the Ontario grand lodge's committee on dues and benefits. In 1899, however, after a winter of confusion, protest, and resistance from the lodges, the grand lodge changed the sliding-scale requirement to a guideline.

In the end the reformers won piecemeal gains, nothing more. In 1906 the SGL banned the widows' annuity benefit. Several grand lodges set maximum weekly amounts for the sick benefit. In Campbell's grand lodge of Ontario the weekly amount was not to exceed 50 per cent of the lodge's per-capita revenue from dues and invested finds. By 1929 about a third of the Ontario lodges charged dues on a sliding scale.[19]

The IOOF's rejection of centrally-imposed reforms raises questions about the financial soundness of its lodges. Despite the IOOFMU's adoption of reforms, six consecutive actuarial valuations reported a net deficit for its lodges. If the British lodges struggled financially with reform, one can imagine a grim prognosis for IOOF lodges without reform. In the meantime, having declined to reform its benefits system, the IOOF began to dismantle it.

THE DECLINE OF THE SICK BENEFIT AFTER 1890 The decline began in the encampment branch. In 1892 the SGL exempted encampments from the minimum benefit law. In 1896 it empowered grand encampments to abolish the stipulated sick benefit or make it optional for encampments. Under SGL resolutions passed in 1906 and 1913, grand encampments could allow subordinate encampments that retained the benefit to establish a non-beneficial class of membership.

To measure the abolition of the encampment benefit, we calculated the encampment-branch sick weeks statistic (the number of sick weeks per patriarch) as a percentage of the lodge branch sick weeks statistic. As Table 3.3 reports, the ratio statistic was 0.96 for 1890 and 1895 when the sick benefit was compulsory for both the encampment and lodge branches.[20] It then fell to 0.58 between 1896 and 1924 when the

Table 3.3
Estimate of Non-Beneficial Membership in the Encampment Branch

| *Year* | *Sick weeks ratio* | *Estimated % of patriarchs who were non-beneficial* | *Ratio for suspensions* |
|---|---|---|---|
| 1890 | 0.96 | 0.00 | 1.27 |
| 1895 | 0.96 | 0.00 | 1.36 |
| 1900 | 0.90 | 0.06 | 1.47 |
| 1910 | 0.86 | 0.10 | 1.49 |
| 1921 | 0.60 | 0.36 | 1.03 |
| 1924 | 0.58 | 0.38 | 1.32 |

benefit was optional for grand encampments but still compulsory for lodges. The differences in members' arrears between lodge and encampment were probably a small influence on the declining trend.[21] Thus our estimate of the proportion of patriarchs who were non-beneficial in 1924 is 38 per cent (0.96 less 0.58).

Although sick benefit was mandatory for lodges before 1925, the SGL permitted reductions to the coverage period for the benefit. In 1896 the grand lodges (or, without legislation by them, lodges) were permitted to require a waiting period of one week or two weeks of sickness before payment of the sick benefit started. In 1917 an amendment to the SGL's minimum benefit law allowed lodges to stop benefit payments after fifty-two weeks.[22] The old law had required lodges to continue the weekly benefit for the duration of the member's illness, albeit at a lower minimum rate of $1 after fifty-two weeks.

As Table 3.4 shows, the IOOF's constant dollar per member expenditure for the sick benefit peaked in 1900 (at 3.5 times the statistic for 1921) and then declined.[23] Lodge and grand lodge reductions to the coverage period for the benefit were one influence on the declining trend after 1900. The more important influence, however, was a drop in the constant-dollar amount of the sick benefit (see right-hand column). Between 1901 and 1924, lodges needed to increase the weekly amount of the benefit by 217 per cent to keep pace with inflation. Instead they reduced it by 3 per cent.

Table 3.5 shows that the sick benefit also slipped in the priorities of the lodges. In 1870 sick claims were 67 per cent of expenses for benefits; by 1929 they accounted for 42 per cent. Conversely, the proportion spent on IOOF "homes and other relief" rose from 3 to 34 per cent.[24] During the nineteenth century, Odd Fellows had declared the

Table 3.4
Constant Dollar Expenditures per Member as a Ratio of Expenditures for 1921

| | *For sick brothers* | *Burials* | *Widows* | *Homes and other* | *Total* | *Mean amount of weekly sick benefit* |
|---|---|---|---|---|---|---|
| 1870 | 1.9 | 1.2 | 7.5 | 0.7 | 1.4 | n.d. |
| 1880 | 3.0 | 1.9 | 7.3 | 1.3 | 2.2 | 3.1 |
| 1890 | 3.3 | 2.4 | 5.8 | 1.8 | 2.5 | 3.1 |
| 1900 | 3.5 | 2.8 | 3.6 | – | – | 2.7 |
| 1910 | 2.0 | 1.8 | 1.3 | – | – | 1.9 |
| 1915 | 1.9 | 1.7 | 1.5 | – | – | 1.7 |
| 1920 | 0.9 | 0.9 | 0.7 | – | – | 0.9 |
| 1921 | 1.0 | 1.0 | 1.0 | 1.0* | 1.0* | 1.0 |
| 1924 | 1.1 | 1.2 | 1.7 | 1.3* | 1.2* | 1.1 |
| 1929 | 0.9 | 1.3 | 1.4 | 1.3* | 1.1* | 1.1 |

* includes estimates of lodge totals for per-capita tax contributions (see Appendix C)

sick benefit to be a "defining feature" of the order. By the 1920s, in contrast, many Odd Fellows saw the home program as the IOOF's "crowning achievement" and the "brightest jewel in [its] diadem."[25]

THE SGL'S ELIMINATION OF THE MANDATORY BENEFIT, 1925–31

In his grand sire's address to the SGL Assembly in 1925, Herbert A. Thompson of Michigan urged the SGL to abolish the stipulated sick benefit. It had become, he insisted, financially ruinous to the lodges. In earlier times a "tremendous" growth in membership and income from investments had enabled lodges "to continue without reaching a financial cataclysm." That was true no longer, as Odd Fellows faced net losses of members and "growing demands upon our treasuries by reason of the constantly increasing age of the member."

Second, "the largest amount that could possibly be paid as a benefit [was] totally inadequate in these days of high standards of living. Perhaps once that amounted to real help; today it is so paltry, even in opulent subordinates, that it makes for criticism rather than for commendation."

Third, the sick benefit had outlived its usefulness. Perhaps it had served a purpose when "there had been little money in circulation;

Table 3.5
Percentage Distribution of IOOF Lodge Expenditures on Benefits

| | *Sick benefits* | *Relief to widows* | *Burials* | *Homes and other relief* | *Total* | *Number of IOOF homes* |
|---|---|---|---|---|---|---|
| 1870 | .67 | .14 | .15 | .03 | 0.99 | 0 |
| 1880 | .69 | .09 | .17 | .05 | 1.00 | 2 |
| 1890 | .67 | .06 | .17 | .09 | 0.99 | 11 |
| 1921 | .50 | .03 | .19 | .29* | 1.01 | 57 |
| 1924 | .46 | .02 | .19 | .32* | 0.99 | 61 |
| 1929 | .42 | .02 | .21 | .34* | 0.99 | 63 |

* includes estimates of lodge per-capita tax contributions (see Appendix C)

population was widely scattered; society was not well organized; government and organized public and semi-public systems of relief had taken little notice of suffering, of disease ... of most of those finer things of life which tend to build up a great people." It did so no longer with the "advancing scale of civilization" and "development of government and quasi-public organizations ... to assist the members of society in the vicissitudes of life."

Finally, the stipulated benefit undermined mutuality, the core value in Odd Fellowship. The IOOF had been founded to promote "human brotherhood," bring "members into closer personal relations," and provide material and personal assistance to needy members out of a fraternal concern "for each other's welfare." By introducing stipulated benefits, the order had departed from true fraternity and entered the realm of a business venture. In many cases, the grand sire contended, the benefit was "not relief, but [was] so much returned to the recipient because he had complied with all the provisions of the contract."

General opinion at the SGL's annual meeting, the Saskatchewan representatives reported, "seemed to be that the stipulated sick benefit system has outlived its usefulness."[26] Nevertheless, the SGL declined the grand sire's recommendation to abolish the sick benefit.[27] Instead, by a vote of 193 to fourteen with five abstentions, it provided a middle ground.[28] Each grand lodge could abolish the benefit or make it optional for lodges. In addition, lodges that retained the benefit could stop payment after thirteen continuous weeks, down from fifty-two weeks under the old law.

Subsequently the SGL permitted a non-beneficial class of membership in lodges that retained the benefit. After 1929 a grand lodge could "provide, or authorize their subordinates to provide ... by law that applicants over 18 years of age may be received into membership as non-beneficial members."[29] After 1931 a lodge could grant a beneficial member's request to transfer to the non-beneficial class.[30]

By 1930, according to information obtained by the grand secretaries for Michigan and Ontario, twelve grand lodges had eliminated the stipulated benefit, twenty-nine had made it optional, and fifteen had retained it. In the optional benefit jurisdictions, the percentage of lodges that had abolished the benefit ranged from two to ninety. It was fifty or more in fourteen of the thirty-three jurisdictions. In all, the grand secretary estimated, 39 per cent of the IOOF's lodges and a third of its members were non-beneficial.[31]

To summarize, Odd Fellows declined to reform their financial practices in response to rising-cost pressures on the sick benefit. Instead, they cut the value of the benefit and dismantled their legislative provisions that made it mandatory.

# 4 The Financial Soundness of the Lodges, 1890–1929

Conventional wisdom blames the IOOF's financial practices for the decline of its sick benefit after 1890. Although a member's sick claims increased with age, all members of a lodge paid the same dues and were eligible for the same amount of benefit. As critics of the system argue, this posed little problem during a lodge's early years when its members were young and had below-average claim rates. As the members aged, however, their claim rates rose. When revenue from level dues became insufficient to cover claims, the lodge's insurance provision collapsed (Gosden, 1961).

The literature makes little distinction between friendly societies and fraternal life insurance orders. It portrays fraternal benefits in general as a flawed experimental stage in the long-term development of insurance. An implicit corollary argument is that commercial insurers survived because their pricing practices were sound. "Ultimately, the insurance fraternities adopted commercial methods or failed and disbanded" (Clawson, 1989: 227).

This interpretation stems from a false opposition between science and culture. Ostensibly commercial insurers correctly understood insurance as a technical or scientific problem; they used actuarial principles to develop their insurance provisions because they were after profit. Fraternal insurers, in contrast, regarded their benefit provisions as a moral project that transcended mere insurance; their goal was the member's moral improvement through the giving of himself, not profit. Thus the IOOF rejected central funds to safeguard the personal contact between the members who received assistance and those who provided it. Level dues expressed the fraternal ideal of mutuality. Meanwhile competition for members discouraged fraternal insurers from raising dues or cutting benefits (Gilbert, 1965).

In the end science prevailed over culture in the insurance industry. As financial realities set in, fraternal life insurers gradually accepted that the "principles they had been taught to believe were erroneous." By the First World War, most of them had reserve funds and age-scaled rates for dues that they calculated from mortality experience tables.[1] A number of fraternal life insurers ended up as mutual life insurance companies.[2]

This chapter rejects the notion that unsound pricing practices were driving friendly societies from the field of sickness insurance. In the process, it rebuts much of the conventional wisdom about commercial and fraternal insurance provisions. British friendly societies, not commercial insurers, pioneered the development of actuarial knowledge for sickness insurance.[3] Commercial pricing practices for sickness insurance were closer to the friendly society model than to the actuarial model. The moral ideology of friendly societies made their insurance provisions more efficient than those of commercial insurers, not less.

## THE EFFICIENCY OF THE IOOF'S BENEFIT SYSTEM

Each lodge paid the sick claims of its members. Subject to requirements of higher bodies, the lodge set the amounts of its weekly benefit, joining fees, and quarterly dues. To claim the benefit, the member had to notify his lodge of his sickness within a week of its onset. Within twenty-four hours of receiving notice of the brother's illness, the lodge sent a member of its visiting committee to render aid to the brother and confirm his disability. Lodge visitors then reported weekly on the brother until he recovered.

The lodge system had important strengths for the sickness insurance market. First, its overhead costs were low. Lodge members, not paid agents, recruited clients. Nominally paid or unpaid lodge officers administered the benefit. For both tasks, the IOOF's emphasis on moral self-improvement encouraged the members to do the work. Second, the intrusive methods of the lodge system helped Odd Fellows avoid an adverse selection of insurance risks. The lodge physician examined each membership applicant's physical condition and health history. The lodge's three-man proposal committee investigated the applicant's moral character, in part to screen out men who would join just for the insurance. Finally, the widespread practice of age-scaled initiation fees discouraged applications from older men, who had above-average sickness risk. Third, the intrusive methods of the lodge system helped Odd Fellows police the moral hazard (malingering) as the visiting committee helped to ward off false claims. In addition, the IOOF's moral ideology discouraged false claims and inspired lodge visitors to detect them.

On the negative side, the fraternal lodge system made little provision for risk diversification; each lodge was responsible for the sick claims of its members. Thus in principle a high local rate of sick claims in a given year could shock a lodge's financial condition. Certain commercial practices might have attenuated the problem. For example, a grand lodge could have pooled the risks from all lodges in a central fund. Alternatively, it could have initiated a scheme of reinsurance, whereby each lodge assumed a portion of the claims in other lodges.

Any centralization, however, stood to weaken the IOOF's management of adverse selection and the moral hazard. In 1908, for example, the IOOFMU in New South Wales, Australia, established central funds for sick and funeral benefits, which in effect turned the lodges into "mere collection agencies." Participation in lodge affairs fell off, and members developed a selfish attitude to claims. "When the lodges administered sick pay," Green and Cromwell observed, "the members knew who was paying – it was the members themselves. But once 'head office' took over, the illusion that someone else was paying made its entry" (Green and Cromwell, 1984: 59–60).

On balance, the IOOF provided an efficient delivery of working-class sickness insurance that commercial insurers could not match. Without the intrusive screening methods and low overhead of the IOOF's decentralized lodge system, commercial insurers could not solve the problems of moral hazard and adverse selection. "The assurance of a stipulated sum during sickness," the president of the Prudential Insurance Company conceded in 1909, "can only safely be transacted ... by fraternal organizations having a perfect knowledge of and complete supervision over the individual members."[4] The introduction of group disability insurance in 1912 allowed commercial insurers to bypass the problems of moral hazard and adverse selection. By 1929, however, group disability insurance was not widespread.

## PROBLEMS WITH THE EVIDENCE OF CRITICS

This section challenges three indictments of friendly society financial practices. First, it rejects the recent scholarly indictment of the societies for declining to adopt "commercial" pricing practices. Second, it challenges the evidence for the grand sire's charge that the IOOF's lodges faced financial ruin in 1925. Third, it questions the validity of the valuation-method appraisals that showed large deficits for the IOOFMU, the IOOF's British-parent order.

FRIENDLY SOCIETY RESISTANCE TO COMMERCIAL PRICING PRACTICES Critics held that fraternal pricing practices were unsound. On the one hand, a lodge's sick claim rate rose as its members aged. On the other hand, none of the lodges scaled dues by the member's age (the *natural premium* method). Most charged dues at a flat rate for all members (the *level dues* method). At best lodges scaled the flat rates by the member's age at joining (the *graded-level dues* method).

The level dues and graded-level dues methods posed little problem during a lodge's early years when its members were young and had below-average sick claim rates. Over time, however, the members aged and their claim rates rose. At some point, the critics argue, the revenue from dues became insufficient to cover claims and the lodge's insurance provision collapsed.

The adoption of commercial pricing practices, the critics argue, could have saved the lodges from ruin. A problem with this argument is that commercial sickness insurers used non-actuarial pricing practices. Like the friendly societies, they did not scale premiums by the insured person's age but charged a flat rate to age forty-nine, and then a sharply higher rate (James, 1947: 262–6; Dublin, 1943: ch. 9). Similarly they charged flat rate premiums for group disability contracts. The amount of the premium depended on details of the contract, such as the amount of the weekly indemnity. It did not vary by the ages of individuals in the insured group, except where persons over sixty years of age constituted 10 per cent or more of the insured group.[5]

THE GRAND SIRE'S EVIDENCE OF FINANCIAL RUIN In 1925 grand sire Thompson warned against the stipulated benefit. His evidence was the "cold figures" that one Ambrose Bruner had prepared for the grand lodge of Kentucky.[6] For calculation, Bruner took each grand lodge jurisdiction's receipts for members' dues and joining fees and subtracted disbursements for "relief" and "current expenses" (benefit claims and lodge operating costs). Over the past decade, he found, lodges had spent beyond their revenues in fifty-three jurisdictions, producing an average loss of $2.74 per member.

In fact, Bruner's figures misread the statistical record and inflated the IOOF's financial problems. On the one hand, they were high for expenses. Some lodges, as Thompson acknowledged, had reported "appropriations for permanent improvements" as current expenses, a category intended solely for "regular and legitimate running expenses."[7] In 1906, for example, Cloverdale Lodge No. 15 in British

Table 4.1
Per-Capita Revenue, Spending, and Profit in Constant Dollars:
Yearly Amounts as a Ratio to the 1921 Amounts

| | *Revenue* | | | | | *Spending* | | | *Profit* |
|---|---|---|---|---|---|---|---|---|---|
| | *From dues* | *Joining fees* | *Rents, investments* | *Other* | *Total* | *Lodge overhead* | *Benefits* | *Total* | |
| 1901 | 2.1 | 2.4 | 1.8 | 1.6 | 2.0 | 1.6 | 2.5 | 1.9 | 2.2 |
| 1910 | 1.8 | 1.8 | 1.5 | 1.5 | 1.6 | 1.4 | 1.8 | 1.5 | 2.2 |
| 1921 | 1.0 | 1.0 | 1.0 | 1.0 | 1.0 | 1.0 | 1.0 | 1.0 | 1.0 |
| 1924 | 1.1 | 0.7 | 1.2 | 1.8 | 1.1 | 1.2 | 1.1 | 1.1 | 1.1 |
| 1929 | 1.1 | 0.6 | 1.6 | 1.1 | 1.1 | 1.2 | 1.1 | 1.2 | 0.8 |

Columbia counted the price of a new hall as a current expense rather than as an addition to assets. On the other hand, Bruner's "cold figures" were low for revenue. His calculations included receipts for dues and joining fees but excluded income from rents and invested funds and all other sources.

With all revenue taken into account, lodges lost money in ten jurisdictions in 1924, not fifty-three as Bruner found.[8] As Table 4.1 shows, the IOOF's net revenue, spending, and profit had declined between 1901 and 1921.[9] During the early 1920s, however, the IOOF's real costs for benefits were stable, not rising. The real value of net lodge profits, moreover, held steady through to 1925, when the sick benefit became optional.

## THE LIMITATIONS OF THE IOOFMU'S VALUATION APPRAISALS

In 1871 the IOOFMU began to use a valuation method to appraise the financial health of its lodges. Its actuary used IOOFMU experience tables to estimate the future morbidity and mortality experience of their current members. Then he estimated whether assets of the lodges (cash on hand and revenues from dues and interest) were sufficient to cover liabilities (sickness and funeral benefits) through to the death of the last member. The IOOFMU's valuations for 1866–70, 1875, 1880, 1884–6, 1889–91, and 1894–6 each estimated a shortfall. Its valuations for 1899–1902 and 1904–7 each estimated a surplus, although 44 per cent of the lodges were in deficiency for the 1904–7 one (Moffrey, 1910: 167, 192).

The valuation measure is appropriate for fully-funded benefit systems, where each member finances his own benefits through lifetime contributions. The measure ignores membership growth because that is irrelevant to what is being measured. In contrast, membership growth matters in a pay-as-you-go system, where the insurer pays current claims out of current revenues. Friendly societies such as the IOOFMU and the IOOF operated pay-as-you-go systems.

Nineteenth-century *ex ante* valuations have five shortcomings for application to the IOOFMU's system. First, actuaries had to make assumptions about future interest rates to obtain present-value estimates of future income and expected liabilities (Moffrey, 1910: 190–1). The present value of future sick pay, for example, was "the amount of money which would have to be invested at compound interest to provide the promised benefit." Similarly, the present value of future dues discounted their face value to reflect interest rates. Assuming a 3 per cent interest rate, for example, a dollar in year 1 was worth $1.03 in year 2. By extension, a dollar expected in year 2 was worth 97 cents in year 1 ($1.00/$1.03). The inaccuracy of *ex ante* assumptions about future interest rates made the first two valuations unreliable. As the IOOFMU's actuary reflected in 1884, the apparent reduction of the deficiency between the two valuations "was not real, for a rate of interest was employed in the computation of assets and liabilities of many lodges which is proved by subsequent experience to have never been realized."[10]

Second, the valuation method made no allowance for new members, who were younger than current members and had below-average sick claim rates. A surplus obtained from the dues of future new members would help to subsidize the liabilities of existing members.

Third, the valuation method made no allowance for changes to the insurance contract between the lodge and its members. As Moffrey notes, the members of the lodge were both creditors and debtors (Moffrey, 1910: 191). Thus they could raise the amounts of their annual dues and joining fees or reduce the amount of the lodge benefit.

Fourth, the valuation method did not allow for members who quit. It assumed that each member would remain a member until death (or a specified terminal age). In reality, many members quit before the age of forty when they began to have above-average sickness risk. When they quit, the lodge's liabilities for their years of above-average risk vanished. Thus the assumption of lifetime membership caused the valuation method to produce a high estimate for a lodge's liabilities.

Fifth, the valuation method did not allow for fluctuations in the size of annual benefit claims, and hence for a lodge's risk of ruin from unusually large claims in a given year. At best, valuations gave crude estimates of a friendly society's long-term financial health and poor appraisals of its immediate financial condition.

## RISING-COST PRESSURES AND THE GEOGRAPHY OF ABOLITION

In 1925 the SGL allowed grand lodges to abolish the sick benefit or make it optional for their lodges. By 1931, the grand secretary for Ontario estimated, 39 per cent of the IOOF's lodges and a third of its members were non-beneficial.[11]

This section investigates the influence of rising-cost pressures on grand lodge responses to the benefit question during the years 1925–9. First, it classes the IOOF's fifty-six grand lodge jurisdictions into "abolition" and "retain" groups, according to how each responded to the benefit question between 1925 and 1929. Then it investigates whether rising-cost pressures differ between the two groups.

CLASSING THE GRAND LODGES We have comprehensive information about grand lodge legislation for the sick benefit during the years 1925–9.[12] Legislation alone, however, is problematic for classification. Where the grand lodge made the sick benefit optional, the percentage of lodges that abolished the benefit ranged from two to ninety.[13] In some cases our sources lack detail about legislation that reportedly abolished the benefit. The Montana grand lodge's abolition of the benefit in 1926, for example, did not produce declining trends for its benefit statistics. Perhaps like the Ontario grand lodge in 1951, this grand lodge banned the benefit for future members but not current ones.[14]

Thus we used three-year trends for the sick weeks statistic (the weeks of sick pay per member) to assist in our classification decisions.[15] We placed a grand lodge in the abolition group if it had abolished the benefit or made it optional by 1929 *and* its sick weeks statistic fell by 50 per cent within two years of the legislation. We classed a grand lodge in the retention group if it did not legislate on benefits through to 1929 *or* its sick weeks statistic fell by less than 25 per cent during the two years following legislation to abolish the benefit or make it optional. We placed all other grand lodges in the middle group. Table D.1 in Appendix D reports our classification decisions and the evidence.

The abolition process showed striking geographical patterns (see Map 4.1 and Table 4.2).[16] None of the twenty-four jurisdictions in the Canada, northeast, and far west regions abolished the sick benefit. Half of the thirty-two jurisdictions in the Old South and middle west regions did so. The relationship between region and abolition of the sick benefit was significant at the .01 level.

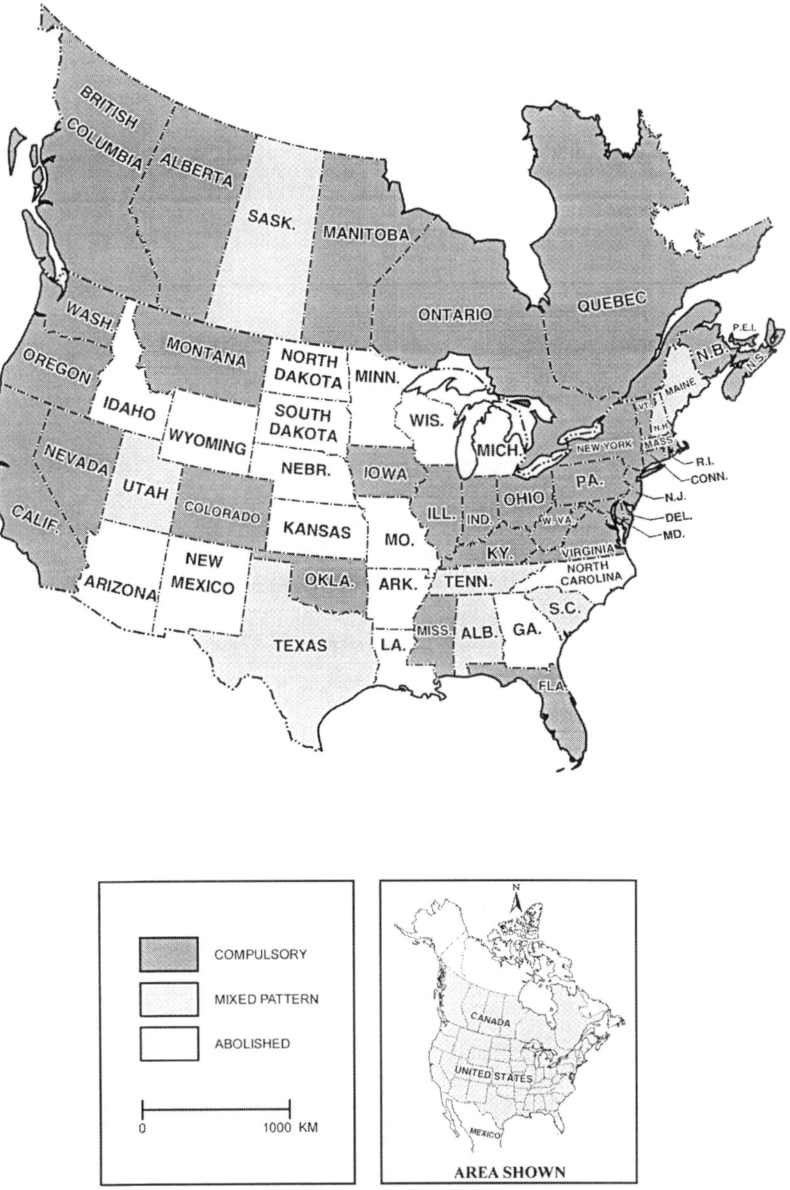


DATA SOURCE: JOURNAL OF PROCEEDINGS OF THE SOVEREIGN GRAND LODGE OF THE I.O.O.F., 1929.
BASE MAP SOURCE: GEOLOGICAL SURVEY OF CANADA
DRAWN BY: M. G DYLKE

Map 4.1
Status of the Sick Benefit
in IOOF Grand Lodge Jurisdictions: 1929

Table 4.2
Grand Lodge Jurisdictions: Benefit Status Groups by Geographical Region

| | *Abolition* | *Middle group* | *Retention* | *Total* |
|---|---|---|---|---|
| Canada | 0 | 1 | 6 | 7 |
| Northeast | 0 | 2 | 11 | 13 |
| Old South | 4 | 4 | 4 | 12 |
| Middle West | 12 | 1 | 7 | 20 |
| West Coast–Nevada | 0 | 0 | 4 | 4 |
| Total | 16 | 8 | 32 | 56 |

Chi square = 25.613 DF=8 significant at .01 level

THE ABOLITION PROCESS IN THE ENCAMPMENT BRANCH The sick benefit was optional for encampments after 1896. If pressure of rising costs caused the SGL to abandon the mandatory lodge benefit in 1925, then one might expect some correspondence between abolitionist grand lodges and grand encampments that had abolished the benefit by 1924. To explore this possibility, we used benefit statistics to class thirty-two grand encampments into abolition or retention groups.

The findings are inconclusive. As Table 4.3 shows, the classifications for grand lodges and grand encampments match for twenty jurisdictions, but differ for seven. Michigan and North Carolina, for example, are abolitionist jurisdictions for the lodge branch, but are retentionist for the encampment branch. The reverse obtains for Maryland, Mississippi, Nevada, Oklahoma, and Quebec. However, although the classifications for the two branches differ somewhat, the difference is not statistically significant.

RATES OF ARREARAGE AND SUSPENSION In 1925 the abolitionist jurisdictions were significantly more likely than retentionists to have had above-average rates of suspension for non-payment of dues during the four preceding years (see Table 4.4).[17] By extension, they also had higher percentages of members who were in arrears for dues and ineligible for benefits.

Group differences in arrearage rates, however, were ambiguous evidence of group differences in rising-cost pressures. On the one hand, suspended members had a lower mean age than all members (see Table 2.9). Thus high suspension rates tended to accelerate the IOOF's rising trends

Table 4.3
Status of the Sick Benefit:
Grand Encampment Classifications by Grand Lodge Classifications

| | *Grand Encampment* | | | |
|---|---|---|---|---|
| *Grand lodge group* | *Abolition* | *Retention* | *Row Total* | *Not classed* |
| Abolition | 7 | 2 | 9 | 7 |
| Mixed pattern | 3 | 2 | 5 | 3 |
| Retain | 5 | 13 | 18 | 14 |
| Total | 15 | 17 | 32 | 24 |

Chi square = 6.433 DF=2 not significant at .05 level

Table 4.4
Grand Lodge Trends for Suspensions by Benefit Status Group, 1921–4

| | *Abolition* | *Middle group* | *Retention* | *Total* |
|---|---|---|---|---|
| Above average SNPD | 13 | 6 | 14 | 33 |
| Below average SNPD | 3 | 2 | 18 | 23 |

Chi square = 7.194 DF=2 significant at .05 level

for membership age and sick claim rates. On the other hand, lodges profited financially from arrearage and suspensions (see chapter 3).

TRENDS FOR MEMBERSHIP Trends for membership are a better proxy for pressure from rising costs on the sick benefit, since the risk of disability increases with age. Thus, to stabilize the cost of claims, lodges require a steady intake of young members (initiates) to offset the aging of current members.

In this regard, the IOOF's lodges were victims of their spectacular success in recruiting new members before 1921. Once in the lodges, the giant new cohorts of the years 1900–21 began to age. Thus lodges needed ever-larger numbers of new members to offset the rising cost of benefits for older members. By the 1920s, however, lodges had "fished out" their recruitment pools and their initiation rates fell off. Therefore they experienced an acceleration of their rising trends for membership age and exposure to the disability risk.

Table 4.5
Grand Lodge Trends for Membership by Benefit Status Group

| *Membership trend* | *Abolition* | *Middle* | *Retention* | *Total* |
|---|---|---|---|---|
| 1901–10 | | | | |
| Above average gain | 14 | 5 | 14 | 33 |
| Below average gain | 2 | 2 | 17 | 21 |
| Chi square = 8.320 DF=2 significant at .05 level | | | | |
| 1911–20 | | | | |
| Above average gain | 8 | 3 | 17 | 28 |
| Below average gain | 8 | 5 | 15 | 28 |
| Chi square = 0.625 DF=2 not significant at .05 level | | | | |
| 1921–29 | | | | |
| Gain or below average loss | 10 | 3 | 20 | 33 |
| Above average loss | 6 | 5 | 12 | 23 |
| Chi square = 2.128 DF=2 not significant at .05 level | | | | |

Effectively, high rising-cost pressures resulted from uneven membership growth: rapid gains followed by a slow gains and then losses. As Table 4.5 shows, the abolitionist jurisdictions tended to have exaggerations of the general trend. They were likely to have had above-average growth rates during the years 1901–10, below-average growth rates during the years 1911–20, and above-average loss of members during the early 1920s. In contrast, the retentionist jurisdictions tended to have a more stable trend for membership. They were likely to have had below-average gains of members during the years 1901–10. Many of them gained members during the early 1920s, a period of loss for all jurisdictions combined.

Thus the abolitionist grand lodges tended to be fading stars in the IOOF constellation. Their glory years for membership growth had come early in the century, and by the 1920s they were experiencing above-average losses of members. Arguably these developments gave them older memberships and above-average rising-cost pressures.

We offer this interpretation with caution. The group differences in lodge growth rates were statistically significant for the period 1901–10, but not for the two later periods. The group differences in the en-

Table 4.6
Net Lodge Profit per Member by Benefit Status Group
(number with net loss shown in parentheses)

| *1924* | *Below average* | *Above average* | *Total* |
|---|---|---|---|
| Abolition | 8 (4) | 8 | 16 |
| Middle | 5 (1) | 3 | 8 |
| Retention | 15 (5) | 17 | 32 |
| Total | 28 (10) | 28 | 56 |

Chi square = 0.625 DF=2 not significant at .05 level

campment branch were not statistically significant for any of the three periods.[18]

*Net Lodge Profits and Abolition* Net lodge profit refers to the sum of the profits and losses of the lodges in a given jurisdiction. For analysis, we determined whether each grand lodge's profit statistic was above or below the mean for the IOOF's fifty-six jurisdictions.

As measured by membership trends, high rising-cost pressures did not spell financial ruin for the lodges. For each of the periods 1901–10, 1911–20, and 1921–4, differences in membership trends for the grand lodges failed to predict which jurisdictions had below-average net lodge profits in 1924.[19] Similarly, net lodge profits failed to predict which jurisdictions were to abolish the sick benefit. As Table 4.6 shows for 1924, the abolitionist and retentionist jurisdictions had similar percentages of grand lodges with below-average net lodge profits. The small group differences for 1924 were not statistically significant, nor were the differences significant for 1901, 1910, 1920, and 1929.

Above-average rising-cost pressures did not translate into financial losses for two reasons. First, after 1890 the lodges changed the sickness insurance contract with their members by reducing the real amount of the benefit and shortening the maximum period for which they paid claims. Second, as discussed below, a rise in their income from investments helped them to remain solvent.

## THE FINANCIAL CONDITION OF LODGES IN BRITISH COLUMBIA

The net lodge profit statistic is a weak measure of financial health. In particular, it does not capture deferred liabilities: that is, the higher claim rates that lodges can expect as their members age. Moreover, lodges, not grand lodges, paid the sick claims. To push the analysis further, therefore, one needs evidence for lodges and actuarial techniques that are appropriate for the IOOF's pay-as-you-go system.

Accordingly, this section examines the financial condition of twenty-seven British Columbia lodges during the years 1890–1929 by using two measures of financial health: the *implicit degree of risk loading* and the *probability of ruin*. The risk-loading measure shows, on an annual basis, whether the lodge's revenues were adequate to cover its overhead costs and expected sick claims. Unlike valuation, it does not assume a closed membership or require information about interest rates. The probability-of-ruin measure shows whether the lodges had a significant chance of ruin from high claims in a particular year. It allows for fluctuations in annual claim size and all lodge assets, not just dues revenue. Although new to economic history, the two measures are used widely in the literature for insurance (Borch, 1990; Beard et al., 1984).

THE SELECTION OF LODGES The twenty-seven lodges listed in Table 4.7 probably had above-average risk of financial weakness in British Columbia. First, they had below-average memberships and hence below-average risk diversification. During the years 1891–1929, their mean size of membership was fifty-nine, compared to 104 for all provincial lodges. Only two of them had an average membership larger than 104, and only eight had a peak membership greater than 104. Second, the twenty-seven lodges include all twenty lodges that closed before 1930. Six of the twenty closed within five years of opening, and twelve closed within ten years.

Thus the twenty-seven lodges provide a strong test of fraternal pricing practices. If these lodges escaped serious financial problems before 1930, then few other lodges should have had them.

THE DATA FOR ESTIMATION The sick benefit was compulsory for lodges and members in British Columbia until 1932. Our evidence from lodge bylaws indicates that all lodges charged flat-rate dues of $12, the minimum allowable under the grand lodge constitution. British Columbia lodges commonly set the amount of their weekly benefit according to the maximum allowed: $10.00 a week for the first six months of illness, $7.50 for the next six months, and $5.00 after one year. In some lodges the coverage period for the benefit started with the onset of disability. Other lodges specified a waiting period of one or two weeks.

The semi-annual returns from the lodges report the number of brothers who made sick claims; revenues from dues, joining fees, rents and

Table 4.7
The British Columbia Lodges Selected for Study and Official Reason (if any) for Closing

| *Lodge No.* | *Lodge name* | *Location* | *Year open* | *Year close* | *Official reason* |
|---|---|---|---|---|---|
| 13 | Royal City | New Westminster | 1890 | 1899 | Fire; merger |
| 14 | Acme | Victoria | 1891 | 1898 | Merger |
| 15 | Cloverdale | Cloverdale | 1891 | 1980 | |
| 17 | Duncan | Duncan | 1892 | 1980 | |
| 20 | Centennial | Nanaimo | 1892 | 1907 | Merger |
| 22 | Gold Range | North Bend | 1892 | 1906 | Members away |
| 25 | Revelstoke | Revelstoke | 1894 | 1904 | Merger |
| 29a | Perseverance | Northfield | 1894 | 1896 | Mines closed |
| 30 | Friendship | Nanaimo | 1894 | 1897 | Merger |
| 31 | Banner | Ladysmith | 1894 | 1904 | Merger |
| 32a | Mission City | Mission | 1894 | 1897 | Members left |
| 33 | Peerless | Victoria | 1894 | 1901 | Merger |
| 35 | Cedar | Cedar District | 1895 | 1902 | Merger |
| 37 | Carson | Carson City | 1896 | 1901 | Few members |
| 38 | Boundary Valley | Greenwood | 1897 | 1922 | Mines closed |
| 39 | Silver City | Sandon | 1897 | 1935 | |
| 40 | Slocan | Slocan City | 1897 | 1971 | |
| 41 | Trout Lake | Trout Lake | 1898 | 1912 | Mines closed |
| 44 | Wildey Lodge | Moyie | 1900 | 1915 | Mines closed |
| 29b | Perseverance | Ladysmith | 1901 | 1904 | Merger |
| 46 | Snowshoe | Phoenix | 1901 | 1920 | Mines closed |
| 49 | Camborne | Beaton | 1903 | 1913 | Mines closed |
| 53 | Maple Leaf | Hosmer | 1908 | 1914 | Merger |
| 56 | Mount Ida | Salmon Arm | 1908 | 1925 | Not given |
| 63 | Prince Rupert | Prince Rupert | 1910 | 1978 | |
| 64 | Corbin | Corbin | 1910 | 1935 | |
| 32b | Maple Ridge | Haney | 1922 | 1980 | |

investments, and other sources; and expenses for sick claims, other lodge benefits, and operating costs. The implicit-degree-of-risk-loading and probability-of-ruin estimates also require information about the lengths of sick spells for claimants. An aggregate sick claim of $100, for example, could arise from the claim of one member for ten weeks, or two or more members for shorter spells of sickness.

IOOF statistics do not show the internal composition for a lodge's aggregate claim. Accordingly we estimate the aggregate claims distribution for each lodge's aggregate sick claim payment and number of claimants. We model the distribution as a Compound-Poisson process. Our method allows for probabilities of different numbers of claims and also the probability that a given number of claims would generate the aggregate claim statistic. Appendix E provides the technical details for estimation of the Compound-Poisson aggregate claims distribution, the application of the implicit risk-loading measure; and the application of the probability-of-ruin measure.

THE FINDINGS The description of the findings includes technical information for readers who have read Appendix E. Other readers can ignore the technical information and pick out the substantive claims.

THE AGGREGATE CLAIMS DISTRIBUTION Table 4.8 reports the estimated coefficients for the Compound-Poisson Aggregate Claims Distribution for the twenty-seven lodges. Each coefficient is statistically significant (the *t*-ratio statistic, the coefficient divided by the standard error, is greater than 2).

As the coefficients for lodge age and lodge age$^2$ show, the amount that a lodge paid for claims (its aggregate claim size) increased the longer it was in operation. Our detailed findings, not reported here, show that the lodge's expected number of claims entered a rising trend in its the twelfth year of operation. The average size of claims rose through to lodge age twenty and then declined. Except for the drop in average claim size after twenty, these findings fit known age-related trends for acute and chronic diseases (see chapter 1). The risk of chronic illness increased with age, and the risk of acute illness peaked at the extremes of age (before age twenty after age sixty-five).

The estimated coefficients for $D_{Open}$ indicate that lodges had below-average claim sizes during their first two years of operation. As the estimated coefficients for $D_{Urb}$ indicate, city lodges had above-average claim sizes. The coefficient on M, the membership size variable in the parameter for expected number of claims, was significantly greater than zero. Although the number of claimants rose with membership size, the claim rate (the number of claims per member) did not.

Table 4.9 shows the predicted and observed sick claims per member. In general the predictions are plausible. The difference between the pre-

Table 4.8
Estimated Coefficients for the Compound-Poisson Distribution[a]

| δ (X) | *Coefficient* | *Standard Error* | *T-Ratio* |
|---|---|---|---|
| M | 0.014318 | 0.00083827 | 17.080 |
| $D_{Open}$ | −2.579 | 0.32041 | −8.049 |
| Age | −0.02748 | 0.0082048 | −3.349 |
| $Age^2$ | 0.0010744 | 0.00022845 | 4.7031 |
| $D_{Urb}$ | 0.37481 | 0.073235 | 5.118 |
| Constant | 0.64514 | 0.075233 | 8.5752 |
| *β (X)* | *Coefficient* | *Standard Error* | *T-Ratio* |
| $D_{Open}$ | 0.28883 | 0.31831 | 0.90739 |
| Age | −0.022599 | 0.0085803 | −2.6338 |
| $Age^2$ | 0.00054215 | 0.0002403 | 2.2558 |
| $D_{Urb}$ | −0.18020 | 0.058781 | 3.0656 |
| Constant | −3.5771 | 0.059144 | −60.481 |

[a] Number of Observations = 397. δ (X) = expected number of claims; β (X) = expected claim size. The −LLF = 7389.096. Under the null hypothesis (all coefficients equal zero except the constants) yields $-LLF_R$= 7803.928. The likelihood ratio test statistic is 829.66 and is distributed $X^2(9)$.

dicted and observed statistics for all twenty-seven lodges ($3.22 and $3.13) is a mere 2.9 per cent. For the lodges individually, the predicted statistic is higher in sixteen cases and lower in eleven cases.

The prediction errors reflect random fluctuations in small numbers. In addition, the algorithm for prediction overstates a lodge's exposure to risk for periods when its members experience unusually high levels of membership arrearage due to unemployment. This helps to explain why the predicted statistic is high for Sandon No. 39, a lodge that paid no benefits between 1911 and 1913 when mining output in the area was negligible (Karlsson, 1989). We cannot explain why the predicted statistic is notably low in three cases (lodges 14, 31, and 22), each of which had one to three years of exceptionally high aggregate sick claims.

Like the known aggregate claims, the estimated aggregate claims consumed a growing proportion of receipts from membership dues as the lodge aged. We turn now to the implications of this rising trend for the financial viability of the lodges.

Table 4.9
Predicted and Observed Dollars of Sick Relief per Member, Average for Years of Operation*

| *Lodge No.* | *Location* | *Predicted* | *Observed* |
|---|---|---|---|
| All lodges, 1890–1929 | | 3.22 | 3.13 |
| 13 (1890–9) | New Westminster | 4.16 | 3.03 |
| 14 (1891–8) | Victoria | 4.14 | 5.42 |
| 15 (1891–1929) | Cloverdale | 3.56 | 3.94 |
| 17 (1892–1929) | Duncan | 3.18 | 2.70 |
| 20 (1892–1907) | Nanaimo | 5.17 | 5.51 |
| 22 (1892–1906) | North Bend | 2.97 | 4.67 |
| 25 (1894–1904) | Revelstoke | 2.59 | 3.37 |
| 29a (1894–6) | Northfield | 2.35 | 4.42 |
| 30 (1894–7) | Nanaimo | 3.70 | 4.08 |
| 31 (1894–1904) | Ladysmith | 2.44 | 4.35 |
| 32a (1894–7) | Mission | 2.46 | 2.02 |
| 33 (1894–1901) | Victoria | 5.26 | 4.77 |
| 35 (1895–1902) | Cedar District | 2.43 | 5.35 |
| 37 (1896–1901) | Carson City | 3.26 | 1.71 |
| 38 (1897–1922) | Greenwood | 2.89 | 2.81 |
| 39 (1897–1929) | Sandon | 3.38 | 2.98 |
| 40 (1897–1929) | Slocan City | 3.41 | 2.74 |
| 41 (1898–1912) | Trout Lake | 3.00 | 2.42 |
| 44 (1900–15) | Moyie | 2.76 | 2.35 |
| 29b (1901–4) | Ladysmith | 2.11 | 2.17 |
| 46 (1901–20) | Phoenix | 2.87 | 3.62 |
| 49 (1903–13) | Beaton | 3.72 | 2.22 |
| 53 (1908–14) | Hosmer | 2.25 | 1.04 |
| 56 (1908–25) | Salmon Arm | 3.43 | 1.25 |
| 63 (1910–29) | Prince Rupert | 2.65 | 2.33 |
| 64 (1910–29) | Corbin | 2.69 | 2.64 |
| 32b (1922–29) | Haney | 2.45 | 1.40 |

* The expected sick relief per member is calculated with the estimated coefficients in Table 4.8, and, in Appendix E, the specifications for $\delta$ (X) and $\beta$ (X) given in (15) and E[Z] from (8). The total expected relief is divided by the number of members.

THE RISK-LOADING ESTIMATES The risk-loading measure shows whether revenues were sufficient to cover operating costs and expected sick claims.[20] A positive risk-loading statistic shows that the revenues are more than adequate, a zero statistic indicates that revenues are barely adequate, and a negative statistic implies that the lodge would need to dip into its reserves to meet the expected costs. Finally, a statistic of less than −1 shows that revenues cannot even meet operating expenses.

Table 4.10 reports the risk-loading estimates for the 1891–1920 period. The risk-loading statistics are extreme for a lodge's first two years, when its dues revenues are unusually low and its revenues from joining fees and operating costs are unusually high. Hence we exclude those years from calculation.

The statistics for dues revenues only (column I) are negative for sixteen of the twenty-seven lodges. For all twenty-seven the expected sick claims would have exceeded dues revenues in 48 per cent of their years of operation. Thus lodge dues were insufficient to meet expected claims. Perforce they were inadequate for accumulating reserves to fund the higher future claim rates that were to come with the aging of members.

Not all lodge revenues came from membership dues, however. The balance came from joining fees (for the four degrees of membership), property rents, and returns on invested funds. When we included revenues from all sources in the risk-loading estimates (Table 4.10, column II), net revenues covered expected claims in all but two lodges. Sick claims exceeded net revenues in only 18 per cent of the total of 397 years of operation for all twenty-seven lodges. This compared to 48 per cent for dues revenues only. By investing these surpluses, the lodges obtained extra-dues revenues to help cover sick claims in later years. Effectively they used profits to subsidize the insurance benefit.

Before judging that the IOOF's pricing practices were financially sound, however, we must investigate whether the lodges were likely to fail because of high claims in a given year.

THE PROBABILITY-OF-RUIN ESTIMATES Table 4.11 presents the average probabilities of ruin for the lodges' years of operation. Clearly the lodges had little chance of becoming insolvent.[21] During the first five years of operation, the probability of ruin for all twenty-seven lodges was a minuscule 0.0008 per cent. With the exception of Prince Rupert Lodge No. 63, it then declined towards zero.

Contrary to conventional wisdom, a lodge was more likely to meet with financial difficulties during its early years of operation rather than in later years when its membership was aging. During the early years, poor business conditions or unusually high claims could cause mem-

Table 4.10
Mean Estimated Risk-Loading Factors Calculated with Net Dues Revenues and Net Total Revenues, 1890–1929, and Percentage of Lodge Years for which the Risk-Loading Measure Was Negative*

| | | *I Dues only* | *% Years negative* | *II All revenue* | *% Years negative* |
|---|---|---|---|---|---|
| ALL LODGES | | −1.41 | .51 | 6.17 | .17 |
| First 2 Years | | −9.18 | .69 | 36.09 | .13 |
| After 2 Years | | −0.19 | .48 | 1.46 | .18 |
| INDIVIDUAL LODGES AFTER 2 YEARS | | | | | |
| 13 (1890–99) | New Westminster | −0.35 | .71 | 1.35 | .00 |
| 14 (1891–98) | Victoria | −0.23 | .60 | 0.26 | .20 |
| 15 (1891–1929) | Cloverdale | 0.29 | .16 | 1.30 | .80 |
| 17 (1892–1929) | Duncan | −0.22 | .42 | 1.96 | .14 |
| 20 (1892–1907) | Nanaimo | 0.24 | .70 | 0.70 | .00 |
| 22 (1892–1906) | North Bend | 1.06 | .80 | 2.16 | .80 |
| 25 (1894–1904) | Revelstoke | 0.96 | .13 | 5.07 | .00 |
| 29a (1894–6) | Northfield | 0.32 | .00 | 0.66 | .00 |
| 30 (1894–7) | Nanaimo | 0.17 | .00 | 0.40 | .00 |
| 31 (1894–1904) | Ladysmith | 1.48 | .00 | 2.69 | .00 |
| 32a (1894–7) | Mission | 0.18 | .00 | 0.42 | .00 |
| 33 (1894–1901) | Victoria | 0.10 | .20 | 0.28 | .20 |
| 35 (1895–1902) | Cedar District | 1.72 | .00 | 2.16 | .00 |
| 37 (1896–1901) | Carson City | −0.81 | 1.00 | −0.11 | .33 |
| 38 (1897–1922) | Greenwood | −0.61 | .54 | 1.90 | .17 |
| 39 (1897–1929) | Sandon | −0.45 | .65 | 0.98 | .19 |
| 40 (1897–1929) | Slocan City | −0.62 | .52 | 1.95 | .13 |
| 41 (1898–1912) | Trout Lake | −0.20 | .46 | 2.55 | .15 |
| 44 (1900–15) | Moyie | −0.33 | .57 | 1.15 | .21 |
| 29b (1901–4) | Ladysmith | 2.04 | .00 | 2.84 | .00 |
| 46 (1901–20) | Pheonix | −0.51 | .76 | 1.66 | .12 |
| 49 (1903–13) | Beaton | −0.31 | .88 | 0.05 | .63 |
| 53 (1908–14) | Hosmer | −1.57 | 1.00 | 0.88 | .25 |
| 56 (1908–25) | Salmon Arm | −0.81 | .92 | −0.40 | .67 |
| 63 (1910–29) | Prince Rupert | −1.16 | .89 | 0.03 | .56 |
| 64 (1910–29) | Corbin | −0.47 | .61 | 1.14 | .28 |
| 32b (1922–9) | Haney | −0.05 | .50 | 2.88 | .00 |

* The risk-loading measure reported in Column I was calculated with net dues revenues, the estimated coefficients in Table 4.8 and, in Appendix E, the specifications of δ (X) and β (X) given in (15). The risk loading measure reported in Column II was calculated with net total revenues.

Table 4.11
Mean Estimated Probabilities of Ruin, 1891–1929*

| | | After | |
|---|---|---|---|
| *All 27 Lodges* | *Overall* *0.00043* | *0–5 years* *0.000823* | *5 Years*† *0.00019* |
| 13 (1890–99) | 0.0 | 0.0 | 0.0 |
| 14 (1891–98) | 0.0000081 | 0.000004 | 0.000034 |
| 15 (1891–1929) | 0.0000038 | 0.0000006 | 0.0000043 |
| 17 (1892–1929) | 0.0 | 0.0 | 0.0 |
| 20 (1892–1907) | 0.000085 | 0.0 | 0.000136 |
| 22 (1892–1906) | 0.0 | 0.00000017 | 0.0 |
| 25 (1894–1904) | 0.0000007 | 0.0000012 | 0.0 |
| 29a (1894–6) | 0.000031 | 0.000031 | – |
| 30 (1894–7) | 0.000002 | 0.000002 | – |
| 31 (1894–1904) | 0.0 | 0.0 | 0.0 |
| 32a (1894–7) | 0.00265 | 0.00265 | – |
| 33 (1894–1901) | 0.00694 | 0.0081 | 0.000001 |
| 35 (1895–1902) | 0.000002 | 0.00000016 | 0.000013 |
| 37 (1896–1901) | 0.000068 | 0.000068 | – |
| 38 (1897–1922) | 0.0 | 0.0 | 0.0 |
| 39 (1897–1929) | 0.0 | 0.0 | 0.0 |
| 40 (1897–1929) | 0.00019 | 0.00106 | 0.0 |
| 41 (1898–1912) | 0.0000019 | 0.0000048 | 0.0 |
| 44 (1900–15) | 0.0000009 | 0.0000025 | 0.0 |
| 29b (1901–4) | 0.0000025 | 0.0000025 | – |
| 46 (1901–20) | 0.0 | 0.0 | 0.0 |
| 49 (1903–13) | 0.0056 | 0.0093 | 0.00016 |
| 53 (1908–14) | 0.0 | 0.0 | – |
| 56 (1908–25) | 0.00025 | 0.000586 | 0.0 |
| 63 (1910–29) | 0.00228 | 0.000001 | 0.00326 |
| 64 (1910–29) | 0.0 | 0.0 | 0.0 |
| 32b (1922–9) | 0.0 | 0.0 | 0.0 |

* Reported revenues from all sources and reported asset values are the data for calculation. The probability-of-ruin statistics state the probability that claims in a given year would exceed total assets and revenues net of operating expenses. The statistics by column are means for all lodge years of operation, the first five years of operation, and all years after the first five years.

† This calculated average excludes the ruin probabilities for lodges 15 and 17 in 1894, the only cases with a ruin probability of 1. Both lodges had unusually high current expenses for the year, probably due to the purchase or construction of a lodge hall.

bers to lose confidence in their lodge. Between 1894 and 1897, for example, Acme Lodge No. 14 in Victoria (1891–8) experienced a 39 per cent loss of members and a 33 per cent decline in assets per member. The apparent catalyst was the high cost of sick claims in 1895: $13.11 per member, compared to under $6 for most lodges and annual dues of $12.

For financial stability in its later years, a lodge needed to amass surplus revenues for investment during its early years of operation. Prince Rupert Lodge No. 63, the only one of the twenty-seven lodges whose probability of ruin increased over time, apparently failed to do this. Of the twenty-seven lodges, this lodge had the lowest per-capita revenues, the highest per-capita operating costs per member, and one of the lowest per-capita statistics for assets.

## CONCLUSION

The financial practices of friendly societies have received a bad press. During the study period fraternal reformers and abolitionists presented them as a recipe for financial ruin. Recent scholarly studies have echoed their indictment. As this chapter shows, however, nineteenth-century British actuaries used a problematic valuation-method appraisal to find that IOOFMU lodges had insufficient revenues to cover deferred liabilities. Similarly, the IOOF's grand sire made selective use of revenue statistics to find that IOOF the lodges were losing money during the 1920s.

Simply put, the critics were wrong. With their intrusive methods, the Odd Fellow lodges managed the problems of moral hazard and adverse selection more efficiently than commercial insurers could. The lodges did not have actuarial pricing, but neither did commercial insurers of the day. Despite rising-cost pressures, most grand lodges reported net profits for their lodges. In any case, net lodge profits predicted poorly which grand lodge jurisdictions were to abolish the sick benefit between 1925 and 1929.

In British Columbia the weakest lodges had adequate revenues to cover deferred liabilities. They also had a negligible probability of ruin from high claims in a particular year. Thus none of the twenty lodge closures before 1930 involved the bankruptcy of lodge assets.[22]

Typically lodges obtained revenue surpluses from dues and joining fees during their early years of operation, when their members were young and had below-average sick claims. This enabled them to use income from assets in later years, when the members were older and had above-average claim rates. Contrary to conventional wisdom, the critical period for lodges was their early years of operation when they needed to amass reserves, not their later years when their high claim rates were rising.

Rising-cost pressures brought the sick benefit to the attention of Odd Fellows. Yet their financial practices were sound. In principle they could have responded by increasing revenues. Why, then, did they reduce the value of the benefit and ultimately abolish it? Perhaps an upsurge of competition gave them direction. Chapter 5 explores this possibility.

# 5 Competition in the IOOF's Insurance Market, 1890–1929

The IOOF lessened its provisions for the sick benefit after 1890. The SGL made the benefit optional for grand encampments in 1896 and grand lodges in 1925. Thirty-eight per cent of the patriarchs had become non-beneficial members of their encampments by 1924, and one-third of the lodge members had become non-beneficial by 1929.

As chapter 4 demonstrated, these developments did not arise from financial weaknesses. The IOOF's moral ideals and decentralized lodge system allowed it to administer its sick benefit efficiently. Rising-cost pressures influenced the declining trend for the benefit, but did not drive the lodges to financial cataclysm. The assets of lodges were adequate to cover their deferred liabilities. The lodges also had a low probability of ruin from high claims in a particular year.

This chapter investigates whether competition crowded the Odd Fellows from the sickness insurance market. Its findings reject the possibility that rival insurers forced the decline of the IOOF's sick benefit. The competition from other insurers intensified before the First World War, but was stable or declining during the 1920s. In contrast, new priorities among the Odd Fellows and in the larger society provided strong opportunity-cost competition for the sick benefit during the 1920s. Even so, rising-opportunity cost is an incomplete explanation for the sick benefit's declining trend.

## THE IOOF'S PRODUCTS AND MARKET

The sick benefit was the IOOF's principal insurance product. A lodge sold the sick benefit in one quantity: the sum and coverage period that its bylaws stipulated. In some localities an Odd Fellow could buy a second quantity of benefit by joining an encampment. By 1924, however, many encampments had discontinued the sick benefit.

Members of a lodge were both sellers and buyers of the insurance contract. Subject to the IOOF's general requirements, the members could alter its terms by passing bylaws for the purpose. They could change the amount of the membership dues, the weekly amount of the benefit, or the coverage period of the benefit. But they could not end the contract; each member remained eligible for the lodge's stipulated benefit as long as he kept his dues paid up.

The price of the sick benefit was the lodge's price of membership. This price included an entry tariff (fees of $20–$25 for the four degrees of membership); regular quarterly dues; and exposure to the risk of fines and per-capita assessments. Some lodges used assessments to fund their funeral benefit. The SGL required a lodge to assess its members if it fell into financial difficulty.

The main purpose of the entry tariff was to discourage older men from joining. To this end, the lodges scaled the amount of their joining fees by the member's age at joining. Once the member had paid the Odd Fellow's entry fee, the entry tariffs of other fraternal orders discouraged him from switching to one of them to get a bigger benefit or lower price. Thus a lodge used benefits as "bait" for new members and joining fees to "set the hook." Its competitive goal was to beat its rivals to the "fish." To assist lodges in the task, the SGL provided for lodges for junior Odd Fellows in 1923 and lowered the minimum age for members in 1924.

THE MARKET The Odd Fellows were white men, largely Anglo-Protestants, from upper working-class and lower middle-class backgrounds. These attributes were the IOOF's template for competition. Conversely, the IOOF did not compete with sickness insurers who had different markets.

## THE IOOF'S RIVALS IN SICKNESS INSURANCE

Disability insurance was available from government programs, commercial insurers, labour unions, employer-sponsored mutual benefit societies, friendly societies, and fraternal life insurance orders. These insurers differed in their combinations of products, the weighting and cost of particular products, and the bundling of products. Unlike the IOOF, commercial insurers sold insurance in different amounts and without fellowship. Also unlike the IOOF, certain friendly societies offered an optional endowment benefit, and life insurance fraternal orders provided a mandatory life insurance benefit with optional sick and funeral benefits.

COMPETITION FROM GOVERNMENT Compulsory government sickness insurance dated from 1883 in Germany and 1911 in Britain.[1] With strong backing from the American Federation of Labor (AFL), eight state commissions, two national conferences, and several state legislatures attended to the issue during the years 1915–18 (Armstrong, 1932: s.II). Despite these initiatives, government sickness insurance did not exist in the United States or Canada.

Workmen's compensation was another matter. Forty-two American states and six Canadian provinces passed workmen's compensation laws between 1911 and 1925 (Weis, 1935; Leacy, 1983). By 1929 only Arkansas, Florida, Georgia, Louisiana, Mississippi, New Mexico, North Carolina, South Carolina, Saskatchewan, and Prince Edward Island were without such a law.

Government workmen's compensation programs provided negligible competition for the IOOF sick benefit. First, industrial accidents accounted for less than 10 per cent of all disability (Armstrong, 1932: 284ff; Britton, 1940; Osborn, 1958: ch. 1).

Second, the laws in place missed much of the labour force. Half of the American state laws in 1917 and one-fifth of them in 1932 applied only to persons in hazardous occupations. None of the laws covered employees of interstate railways. In thirty-two states, workmen's compensation was optional for employees. The law exempted small businesses in twenty-four states and public employees in five states. Some state laws were so hedged about with restrictions that payment of the benefit was uncertain. Although comprehensive by American standards, Ontario's law omitted persons in farming, wholesale and retail establishments, and domestic service (Guest, 1980: 45).

COMMERCIAL INSURANCE Commercial insurers sold policies to individuals and group plans to employers. Casualty insurance companies dominated commercial sales to individuals, while life insurance companies controlled sales of group plans. Neither individual nor group plan sales offered severe competition for the IOOF's sick benefit before 1930.

During the late nineteenth century, casualty insurers began to insure against selected diseases, as a free addition to their profitable accident insurance policies. In time, they extended the additional coverage to all diseases, due to difficulties in distinguishing between covered and non-covered diseases (Osborn, 1958: ch. 4). Both casualty and life insurers sold one-year term policies to individuals. They sold different amounts of weekly indemnity, provided always that the amount was less than full income replacement. They charged premiums at a flat rate to age forty-nine, and then a sharply higher rate (James, 1947: 262–6; Dublin, 1943: ch. 9).[2]

Commercial sales to individuals were minor competition for the IOOF sick benefit. First, the volume of commercial sales was small. Although during the years 1921–8 Metropolitan Life, for example, increased the number of its policies in force from 9,071 to 117,984, its twenty thousand agents sold only 49,801 new policies in 1928 – that is, about two per agent (James, 1947: 262–6; Dublin, 1943: ch. 9). By our estimate, commercial policies captured only 30 per cent of the Canadian market during the years 1917–18.[3]

Second, commercial insurers sold to upper middle-class men, not the IOOF's lower middle-class and working-class market. The commercial product provided for a much higher amount of weekly benefit at substantially greater cost. In 1921, for example, a commercial policy commonly paid a weekly indemnity of $25 for an annual premium of $60 (Epstein, 1933: ch. 23; Rubinow, 1913: ch. 18). In contrast, the sixteen thousand IOOF lodges had a mean weekly benefit of $2.85 and mean annual dues of $6.38. Differences in social-class culture reinforced this market segregation. Unlike working-class Odd Fellows, for example, the high-income men who bought commercial policies preferred market insurance without fellowship.

High overhead costs also kept the price of the commercial product out of the reach of wage workers. Commercial insurers used paid agents to recruit new business and paid officials to administer the business. In contrast, lodges of friendly societies used their members to recruit new business and unpaid and nominally paid officers to administer the sick benefit. Commercial insurers also lacked the lodge's intrusive methods of monitoring sick claims. Thus they suffered more from the problems of moral hazard and adverse selection.

COMMERCIAL GROUP DISABILITY INSURANCE Group insurance originated in 1912 when the Equitable Life Insurance Company bought group life and group disability insurance for its employees.[4] Subsequently life insurance companies established group insurance branches to specialize in the sale of group plans to corporate customers. Employers bought group plans to show goodwill, win the loyalty of their employees, and secure labour peace. Employees viewed them as a form of wages and potentially an object for collective bargaining.

Canadian insurance law delayed the entry of group insurance into Canada. In 1919 the Dominion Insurance Superintendent ruled that group insurance was permissible under the Dominion Insurance Act

(Campbell, 1966). Life companies, however, could not insure risks other than life until 1922, when an amendment to the Dominion Act removed the restriction.[5] Only then could life companies write group disability policies for the Canadian market.

Group insurance used an employer's mass purchasing power to provide low-cost coverage without a medical examination. The insurer sold group disability plans on a one-year renewable term basis. The insurer made the contract with the employer, and the employer issued certificates to employees in the plan.[6] The employer paid the premium in a non-contributory plan, whereas in the alternative contributory plan, the employees paid part or all the premium through payroll reduction. The insurer's overhead costs were low because the employer kept the records, paid claims, and made payroll deductions in contributory plans.

The employer chose the type of group plan insurance (life, disability, annuity, death, and dismemberment). He could also select two or more plans for a group plan package. Group life plans were the primary product, but disability plans commonly were a secondary feature in packages that featured life insurance. Alternatively, the insurer used disability plans as a Trojan horse for the sale of group life plans (*Gold Dust*, March 1929; Ilse, 1953: 174).

The insurer restricted participation in a group plan to full-time employees, and the minimum size for a group was twenty-five. For a contributory plan to take effect, the participating employees had to be 75 per cent of those eligible. In the London Life Insurance Company, the percentage was 85 if the group had less than fifty members. A non-contributory plan insured all eligible employees on the date the contract took effect. A contributory plan allowed the employee thirty-one days to enter the group without medical evidence of insurability.

The insurer limited the amount of the weekly indemnity to two-thirds of the employee's average weekly earnings, to a maximum of $40. The coverage excluded workplace accidents that workmen's compensation covered. It also excluded disability that a physician had not treated. London Life issued forty-one contracts during 1928 and 1929. The maximum period of coverage was thirteen weeks in thirty-one cases (76 per cent), six weeks in five cases, twenty-six weeks in four cases, and ten weeks in one contract. The contract specified a waiting period of three, four, seven, or fourteen days of sickness. According to Ilse, the usual practice was a seven-day waiting period. A three-day waiting period was common in contracts issued by London Life.

Some contracts set the weekly indemnity at a flat rate, such as $10. More commonly, the contracts tied the amount to the employee's earnings or position in the company. One London Life contract, for example, set the indemnity at $40 for executives, $25 for branch managers, $15 for foremen, and $10 for others. The usual lowest amount was $10. One London Life contract, however, set the indemnity at $8 for apprentices and women; another contract set a $5 rate for employees with weekly earnings of between $8 and $10.

The insurer charged the same premium for each person in the insured group, and the amount of the premium depended on the details that the employer selected for the plan. During the early 1920s insurers used IOOFMU tables for 1893–7 to calculate their premiums. One large insurer charged a monthly premium of 88 cents ($10.56 per annum) for a $10 weekly indemnity with a seven-day waiting period, and a coverage period of twenty-six weeks. Based on experience, the company lowered its price to 86 cents ($10.32 per annum) in 1927 (Ilse, 1953). In Canada, London Life's price for such a policy would have been $10.24 (*Gold Dust*, 1928: 53ff).

Group insurance potentially was serious competition for the IOOF's member-funded flat-rate sick benefit. A non-contributory employer's plan automatically covered all employees, including any Odd Fellows among them. Where the employee's participation was voluntary (contributory plans), the employer paid part of the premium. Plans of both types tied the amount of the indemnity to the employee's earnings or position.

Despite its attractions, group plans compared poorly to the IOOF's sick benefit in some respects. The IOOF's price included a range of benefits, not just sickness insurance, and the sick benefit was in force as long the member paid his dues. In contrast, the employee's group coverage ended if either the employer or insurer did not renew the contract, or if the employee changed jobs. Job turnover was primarily a problem for young men in the early stages of their working lives (James, 1994: 185–204). Young men, in turn, headed the demand for market insurance.

What is more important, group disability plans were not sufficiently widespread during the 1920s to have crowded the IOOF out of the sickness insurance field. Contracts issued by Metropolitan Life, by far the largest of the group disability insurers, covered just 26,000 Americans in 1921 and 615,454 Americans in 1928.[7] Group disability plans were unavailable in Canada until 1925, when Metropolitan Life introduced them. By our estimate, group plans covered just 39,000 Canadians by 1929.[8] The small numbers in American and Canadian group plans, moreover, included women, Roman Catholics, low-income workers, persons with poor health, men of colour, and others outside the IOOF's insurance market.

LABOUR UNIONS Unions traditionally used benefits to attract members and hold the loyalty of existing members (Boyer, 1988). During the 1850s, for example, British unions such as the Amalgamated Society of Carpenters and Joiners used benefits to recruit Canadian members (Logan, 1948: 28, 76). During the 1890s miners' unions in the American west and British Columbia reportedly devoted more time to mutual aid than to collective bargaining (Derickson, 1988: ch. 3).

By 1907 nineteen unions, accounting for 25 per cent of organized labour in the United States, offered a sick benefit (Rubinow, 1913: ch. 18). By 1930 forty-six of 105 AFL unions had a sick benefit.[9] In 1916 28 of 78 international unions in Ontario (37 per cent) paid sick claims.[10] In 1913 fourteen of thirty-one unions in Hamilton, Ontario, had a sick benefit; another had an optional sick benefit; another gave its sick members discretionary assistance; and another remitted the member's dues for the period of sickness. The amount of the weekly benefit in Hamilton's unions ranged from $2.50 (the Amalgamated Society of Engineers) to $8.00 (one of the four boot and shoe workers' internationals). The most common amount, $5.00, was paid in five cases, one of them a female boot and shoe workers' international.[11]

Competition from unions, however, did not force the IOOF from the sickness insurance market. First, unions with a sick benefit included Roman Catholics, Jews, women, and others who were outside the IOOF's market. Second, after years of steady growth, the union movement declined during the 1920s (see Table 5.1).[12] The declining trend was steeper for American unions than for Canadian ones, and steeper in either country than for the IOOF. In line with the trend for Canadian union membership, the membership of Ontario's six registered union sick benefit societies fell by 21 per cent between 1921 and 1925. Although membership in four of them increased by 12 per cent between 1925 and 1929, the two others ceased operation.[13]

In a few cases, unions abandoned the direct union provision of sickness insurance in favour of collective bargaining agreements that included commercial group disability insurance. In 1926 the Street Railway Workers' Union in Newburgh, New York, was the first union to obtain sickness insurance in this fashion (Ilse, 1953: ch. 13). In a second case, the Chicago Surface Lines and Elevated Railway Lines Company agreed to contributory group life and group disability plans for its eighteen hundred employees in 1928 (*Gold Dust*, April 1928).

EMPLOYER-SPONSORED SICK BENEFIT SOCIETIES Employer-sponsored sick benefit societies originated in a tradition of corporate paternalism during the 1870s. By 1908 the United States had over five hundred such societies, compared to twenty-two in Ontario. Before the

Table 5.1
IOOF and Union Membership in the United States and Canada: Ratio to Peak Year

| | *United States* | | *Canada* | |
|---|---|---|---|---|
| | *IOOF* | *Union* | *IOOF* | *Union* |
| 1911 | 0.82 | 0.46 | 0.73 | 0.35 |
| 1912 | 0.84 | 0.49 | 0.79 | 0.42 |
| 1913 | 0.85 | 0.54 | 0.74 | 0.47 |
| 1914 | 0.85 | 0.53 | 0.87 | 0.44 |
| 1915 | 0.84 | 0.51 | 0.87 | 0.38 |
| 1916 | 0.85 | 0.55 | 0.86 | 0.42 |
| 1917 | 0.86 | 0.61 | 0.87 | 0.54 |
| 1918 | 0.86 | 0.69 | 0.87 | 0.66 |
| 1919 | 0.91 | 0.82 | 0.93 | 1.00* |
| 1920 | 0.98 | 1.00* | 0.98 | 0.99 |
| 1921 | 1.00* | 0.95 | 1.00* | 0.83 |
| 1922 | 0.98 | 0.80 | 0.99 | 0.73 |
| 1923 | 0.96 | 0.72 | 0.98 | 0.74 |
| 1924 | 0.95 | 0.70 | 0.97 | 0.69 |
| 1925 | 0.94 | 0.70 | 0.97 | 0.72 |
| 1926 | 0.91 | 0.69 | 0.96 | 0.73 |
| 1927 | 0.89 | 0.70 | 0.95 | 0.77 |
| 1928 | 0.85 | 0.69 | 0.93 | 0.80 |
| 1929 | 0.80 | 0.68 | 0.91 | 0.85 |

* peak year

First World War the company societies typically obtained most of their funds from employee dues. The Lysaght Dominion Sheet Metal Company in Hamilton, Ontario, for example, limited its contribution to revenues obtained from salvaging waste paper in the plant (McCallum, 1990: 54). In this fashion, the company encouraged its employees to be self-reliant.

Employee participation was voluntary in 85 per cent of American societies surveyed on the eve of the First World War.[14] Eligibility for membership commonly required a waiting period, such as a minimum period of permanent employment. The coverage ceased when the employee left the firm. The benefit, \$5–\$6 per week for up to thirteen weeks, was similar to that of IOOF lodges, and the dues commonly were \$2.50 to \$6 per annum (Millis, 1937: ch. 1; Rubinow, 1913). Funds connected with certain American railway companies were an exception. Because railway employees had high wages, their benefit ranged up to \$17.50 a week and the dues ranged up to \$60 annually.

On balance, the company society and IOOF benefits were comparable for price and the amount. From an employee's viewpoint, a company society compared poorly in some ways. Eligibility for membership commonly required a waiting period and classification as a full-time worker. The benefits stopped if the worker left the firm, which might happen when he was too old or unhealthy to find coverage elsewhere. The employees had no voice in some societies. In the Endicott-Johnson Company's society in Binghamton, New York, during the years 1896–1916, autocratic department foremen ruled whether the member was truly sick and qualified for benefits (Zahavi, 1988: ch. 1). In the circumstances, some men with access to a company society preferred to be Odd Fellows. Using information for Toronto in 1911, for example, we identified fifty Odd Fellows whose employer had a sick benefit society.

The conditions for company sick benefit societies changed during the First World War (Jacoby, 1985: ch. 5). Wartime conscription and curbs on immigration created a shortage of labour. Union membership soared and worker militancy, marked by absenteeism and strikes, increased. To maintain production, government helped unions to recruit members without company interference, supported collective bargaining, and developed industry-wide standards for wages and working conditions.

In these circumstances, employers set out to win the loyalty of their workers. They developed hitherto piecemeal and paternalistic welfare provisions into a structured, coherent labour policy known as corporate welfarism. Elements of the new policy included industrial councils (company unions) with joint labour-management participation; personnel departments that standardized hiring and firing; profit-sharing and stock-purchase plans; pension plans; death and sick benefits; company recreational facilities; and housing assistance (Brandes, 1976; McCallum, 1990).

In the meantime, union leaders shifted their strategy from confrontation to cooperation (Bernstein, 1960: ch. 2). Samuel Gompers, head of the AFL, linked wages to productivity, which he believed was rising and could accelerate through cooperation. His successor, William Green, past president of the United Mine Workers and an Odd Fellow, also promoted cooperation, to raise wages and make unions respectable with the American public.

Non-union workers embraced welfare capitalism for their own reasons. At the Endicott-Johnson shoe company in Binghamton, New York, workers regarded corporate benefits as a form of wages that they had earned (Zahavi, 1988: ch. 4). Subsequently they used benefits obtained during the war as a benchmark for judging company policies during the 1920s, when the supply of labour was abundant again. Thus the company negotiated for its workers' loyalty and obtained it with strings attached.

During the 1920s welfare capitalism lost much of its attraction for businessmen. At the war's end, the economy slumped, the supply of labour became abundant, unions were cooperative and losing members, and wartime economic controls ended. These circumstances relieved the pressure on businessmen to promote welfare programs. Consequently welfare capitalism was a minority phenomenon during the 1920s. Although common in large firms, it never reached more than one worker in seven. In 1929 sick benefit societies existed in 30 per cent of large firms, but in just 4.5 per cent of small firms, which accounted for half the industrial work force (Jacoby, 1985: ch. 6). In 1931 the number of workers in company societies was higher than in 1908 (825,000 compared to 640,000), but the number of societies was down (Brandes, 1976: ch. 10).

The evidence for Ontario fits the American trends. The provincial insurance department registered thirty-one new company societies during the period 1885–1914, seventeen in the years 1918–20, and seven during the years 1921–9. Forty of the fifty-five societies (73 per cent) involved Toronto firms, and all but one involved firms in cities. In 1925 the memberships of forty-two societies ranged from seventy to eighteen hundred. During the 1920s the memberships in the province's registered societies followed a flat trend: seventeen thousand in 1921, twenty-one thousand in 1925, and twenty thousand in 1929.

On balance, the company sick benefit societies were important competition for the IOOF's sick benefit mainly in cities. This helps to explain why Ontario Odd Fellows were a lower proportion of the population in cities than in smaller urban places. Although important, competition from company societies was stable, not rising, during the 1920s.

## FRIENDLY SOCIETIES AND LIFE INSURANCE FRATERNAL ORDERS

The IOOF's chief friendly society rivals were the Knights of Pythias, the Loyal Order of Moose, the Fraternal Order of Eagles, and the Foresters of America (an American offshoot of the Ancient Order of Foresters that did not operate in Canada). The IOOF also faced competition from life insurance orders that offered an optional sick benefit. The Woodmen of the World, the Maccabees, the Independent Order of Foresters, and the Royal Arcanum were the largest organizations in this group.

In the life insurance orders, a member qualified for the optional disability benefit by joining a "sickness and funeral branch," subject to passing a medical examination. The branch benefit was much like commercial insurance and contrasted sharply with arrangements in friendly societies.[15] Whereas the lodges paid sick claims in a friendly society, a central office paid claims from a "sick and funeral fund" in the life insurance orders. This helped to diversify the risk, but had drawbacks for overhead costs and the problems of adverse selection and moral hazard. Like commercial insurers, the central office charged monthly premiums, paid in advance, not by quarterly dues. The central office could cancel the member's sickness insurance by giving him notice. This was closer to the commercial practice of renewable one-year term contracts than to the IOOF provision, whereby the member remained eligible for the benefit as long as he paid his dues. The member could draw benefits for a maximum of twenty-six weeks in the Maccabees but only for twelve weeks in the Independent Order of Foresters and the Canadian Order of Foresters.[16] An Odd Fellow, by contrast, could draw benefits for the duration of his illness until the rules changed in 1917, and then up to a maximum of one year during the years 1917–25.

The competitive mix for friendly societies varied by region and locality. Although the Odd Fellows had twice the membership of the Knights of Pythias, for example, the Knights were the more numerous in Florida, Louisiana, Mississippi, North Carolina, and South Carolina. The Fraternal Order of Eagles, founded in Seattle in 1898, drew most of its members from the Mississippi valley and Rocky Mountain regions (Preuss, 1924: 133). In 1892 the Improved Order of Red Men drew 66 per cent of its members come from Pennsylvania, Massachusetts, New Jersey, New York, and Indiana (Litchfield, 1893). Neither the Redmen nor the Foresters of America had lodges in Canada. Neither the Ancient Order of Foresters nor the Sons of England had lodges in the United States.

The major orders were only part of the IOOF's fraternal competition. In 1897, for example, Ingersoll, Ontario, a town with a population of forty-five hundred, supported no less than fifteen fraternal lodges that provided a sick benefit. Besides its two IOOF lodges, the town had lodges of the Canadian Order of Odd Fellows, Ancient Order of Foresters, Canadian Order of Foresters, Independent Order of Foresters, Royal Arcanum, Canadian Order of Home Circles, Maccabees,

Table 5.2
Number of Odd Fellows for Each Member in Other Societies with a Sick Benefit

| *Friendly Societies* | *1915* | *1920* | *1925* | *1929* |
|---|---|---|---|---|
| IOOF | 1.0 | 1.0 | 1.0 | 1.0 |
| Knights of Pythias | 2.2 | 2.5 | 2.1 | 1.8 |
| Loyal Order of Moose | 2.6 | n.d. | 2.9 | 2.6 |
| Fraternal Order of Eagles | 4.1 | 4.4 | 3.5 | 3.4 |
| Improved Order of Red Men | 3.4 | 3.7 | 3.6 | 4.2 |
| Foresters of America* | 7.9 | n.d. | 7.2 | 9.5 |
| LIFE INSURANCE ORDERS | | | | |
| Knights of the Maccabees | 4.9 | 5.6 | 8.9 | 5.0 |
| Independent Order of Foresters* | 7.4 | 9.9 | 11.7 | 8.7 |
| Royal Arcanum | 6.6 | 12.1 | 15.1 | 11.3 |

* benefits available to women

Ancient Order of United Workmen, Woodmen of the World, Royal Templars of Temperance, Orange Order, the Sons of England, and the Catholic Mutual Benefit Association (a Roman Catholic friendly society).[17]

During the early twentieth century, however, the IOOF's competition from fraternal rivals was stable or declining. First, there is evidence from membership trends. As Table 5.2 shows, the Odd Fellows had twice the membership of the Knights of Pythias, the second-largest friendly society in 1925. They also had 3.5 times the membership of the Woodmen of the World, the largest life insurance order with an optional sick benefit.[18] Although the Odd Fellows lost some ground to the Loyal Order of Moose and Fraternal Order of Eagles during the 1920s, they held their own against other orders.

Second, like the IOOF, two major friendly societies were withdrawing from the sickness insurance field. In 1894 the supreme lodge of the Knights of Pythias enabled grand lodges to require or abolish sick benefit or make it optional for lodges. It also enabled a lodge to abolish the benefit if its grand lodge did not require it.[19] By 1902 the grand lodge of Minnesota had abolished the sick benefit. In 1914 the grand chancellor for British Columbia "believed, though [he had] not checked it, that the majority of subordinate lodges in [British Columbia] have dis-

Table 5.3
Ontario: Number of Odd Fellows for Each Person with a Sick Benefit in Other Largely Protestant Orders

| | *1921* | *1925* | *1929* |
|---|---|---|---|
| Independent Order of Odd Fellows | 1.0 | 1.0 | 1.0 |
| Canadian Order of Foresters | 2.8 | 4.2 | 4.2 |
| Sons of England | 3.7 | 4.5 | 4.7 |
| Independent Order of Foresters | 5.3 | 6.5 | 5.6 |
| Ancient Order of Foresters | 5.6 | 7.2 | 5.9* |
| Canadian Order of Chosen Friends | 17.1 | 26.2 | 18.9 |
| Canadian Order of Oddfellows | 24.1 | 28.1 | 34.4 |
| Loyal Order of Moose | 25.5 | 14.3 | 6.7 |
| IOOF, Manchester Unity | 40.7 | 32.3 | 26.4 |
| Knights of Pythias | 13.6** | 11.5 | 11.2 |
| Other Protestant orders | 8.0 | 15.6 | 20.0 |
| Total, all orders | 149,516 | 129,339 | 126,226 |
| IOOF total | 62,035 | 62,219 | 57,205 |
| IOOF % of total insured | 0.42 | 0.48 | 0.45 |

* estimate from data for proximate years
** all members; no data for beneficial members only

pensed with the compulsory sick benefit system."[20] Another friendly society, the Fraternal Order of Eagles, made its sick benefit optional in 1927 (Schmidt, 1980: 95).

Third, our detailed evidence for Ontario confirms that the IOOF's fraternal competition was stable or declining during the 1920s. As Table 5.3 shows, the IOOF's share of the fraternal sickness insurance market increased from 42 to 45 per cent between 1921 and 1929.[21]

## THE RISING OPPORTUNITY COST OF IOOF MEMBERSHIP

The Odd Fellows had an opportunity cost along with money costs for membership. Time and money committed to the lodge was time and money forgone for other purposes. Membership in a lodge, moreover, was a multiple-faceted product that included the sick benefit, social benefits, and direct and indirect economic benefits. In this context, the opportunity cost of membership soared after the First World War. The value placed on certain lodge benefits declined, while the value placed on extra-lodge attractions rose. The upshot was a drop in the relative value of lodge membership.

Several developments debased the social currency of lodge night during the 1920s. The diffusion of the automobile, radio, and cinema diminished lodge night as a source of fellowship and entertainment. The development of instalment buying and consumerism undermined fraternal values such as mutuality and altruism. Changes in sex relations weakened lodge attractions such as all-male fellowship and fraternal ritual to express traditional male-gender constructions. As attendance at lodge meetings declined, lodge night became less useful an occasion for making business contacts. The rising popularity of luncheon club organizations (Kiwanis, Lions, Kinsmen) signalled a rising popularity for a community-service orientation. This contrasted with the fraternal tradition of service to members.

The sick benefit, as well as lodge membership, had a rising-opportunity cost. After 1890 its real dollar value fell. Its value also fell relative to other benefits of membership. With the development of grand lodge home programs, the sick benefit accounted for a smaller proportion of IOOF expenditures on benefits. Meanwhile real wages and rates of savings were rising in the larger society. Although rise in real wages raised the lost-income cost of sickness, the rising rates of savings helped men to self-insure for the sickness risk rather than buying the IOOF's market insurance.

By the 1920s the sickness risk itself was undergoing a major transformation. Specifically, health care was supplanting lost income as the major cost of sickness. Whereas the risk of income loss focused on the male breadwinner, any family member could incur health-care costs for physician's services, hospital beds and diagnostic services, and drugs.

Throughout the nineteenth century, the breadwinner's lost income was the chief cost of sickness. By 1914, however, the costs of family health care and lost income were about equal. By the 1920s family health care was the chief cost, as medical costs rose by 20 per cent for families with less than $1,200 income and 85 per cent for families with incomes between $1,200 and $2,500. The medical costs were highly variable as well as rising. In 1919 the average medical bill for urban families with incomes in the $2,000–3,000 range rose from $67 to $261, should the family experience a hospitalized illness. "A small but significant number of families," notes Starr, faced bills that amounted to a third to a half of their annual incomes.[22]

IOOF lodges made two types of provision for health-care costs. First, the SGL *Code* entitled all members, even those in arrears for dues, "to be visited by the officers of his lodge and cared for in sickness." Where necessary, the attentive benefit supplied round-the-clock visitation in the brother's home or hospital. Lodge members either supplied unpaid watchers for the purpose or used lodge funds to hire a nurse or a paid watcher.

Second, the *Code* allowed a lodge to elect a physician "whose duty it shall be to attend and render medical assistance to members" in return for payment from lodge funds. In 1931, for example, the Thamesford, Ontario, lodge bylaws provided for the annual election of "a physician whose duty it shall be to professionally attend each beneficial member ... if called upon to do so by the member or the lodge, and to supply necessary medicines ... For such service the physician shall be paid at the rate of $3.00 per annum for each member in good standing in the beneficial list."

The IOOF's price of membership, however, covered only a small portion of the health-care risk. Judging by anecdotal evidence, lodge practice agreements with physicians were widespread before the First World War, but were less common by the 1920s (Rosen, 1977; Naylor, 1986: ch. 3). What is more important, lodge practice agreements and the attentive benefit covered members but not their dependants.

Meanwhile, market insurance for the health-care risk was largely unavailable from any source because of the extreme moral hazard involved.[23] As with income replacement insurance, sickness was a poorly defined condition. In addition, the cost of treatment was within the insured's control. It also was within the control of the physician and hospital, who stood to benefit from additional services and could raise prices where insurance increased the patient's ability to pay.

Perforce families used savings (self-insurance) to cover the health-care risk. Thus in families with finite resources, the accumulation of savings for health care became more pressing than the purchase of market insurance for lost income. In other words, the opportunity cost of the IOOF's sick benefit was rising.

The IOOF sick benefit's rising-opportunity cost clearly hastened its decline during the 1920s, but this leaves important questions unanswered. Why had the decline of the sick benefit begun in the 1890s, three decades earlier? Why did the IOOF's aging members choose to weaken the sick benefit when their exposure to the disability risk was rising and the price of the benefit was subsidized for older men?

## CONCLUSION

Competition from rival sickness insurers cannot explain why the IOOF weakened its provisions for the sick benefit. By the 1920s the IOOF's competition from rival insurers was stable or declining. Commercial group insurance was the only dynamic source of competition during the decade. By 1929, however, the volume of group plan sales was small, and persons in the plans included individuals who were not in the IOOF's market.

The weakness of competition as an explanation is intuitively obvious from a comparison of jurisdictions that retained stipulated benefits with jurisdictions that had abolished the sick benefit or made it optional by 1929 (see Map 4.1). As chapter 2 demonstrates for Ontario, the IOOF's competition was most intense in large cities. By extension, the IOOF faced its most intense competition in states and provinces with above-average industrial economic development. The grand lodges, however, retained the mandatory benefit in the heavily-industrialized northeast (New York, Pennsylvania, New Jersey, Delaware, Maryland, all New England states except Vermont, and Ontario). By contrast, grand lodges had abolished the benefit in several predominantly rural states in the American southeast and middle-west regions (Idaho, Wyoming, Montana, North Carolina, North Dakota, and South Dakota, and Missouri).

During the 1920s opportunity-cost competition clearly hastened the decline of the sick benefit. What is more important, the opportunity-cost influence leaves unresolved the conundrum of the old man's benefit. Why did the IOOF's aging members elect to weaken their provisions for the sick benefit when their exposure to the disability risk was rising? The next chapter presents our solution to the problem.

# 6 A Young Man's Benefit, 1856–1929

The cost pressures on the sick benefit rose as the IOOF's members aged. But rather than changing their pricing practices, the Odd Fellows cut the value of the sick benefit. Neither internal weakness nor external pressure determined the IOOF's course of action. The IOOF's lodge system was financially sound, and competition from rival insurers was stable during the 1920s. Thus, it was a change in attitude that caused the decline of the sick benefit. In 1863 the SGL had described the sick benefit as "a distinguishing characteristic of the Order and one of its fundamental principles." In 1925, in contrast, its assembled grand representatives held "the general opinion ... that the stipulated sick benefit system [had] outlived its usefulness."[1]

Although the opportunity cost of the sick benefit was rising during the 1920s, this was too late to provide a strong explanation for the decline of the sick benefit. What is more important, it does not resolve the conundrum of the old man's benefit. Old members had a greater risk of disability than young members and a subsidized price for membership. The sick benefit, in other words, appeared to be an old man's benefit. At the same time the average age of the Odd Fellows was rising. In the circumstances, why did the IOOF's aging members cut the value of the sick benefit and make it optional for the lodge branch in 1925?

This chapter gives our solution to the conundrum. It shows that young men, not older men, headed the demand for market insurance. Contrary to conventional wisdom, in other words, the IOOF's sickness insurance was a young man's benefit. Similarly the SGL's sick benefit legislation of 1925 was a long-term outcome of the aging trend for membership.

## TWO CONTRASTING THEORETICAL MODELS

Before the 1920s, the breadwinner's lost income was his family's chief cost of sickness. Depending on its circumstances, his family could cover the risk with market insurance, family insurance, or self-insurance. Market insurance was available from commercial insurers, friendly societies, life insurance fraternal orders, labour unions, and company-sponsored mutual benefit societies.

According to the old man's model, a man's demand for market insurance increased as he aged. His probability of making a sick claim became above average as he passed the age of forty. At the same time, insurers charged flat-rate premiums. Thus the longer a policy was in force, the greater its value for the insured person. Effectively, the young man's premium subsidized the old man's sick claim.

According to the young man's model, on the other hand, a man's demand for market insurance declined as he aged. Like older men, young men had a risk of disability, albeit a lesser one. Unlike older men, they lacked alternatives to market insurance.[2] At the start of their working lives, they had no older children for family insurance (secondary incomes). They also had too little savings to cover the risk (self-insurance).

As they aged, however, men acquired savings and working children. In the process, self-insurance and/or family insurance became viable substitutes for the fraternal sick benefit. In general, they preferred the alternatives, since family insurance and self-insurance had lower transaction costs and kept resources within the family (Kotlikoff and Spivak, 1981).

Cultural considerations possibly influenced some members' decisions to quit. As Johnson noted for Britain, a man could express respectability by joining a lodge (Johnson, 1985). By joining he showed his peers that he could afford the joining fees and annual dues. By the same logic, a man could express respectability by letting his membership lapse some years later. This action would signal that he no longer needed market insurance. Unlike Anglo-Protestant men at the start of their working lives, and "foreigners" in ethnic benefit societies, he had savings to cover the risk.

The social message of quitting, of course, depended on the member and circumstances. Quitting meant a loss of face for the Odd Fellow who was unable to pay his dues. For well-off members, quitting may have implied a disrespect for peers and a highly-regarded community institution. As a selfish act, quitting violated the IOOF's moral ideals. Finally, just as peer pressure encouraged the decision to join, so it discouraged a decision to leave.

In any case, an Odd Fellow's method of quitting was to let his dues lapse. When he was in arrears for one year's dues, his lodge could suspend his membership or declare him "ceased." The lodge, in turn, had an incentive to act. As long as it kept the member on the books, it had to pay the grand lodge per-capita tax for him.

The average spell of membership for a suspended member was five to seven years. In Ontario during the years 1895–1914, suspended members on average were five to seven years older than initiates.[3] Similarly 894 suspended members in six British Columbia and Ontario lodges had been members on average for five years. The member was in arrears for dues and ineligible for benefits during the last year of his spell. Thus the average length for an insured spell of membership was four to six years.

Self-insurance was feasible for most middle-income workers after four years of membership. The average sick spell for disabilities lasting more than a week was about five to eight weeks.[4] At the same time, a household's average yearly savings were equal to 2.8 weeks of the husband's weekly earnings, according to a United States Bureau of Labor cost of living survey for 1917–19.[5] At this rate, four years of savings were equal to eleven weeks of the breadwinner's income. The sick benefit, moreover, provided only partial replacement of a breadwinner's lost income. Thus four years of savings easily replaced the IOOF's partial-income replacement benefit over five to eight weeks of disability.

Between 1890 and 1929, the Odd Fellows needed the sick benefit for increasingly shorter periods of time. The decline in the constant-dollar value of the benefit reduced the amount of savings required to replace it. Meanwhile, the worker's accumulation of savings accelerated. During the years 1900–29, men of all ages benefited from a rising trend for real wages (Grantham, 1994; MacKinnon, 1996). Moreover, earnings increased with age for men born in the late nineteenth century (Gratton, 1996: 52). In the process, self-insurance gradually displaced family insurance as the preferred alternative to the sick benefit. With the rise in the family breadwinner's wages, the family had less need for secondary incomes from other family members (Gratton, 1996).

Individual workers did not always amass savings at the rate of the statistical average. In England low-income working-class families saved in short bursts to spend rather than over the long term to accumulate (Johnson, 1985). North American Odd Fellows were better off than low-income English workers. Even so, higher earnings did not necessarily make them savers. Between 1922 and 1929, for example, real wages rose by 15 per cent for American workers. At the same time, electricity, central heating, indoor sanitation, home appliances, radio, phonograph, the automobile, and credit purchases on the instalment plan became available to their families. In the circumstances, many working-class families consumed to the limit of their incomes (Brody, 1980: 62–6). Effectively, they chose a qualitative leap in living standards over building up their financial reserves.

THE SICK BENEFIT AND IOOF MEMBERSHIP A narrow insurance model predicts that young men joined for the sick benefit and quit five years later when they no longer needed it. Such logic is intuitively flawed. If men joined for a young man's benefit, why was the IOOF's membership aging? Why did Michigan lodges continue to have members after 1925 when their grand lodge abolished the sick benefit?

In fact, several benefits came with the purchase of membership. All lodges offered a funeral benefit. Less commonly, they offered widows' and orphans' benefits, discretionary aid to members in distress, and access to IOOF homes for widows and orphans of members and aged indigent members. In an era of high geographical mobility, networks of lodges helped men to locate employment, business contacts, and sources of credit. Finally, the lodges provided social benefits such as fellowship, entertainment, respectability, and ritual to combat male-gender anxiety.

Effectively membership of an Odd Fellow lodge was a bundled good.[6] By paying his dues, a member secured a range of benefits as a package, but could not buy them separately. The bundling of social and economic benefits, in turn, offered important advantages for the lodge. On the one hand, social interaction helped the members to mitigate the problems of moral hazard (malingering) and adverse selection. On the other hand, insurance benefits helped a lodge to sell its social products to a wider set of consumers.

Thus the sick benefit was an insurance product within a larger membership product. By extension, the lodges had different types of members. Some long-term members kept up their memberships for the social benefits. Some short-term members quit because they had fallen on hard times, not because their demand for the sick benefit had lessened. Other short-term members were new men in town who joined to make contacts and left after they had made some. Accordingly, we do not base our empirical strategy on the narrow insurance model. As discussed below, we allow for the multiple attractions of membership and different types of members.

## THE DATA

To test the model for the young man's benefit, we compiled membership histories for 1,808 initiates in six lodges. Four of the six lodges were in

British Columbia. Lodge No. 15 (1891–1929) was in Cloverdale, a farm service centre to the south of Vancouver.[7] Lodge No. 63 (1910–29) was in Prince Rupert, a northern port and railway terminus. Lodges nos. 39 (1897–1929) and 64 (1910–29) were in Sandon and Corbin, both Kootenay mountain mining towns in the south-central part of the province. The last two lodges (Samaritan No. 35, 1856–1925, and Oxford No. 77, 1871–1902) were in Ingersoll, a manufacturing and farm service town in southwestern Ontario (Emery, 1993: 51–3).

Lodge membership registers and semi-annual returns are the chief documentary sources. These records state the member's name, date and means of joining (initiation, transfer from another lodge); date and means of exit (death, suspension, expulsion, transfer to another lodge, or membership still in progress at the end of our observation). In 1902 the Ingersoll lodges merged and continued under the Samaritan name. In the course of their protracted negotiations for merger (1890–1902), officers of the lodges compiled a third documentary source: lists of their members for the years 1890, 1896, and 1902.

A *membership spell* is the interval between initiation and exit from observation. The membership spell is a year longer than the member's *insured spell* of membership. A British Columbia Odd Fellow became ineligible for benefits when he fell into arrears for one quarter's dues. Thirty days was the period of grace for Ontario Odd Fellows.

A *completed* membership spell ends with the member's first suspension for non-payment of dues. We disregard reinstatements of suspended members. That is, we do not treat reinstatement as the resumption of a suspended member's membership spell. Nor do we treat it as the start of a new spell.[8] As SGL statistics show, reinstatements were equal to 20 per cent of suspensions during the years 1900–10. The percentage fell from 32 to 7 between 1921 and 1929.

The membership spells are for initiates only. The data file excludes charter members and transfers from other lodges. Those membership spells are *left-censored*. As the observer scans from left to right, they begin before the records bring them into view. In contrast, the file includes *right-censored* spells. These are still in progress as they pass from observation in the records. Some continue after our end-years for observation: 1929 for the British Columbia lodges and 1925 for the Ontario lodges. Some transfer to another lodge. Other spells end with the member's death. We treat deaths as right-censored because the member's exit is involuntary and unrelated to insurance.

MISSING INFORMATION If our sources do not report that a member exits through death, transfer, expulsion, or suspension, then we assume that he was still a member at the end of observation. As we discovered, however, our information for Ingersoll members is incomplete for exits.[9] Although our records show 106 no-exit men who joined Samaritan Lodge before 1888, only sixty show up on the lodge's list of members for 1890. Clearly the forty-six others exit before 1890.

Our three membership lists minimize the problem of unreported exits for the years 1890–1902, but not for later years. In 1925 the semi-annual returns for Samaritan Lodge report 262 members. Information in the lodge register indicates that up to eighteen of them are transfers from other lodges. It also shows fifty-five men who exit from the lodge after 1925. This leaves 189 spots in 1925 for other men in the lodge register who are on the 1902 membership list or join through initiation during the years 1903–25. The membership register, however, does not report an exit for 282 such men. Thus it shows ninety-three excess members for 1925.

The 139 excess survivors for the pre-1890 and 1903–25 periods inflate the presence of long-term members and bias the evidence towards the model for the old man's benefit. Accordingly, we make two corrections to the data file. First, we eliminate the forty-six excess survivors from the pre-1890 period. We know that the membership spells for these men ended before 1890, but we do not know their exit years. The second correction is for members who have no reported exit and who are on one or more of the three membership lists. In these cases, we right-censor the membership spell in the year of the last membership list that included them (1890, 1896, or 1902).

The corrections are conservative. In particular, they to not apply to initiates for the years 1903–25. Thus, even with the corrections, the data file overrepresents long membership spells. Precisely for this reason, it provides a stiff test for the hypothesis that young men headed demand for the sick benefit.

SUMMARY STATISTICS Table 6.1 summarizes the outcomes of 1,808 membership spells. Compared to the British Columbia spells, the Ingersoll spells have a higher proportion of suspension outcomes and a lower proportion of "in progress at end-year" outcomes. This arises primarily from the longer period of observation for them.

Table 6.2 reports the age profiles for age at joining and at exit for 894 suspended members for whom we have information about age. A majority of these initiates joined when they were under thirty years of age. On average they quit their lodges after five years of insured membership. Their mean age at joining was 27.4, and their mean age at suspension was 33.8.

These findings alone fail to demonstrate the model for the young man's sick benefit. The young ages of the joiners, for example, could

Table 6.1
Modes of Spell Termination for Initiates in Four British Columbia and Two Ontario Lodges

| | Suspension | Right-Censored Cases: Death | Right-Censored Cases: Out transfer | Right-Censored Cases: Other right-censor* | Total |
|---|---|---|---|---|---|
| All six lodges | 894 | 108 | 199 | 607 | 1,808 |
| % distribution | .49 | .06 | .11 | .34 | 1.00 |
| Four BC lodges | 258 | 35 | 68 | 251 | 612 |
| % distribution | .42 | .06 | .11 | .41 | 1.00 |
| Two Ontario lodges | 636 | 73 | 137 | 350 | 1,196 |
| % distribution | .53 | .06 | .11 | .30 | 1.00 |

* Includes four expelled members, seventy-seven Oxford Lodge members whom the Samaritan Lodge rejected in the 1902 merger, and spells that were still in progress at the end-year of observation (1925 for Ontario and 1929 for British Columbia).

express the attraction of other lodge benefits for young men. Conversely, the six lodges had age-related initiation fees that discouraged older men from joining. Finally, the right-censored cases require consideration. The high quit rates in the younger age groups, for example, may indicate that old men headed the demand for the sick benefit. Alternatively, they could show that the demand declined with the member's age.

To summarize, two offsetting life-course influences acted on demand for the sick benefit. The one was the development of alternatives to market insurance. The other was the rise in exposure to the disability risk and the subsidized price for older men. In the circumstances, we need an empirical strategy that can show which of the two influences was the more dominant.

## THE EMPIRICAL STRATEGY

We use *hazard rates* to measure an Odd Fellow's attachment to membership. These rates state the member's conditional probability of exit for each year that he remains a member.[10] If old men headed demand for the sick benefit then, all else being equal, the probability of exit would drop as the spell of membership lengthens. Conversely, if young men headed the demand, the hazard rates would rise.

Table 6.2
Age at Joining and Age at Exit for Suspended Members, 1856–1929: Percentage Distribution by Age Group

| *Age group* | *Six lodges* | | *Four BC lodges* | | *Two Ingersoll lodges* | |
|---|---|---|---|---|---|---|
| | *Entry* | *Exit* | *Entry* | *Exit* | *Entry* | *Exit* |
| 19–24 | .44 | .05 | .26 | .05 | .51 | .07 |
| 25–29 | .26 | .31 | .30 | .21 | .24 | .35 |
| 30–34 | .16 | .25 | .20 | .28 | .15 | .24 |
| 35–39 | .08 | .18 | .13 | .18 | .06 | .17 |
| 40–44 | .05 | .11 | .09 | .15 | .03 | .09 |
| 45–49 | .007 | .06 | .02 | .08 | .006 | .04 |
| 50+ | .003 | .04 | .00 | .05 | .004 | .04 |
| Total | 1.00 | 1.00 | 1.00 | 1.00 | 1.00 | 1.00 |
| N = | 894 | 894 | 258 | 258 | 636 | 636 |
| Mean age | 27 | 34 | 30 | 35 | 26 | 32 |
| Median age | 25 | 32 | 28 | 34 | 24 | 31 |

To isolate demand for the sick benefit, we class the benefits of membership into two categories: Good E and Good S.[11] Good E, the primary economic benefit, is the sick benefit. Good S is a residual category for social and other benefits.

With the purchase of membership, the buyer secured one unit of Good E and one unit of Good S. A lodge member could buy an extra unit of each good by joining his local encampment. In the lodge alone, however, he could not buy a second unit of either good. Perforce the marginal utility of a second unit of a lodge good was zero.[12] IOOF constitutions and lodge bylaws fixed the amounts of the units. Although the amounts varied from one lodge to another, a man could join only that lodge in whose territory he lived. Thus lodge shopping was possible between lodges of different orders, but not between two IOOF lodges.

At a given movement, a man had a maximum amount that he was willing to pay for each good. These amounts were his *reservation prices*, $r_E$ and $r_S$. We assume that the two reservation prices were independent of each other. Hence his reservation price for the bundled good, $r_B$, was the sum of $r_E$ and $r_S$. Thus he paid his membership dues as long as his reservation price, $r_B$, exceeded the price, $p_B$, that the lodge asked for its bundled good.[13] We assume that his reservation price for the social good was stable over his life course. Hence any change in $r_B$ expressed a change in $r_E$, its insurance component.

THE OLD MAN'S MODEL If the sick benefit was old man's insurance, then the member's reservation price (willingness to pay) for membership would increase as he aged and his risk of disability rose ($r_E$ increases, hence $r_B$ increases). At the same time, he would be reluctant to give up future entitlements at a subsidized price after years of paying a high price. Thus the longer he remained a member, the less likely he would become to quit. Implicitly, his demand for market insurance over the life course would be insensitive to alternatives such as self-insurance or family insurance.

THE YOUNG MAN'S MODEL If, on the other hand, the sick benefit was young man's insurance, then the member's reservation price would fall as he aged and alternatives to market insurance opened up to him ($r_E$ decreases, hence $r_B$ decreases). At some point the reservation price ($r_B$) would fall below the purchase price ($p_B$), and the individual would stop paying dues and exit from membership.

Implicitly, the long-term Odd Fellows tended to have above-average social reservation prices ($r_S$). We do not rule out insurance reasons for becoming long-term members, however. Doubtless some men failed to accumulate enough savings for self-insurance (or older children for family insurance). Consequently, their reservation price for the sick benefit ($r_E$) remained high as their membership duration increased. Possibly in other cases, the long-term Odd Fellow had savings, but stayed in the lodge to get the sick benefit at the subsidized old man's price.

OTHER INFLUENCES ON QUITTING Our chief interest is in how the length of the membership spell influenced the member's probability of quitting. To check for other influences on quitting, we calculate separate hazard-rate estimates that included the member's age at joining and year of joining. The age variable, for example, can show whether forty-year-old joiners and twenty-five-year-old joiners had different probabilities of quitting after five years of membership. The year variable captures the influence of time on the trends for quitting.

We also calculated hazard-rate estimates for each of the six lodges separately to check for lodge-specific patterns and aggregation errors. Did the quitting behaviours differ, for example, between the miners of

Sandon Lodge and the farmers of Cloverdale Lodge? Would our statistical findings at the general level hold for the six lodges individually? If not, would our general findings be an artifact of the aggregation of dissimilar lodge-level behaviours?

Finally, we allow for the unobserved heterogeneity of attachment to social benefits (Good S). As noted above, we assume that a member's reservation price for social benefits ($r_S$) was stable over his life course. Although stable for individuals, the reservation price varied among individuals. Members with high $r_S$ were less likely to exit than members with low $r_S$.

The unobserved heterogeneity of demand for Good S biases the estimated hazard rates towards *negative-duration dependence*: in other words, the hazard rate falls as the spell lengthens (Heckman and Singer, 1984). Let us suppose, for example, that lodge members fall into two groups. The one has a low $r_S$ and a high rate of exit. The other has a high $r_S$ and a low rate of exit. Assuming that each group's exit rate is stable, the high-exit members leave the membership more quickly than the low-exit members. Thus the probability of quitting may drop as the membership spell lengthens. At first glance, this supports the hypothesis that the sick benefit was the old man's insurance. In reality, the members did not have rising reservation prices for the sick benefit ($r_E$) as they age. Rather the low-exit men are becoming a larger proportion of membership as the high-exit men leave.

Appendix F provides the technical details for the calculation of the hazard rates. The statistic on which we focus is the Weibull duration-dependence parameter ***b***. We use a Gamma-mixing distribution to control for the negative influence on duration dependence of the unobserved heterogeneity of demand for Good S. This furnishes two hazard-rate statistics for interpretation: the Weibull duration-dependence parameter ***b*** without the Gamma-mixing distribution, and the Weibull duration-dependence parameter ***b*** with mixing.

In both cases, if $b>1$, then the hazard function displays *positive-duration dependence.* As the young man's model predicts, in other words, the Odd Fellow's probability of exit increases with the length of his membership spell. If, however, $b<1$, then the hazard function displays negative-duration dependence. As the old man's model predicts, in other words, the Odd Fellow's probability of exit falls as his membership spell lengthens.

## THE FINDINGS

The findings show that the sick benefit was primarily a young man's insurance. As noted above, the unobserved heterogeneity of demand for Good S gives a negative bias to the estimated hazard rates without mix-

Table 6.3
Estimated Coefficients for Weibull and Weibull-Gamma Mixing Specifications (excluding lodge-specific effects)

| *Parameter* | *Covariate* | *I* No *Mixing* | *II* *Mixing* | *III* *Mixing* |
|---|---|---|---|---|
| b | | 1.21 (0.03)† | 5.46 (0.40)† | 5.08 (0.36)† |
| $a(X)=e^{X\phi}$ | Constant | −2.76 (0.028)* | −1.51 (0.04)* | −1.01 (0.09)* |
| | Age at initiation | | | −0.012 (0.003)* |
| | Year at initiation | | | −0.006 (0.001)* |
| δ | | | 8.9 (0.89)* | 7.73 (0.77)* |
| LLF | | −3390.1 | −3119.0 | −3093.2 |
| N = | | 1,808 | 1,808 | 1,808 |

Notes: Standard errors of the estimated coefficients are in parentheses. The estimated coefficient is significantly greater than zero if the ratio of the estimate to its standard error exceeds 2. To test if the duration dependence parameter is significantly greater than 1, calculate the *t* ratio=(b − 1)/(Standard error of b). Compare this value to the critical values for a Student's *t* distribution.
* indicates significantly different from 0 at 5 per cent level of significance.
† indicates significantly different from 1 at 5 per cent level of significance.

For the a(X) parameter, a negative coefficient shows a unit increase in the covariate that decreases the probability of exit at all spell lengths. Blank cells indicate that the parameter or covariate was excluded from the specification reported in the column.

ing. Despite the negative influence, the estimated Weibull duration-dependence parameter *b* (1.21) is significantly greater than 1 (Table 6.3, column 1). This shows positive-duration dependence for the estimated hazard rates without mixing. Thus the estimated probability of exit from membership rises as the membership spell lengthens.

The estimated probability of exit is much higher when we use the Gamma-mixing distribution to control for the unobserved negative influence. With mixing, the estimated Weibull duration-dependence parameter *b* is 5.46 (Table 6.3, column II).[14] This statistic shows strong positive-duration dependence.

The mixing statistics also show strong positive-duration dependence for each of the six lodges. The duration year and magnitude of the peak hazard rate vary from lodge to lodge. The peak rate occurs as early as the third year (Samaritan) and as late as the sixth year (Corbin). The peak magnitude ranges from 6 per cent (Cloverdale) to 16 per cent (Oxford and Corbin). In each case, however, the lodge-specific pattern accords with the general pattern: its hazard rates rise to a peak within six years of membership and then decline. Like the general pattern, the lodge-specific patterns are consistent with the model for the young man's benefit.

Whereas the estimated hazard rate states the conditional probability of exit from membership, the estimated survival rate states the conditional probability of staying. Figure 6.1 shows the estimated hazard rates and survival rates, with mixing, for the six lodges combined.[15] Note that the hazard rates are plotted on the left-hand scale for the Y-axis (0 to 14 per cent), whereas the survival rates are plotted on the right-hand scale (0 to 100 per cent).

The probability of exit rises from 0 to 12 per cent after four years of membership and then declines. We interpret this pattern as showing two groups of members. Men in the first group join primarily for the insurance and have a rising exit rate, whereas men in the second group join primarily for Good S and have a low probability of exit. As the survivor rates show, half the initiates stay in the membership for ten years and 25 per cent stay in for thirty years.

As discussed above, we do not rule out insurance considerations for long-term members. Failed self-insurers retained a high reservation price for the Odd Fellow benefit. Possibly some long-term members who had savings stayed in the lodge to get the sick benefit at its subsidized old man's price. For this hypothetical second group of long-term members, the old man's model applies.

If such men existed, then they were a minority in the Oddfellowship. On average, only a third of the joiners lasted until age forty-five, when the subsidized price came into play. Ultimately the old man's model fails on intuitive grounds. It cannot explain why young men joined at a high price and quit before they qualified for the subsidized price. Nor can it explain why an order with aging members turned against a sick benefit that had a subsidized price for older men.

THE ESTIMATIONS WITH COVARIATES Both age at joining and year of joining have statistically significant negative influences on the estimated hazard rate (Table 6.3, column III). With the covariates included, the estimated Weibull duration-dependence mixing parameter $b$ drops from 5.46 to 5.08. Thus at first glance, the probability of exit is lower for a man who joined at age thirty than for a man who joined

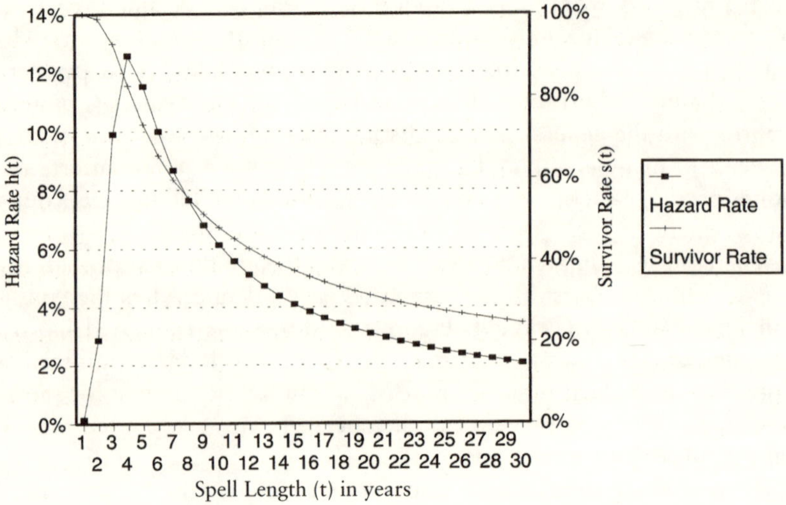


Figure 6.1
Estimated Hazard and Survivor Rates for All Six Lodges

at age twenty-one. Similarly, it is lower for a man who joined in 1900 than for a man who joined in 1870. The hazard-rate estimations for each year of membership (not reported here) show that both negative influences vanish by the tenth year. In other words, they obtain for short spells of membership, but not for long-term ones.

The two negative covariate influences, and their attenuation by the tenth year of membership, are consistent with our model for the young man's benefit. Older joiners, for example, were more likely than young joiners to be past their need for the sick benefit. They had a lower probability of exit because their social reservation prices ($r_S$) were likely to be high.[16]

Similarly the negative influence for joining year matches the known trend for the sick benefit. The benefit was in its heyday before 1890 and then declined. After 1890, therefore, Good s gradually became the IOOF's primary attraction. By extension, the joiners were increasingly likely to have high social reservation prices and a low probability of exit. For the same reason, men with high social reservation prices were becoming a growing proportion of the membership.

Finally, the disappearance of both negative influences by the tenth year of membership makes sense. The men who remained members for ten years were likely to have high social reservation prices regardless of their age at joining or their joining year.

Despite their compatibility with our model for the young man's benefit, neither of the negative covariate influences held up at the lodge level of analysis. As expected, the influence of age at joining was negative for all six lodges. The influence of joining age, however, was not statistically significant for any of them. The influence of year of joining was positive rather than negative for three lodges. The influence of joining year was statistically significant for only two lodges, and for one of them, Cloverdale, the influence was positive.

Simply put, the effects of both age and year of joining for all six lodges are statistical artifacts. They result from the aggregation of rather dissimilar patterns for the individual lodges. Compared to the Ingersoll lodges, for example, the British Columbia lodges had older joiners and later peak hazard rates. Thus the aggregated hazard-rate estimations show a spurious correlation between the older joiners and lower hazard rates during the first three or four years of membership duration.

## CONCLUSION

Young men, not old men, headed demand for the sick benefit. The dominant influence on demand over the life course was not the rising exposure to the disability risk and the subsidized old man's price, but rather the emergence of alternatives to market insurance. Thus the sick benefit was primarily young man's insurance in an order that had two principal types of members. Men of the first type joined primarily for the insurance and quit when they were able to use self-insurance or family insurance to cover the risk. Thus high rates of membership turnover in the lodges did not show that the IOOF's provision of insurance was fundamentally flawed. Rather they showed that the Odd Fellows did not need market insurance after five to ten years.

Men of the second type joined for a range of membership benefits (Good S), not just for the insurance (Good E). As with men of the first type, their demand for insurance declined as they aged. In contrast, their demand for Good S was high enough that they did not quit when their need for market insurance passed. These men gradually became a majority of the IOOF's members. The decline in the real value of the sick benefit and the long-term rise in rates of saving allowed the high-exit men to quit after increasingly shorter intervals, so that the aging trend for the IOOF's members shifted the weight of numbers towards men of the second type.

Thus the change in the character of the membership explains why the IOOF's supreme body allowed subordinate bodies to abolish the benefit in 1925. What influenced Odd Fellows, moreover, influenced others. In both the United States and Canada population was aging, its rates of savings were rising, and sickness insurance was falling out of its market.[17] This helps to explain why government in the two countries declined to enact compulsory sickness insurance, as Germany had done in 1883 and Great Britain in 1911. A strong American campaign for government sickness insurance collapsed after the First World War. Subsequently, the United States Social Security Act of 1935 provided for old age pensions and unemployment insurance, but not sickness insurance. New priorities now came to the fore and sickness insurance was dropping from sight.

# 7 Epilogue

Between 1929 and 1960 the IOOF's sick benefit continued to decline in a stagnate market. In this context, commercial group insurers displaced friendly societies as the principal source of disability insurance. The group insurers became dominant, however, by developing a new mass market rather than increasing their share of the traditional market that friendly societies were abandoning. Conversely, self-insurance was always the chief competition for the friendly society sick benefit.

## THE DECLINE OF THE IOOF'S SICK BENEFIT AFTER 1929

During the years 1930–60 the IOOF continued its transition from a friendly society to a social organization like the Masons or Elks. By 1931 the IOOF's provisions for the stipulated sick benefit could weaken in three basic ways. First, under the SGL's enabling legislation of 1925, grand lodges could abolish the benefit or make it optional for their lodges. By 1929, thirty-two grand lodges (57 per cent) still required the sick benefit. In sixteen jurisdictions (29 per cent), the grand lodge, or most of its lodges, had abolished it. In eight jurisdictions (14 per cent), lodge decisions about the benefit showed a mixed pattern.

Second, grand lodges could permit their lodges to introduce a non-beneficial class of membership. In 1929 the SGL had allowed grand lodges to "provide, or authorize their subordinates to provide" for the initiation of applicants into a non-beneficial class of membership. In

Table 7.1.
Grand Lodge Legislation on Benefits in Six Jurisdictions, 1925–60

| | *Legislation* | | | | | |
|---|---|---|---|---|---|---|
| | *B.C.* | *Alta.* | *Sask.* | *Man.* | *Ont.* | *Mich.* |
| Optional for lodges | 1931 | 1928 | 1927 | 1939 | – | 1930 |
| Non-beneficial initiates | 1953 | 1930 | 1937 | – | 1932 | – |
| Abolition of benefit | – | – | – | – | 1951 | 1925 |

1931 it allowed lodges to grant any beneficial member's request to transfer to the non-beneficial class.

Third, lodges could reduce the real value of the sick benefit. They could allow inflation to reduce its real amount or they could shorten the maximum period for which they paid their benefit. In 1896 the SGL had allowed grand lodges or lodges to provide for a waiting period of one week or two weeks of sickness before payment commenced. Under the 1925 legislation, grand lodges could permit their lodges to adopt a maximum coverage period of thirteen weeks, compared with fifty-two weeks under the old law.

The decline of the sick benefit after 1929 is hard to document. Our information about grand lodge legislation for the sick benefit is comprehensive for 1927 and 1930, but piecemeal for later years. In any event, this legislation alone does not capture developments at the lodge level. In the circumstances, we track legislative changes in the grand lodges of British Columbia, Alberta, Saskatchewan, Manitoba, Ontario, and Michigan. We also use SGL benefit statistics to show developments in the six jurisdictions and throughout the IOOF.

DEVELOPMENTS IN SIX JURISDICTIONS As Table 7.1 shows, all six grand lodges had abolished the benefit or made it optional for lodges by 1951 although their specific provisions varied. Before 1951, for example, the Ontario grand lodge required its lodges to offer the benefit, but allowed them to initiate non-beneficial members. In contrast, the Manitoba grand lodge made the benefit optional for its lodges in 1939, but did not allow initiations to non-beneficial membership in lodges that retained the benefit.

THE GRAND LODGE OF MICHIGAN Michigan was the home state of Grand Sire Thompson, who had campaigned for the abolition of the sick benefit. In 1925 the grand lodge abolished the sick benefit by a vote of 606 to 49.[1] This legislation stated in unequivocal language that "On and after January 1, 1926, no Subordinate Lodge shall pay, or be required to pay, any stated weekly sick benefits." In 1926 the grand lodge reaffirmed its decision by voting 577 to 23 against an amendment to make the benefit optional for lodges. In 1929, however, the grand master called for legislation to make the stipulated benefit optional for lodges and the following year an amendment for this purpose was passed by a two-thirds majority.

We have two observations about the effects of the legislation. First, the abolition of the stipulated benefit did not end the payment of sick benefits. After 1925 the lodges aided sick brothers on a discretionary basis. Evidence of this lies in the grand secretary's annual reports of the subordinate lodges for the years 1926–9. Although he discontinued reporting lodge statistics for "weeks benefits paid," which applied only to the stipulated benefit, he continued to report statistics for number of "brothers relieved" and "amount [paid for the] relief of brothers," which applied also to discretionary benefits. During those years the sick claim rate (the percentage of brothers who received relief) was 38 per cent of that for 1924, the last year for the mandatory stipulated benefit.

Second, the 1930 legislation did not bring back the stipulated benefit. Of sixty Michigan lodges whose bylaws we examined for the period 1931–50, only two restored the sick benefit.[2] The sick claim rate for the years 1930, 1935, 1940, and 1950, moreover, held at about 40 per cent of the 1924 rate for the stipulated benefit. This is approximately the proportion for the discretionary benefit during the years 1926–9. Despite the legislation for lodge choice in 1930, in other words, few lodges restored the stipulated benefit.

THE GRAND LODGE OF ONTARIO During the 1930s and 1940s the grand lodge of Ontario declined to abolish the sick benefit or make it optional for lodges. In 1932, however, it allowed its lodges to initiate non-beneficial members. In 1935 the grand lodge enacted lower minimum joining fees and annual dues for non-beneficial members ($12 and $4 respectively, compared to $16 and $6 for beneficial members). In 1938 the grand master stressed "the importance of this class of membership" when launching an intensive membership-recruitment campaign.[3]

Thus while the sick benefit was compulsory for lodges, a growing proportion of their members was non-beneficial. By 1943, 11.5 per cent of the members were non-beneficial, up from 5.4 in 1938. The semi-annual returns for later years omitted this information for membership, but reported it for initiations. In 1944, 53 per cent of the initiates were non-beneficial. By 1950, the statistic was 69.[4]

Finally in 1951 the grand lodge voted to phase out the sick benefit. Its method was to abolish initiations into beneficial membership, while allowing existing members to choose whether to remain beneficial. Its lodges last reported payments for sick claims in 1983.

THE GRAND LODGE OF MANITOBA This grand lodge declined to permit initiations into non-beneficial membership. Although it made the sick benefit optional for lodges in 1939, this was an emergency depression measure to allow lodges to suspend the payment of sick claims until their financial condition had recovered. Few lodges abolished the benefit for the long term. Of twenty-eight lodges whose bylaws we examined for the years 1943–50, only one abolished the benefit.

According to Lloyd Shelvy, the Manitoba grand secretary in 1994, the turning point for the benefit came during the 1950s.[5] One after another, the lodges discontinued initiations into beneficial membership, while giving existing members the choice of remaining in the beneficial class. In Shelvy's lodge, Rapid City No. 18, all but two of the current members transferred to the non-beneficial class. The benefit statistics for Manitoba are consistent with Shelvy's recollections. Between 1950 and 1955 the sick claim rate fell by 54 per cent.[6]

GENERAL TRENDS FOR THE SICK BENEFIT We use trends for two IOOF benefit statistics to survey the abolition process in all fifty-six jurisdictions. The first is the sick claim rate (the proportion of members who made a claim in a given year). The second is the sick week rate (the weeks of sick claims per member in a given year). If abolition of the stipulated benefit was spreading after 1929, then one would expect to find declining trends for both these statistics after 1924, the last year for the compulsory stipulated benefit.

One must interpret any declining trends with caution because of two offsetting influences on the statistics. First, as our evidence for Michigan reveals, the grand lodge statistics include discretionary benefits in lodges that no longer had the stipulated benefit. Such discretionary benefits, in other words, mask some of the declining trend for the stipulated benefit.

Second, high rates of arrearage for beneficial members during the 1930s inflated the declining trends for IOOF benefit statistics. The lodges suspended between 8 and 11 per cent of their members for nonpayment of dues during the years 1930–40, compared to 6 per cent in 1924. Between 29 and 47 per cent of Ontario Odd Fellows were in arrears during the years 1930–44, compared to 28 per cent in 1924. The arrearage of non-beneficial members, of course, did not influence the trends for the benefit statistics after 1924.

Table 7.2
IOOF Sick Claim Rate and Sick Week Rate as a Proportion of the Rates for 1924

| | A. Sick Claim Rate | | | | | |
|---|---|---|---|---|---|---|
| | *1924* | *1930* | *1940* | *1950* | *1960* | *1970* |
| TOTAL | 56 | 56 | 55* | 56 | 56 | 56 |
| <.50 1924 Rate | 0 | 15 | 29 | 38 | 49 | 51 |
| <.25 1924 Rate | 0 | 7 | 10 | 25 | 33 | 39 |
| Rate of 0.0 | 0 | 3 | 3 | 3 | 1 | 11 |
| SGL | 1.00 | .85 | .71 | .47 | .32 | .18 |

| | B. Sick Week Rate | | | | | |
|---|---|---|---|---|---|---|
| | *1924* | *1930* | *1940* | *1950* | *1960* | *1970* |
| TOTAL | 56 | 56 | 55* | 56 | 56 | 56 |
| <.50 1924 Rate | 0 | 18 | 34 | 42 | 48 | 52 |
| <.25 1924 Rate | 0 | 12 | 21 | 33 | 40 | 44 |
| Rate of 0.0 | 0 | 9 | 13 | 19 | 18 | 22 |
| SGL | 1.00 | .90 | .75 | .40 | .25 | .13 |

* charter for Tennessee suspended

Keeping in mind the offsetting influences, Table 7.2 shows sharp drops for the two benefit statistics after 1924. By 1960 the sick claim rate was less than half the 1924 rate in forty-nine grand lodge jurisdictions and less than 25 per cent in thirty-three cases. Similarly, the sick week statistic was less than half the 1924 statistic in forty-eight jurisdictions and less than 25 per cent in forty cases. The declines in the benefit statistics indicated that the abolition of the sick benefit was widespread by 1960. At least one lodge, Alberta's Lethbridge Lodge No. 2, still had the stipulated sick benefit in 1994 when we undertook our research for that province.

## MARKET STAGNATION AND MARKET SHARES, 1930–60

Market insurance for the sickness risk stagnated during and after the 1920s. This was influenced both by the rising opportunity cost for market insurance and the trend for savings and self-insurance in breadwinner families.

Information in American and Canadian statistical yearbooks gives a false impression of market growth for the disability risk. In Canada the constant dollars of premiums per 1,000 population doubled between 1920 and 1942 and rose 4.9 fold between 1920 and 1947. Although the American statistic did not change between 1920 and 1939, it increased 1.7 fold between 1939 and 1947.[7] The rising trends for the premium statistics, however, express rising trends for health insurance premiums and mask flat trends for sickness insurance premiums. Health insurance entered the market about 1935 and grew rapidly after 1940.[8]

INSTITUTIONAL MARKET SHARES IN THE STAGNANT MARKET

Commercial group plans displaced friendly societies as the chief source of disability insurance. The market share for group plans rose steadily after 1929. In contrast, the market shares were declining for friendly societies, life insurance fraternal orders, labour unions, mutual benefit associations, and government programs.

*Friendly Societies* Clearly the market share of friendly societies was shrinking. With the decline of its sick benefit and membership after 1925, the largest friendly society, the IOOF, moved to the sidelines of the marketplace. Two other large friendly societies, the Knights of Pythias and the Fraternal Order of Eagles, had an optional sick benefit by the 1930s. The Improved Order of Red Men, the Knights of Pythias, and the Foresters of America lost over 60 per cent of their members between 1929 and 1958. Only the Loyal Order of Moose and the Fraternal Order of Eagles, with gains of 55 and 27 per cent, bucked the trend.

*Life Insurance Fraternal Orders* Canadian evidence suggests a declining trend for sickness insurance in the life insurance orders. The largest such order in Canada, the Independent Order of Foresters, had 11,941 certificates in force in 1950, a 50 per cent drop from 1925. With its American business included, the drop was 59 per cent. As a ratio to population, the certificates in force for Dominion-registered fraternal benefit societies fell by 43 per cent between 1925 and 1935 and 27 per cent between 1925 and 1950.

*Mutual Benefit Associations* In the United States the insurance business of "mutual accident and sick benefit associations" stagnated during the years 1920–48. Its number of certificates in force per 1,000 population in 1940 was only 1.1 times the statistic for 1920 and by 1948 it was 1.4.[9]

*Labour Unions* During the Second World War most labour unions abandoned the direct provision of benefits. Instead, with government encouragement, they obtained commercial group plan benefits through collective bargaining agreements. In the United States, the national government limited salary increases through its wage stabilization program. At the same time, it allowed benefits to enter into collective bargaining agreements. By 1950 a third of all such agreements had group insurance provisions (Ilse, 1953: 332–50). By 1959 employee benefit plans covered 36 million persons, representing 86 per cent of union members and their dependants (Follmann, 1965).

*Government programs* Government's place in the sickness insurance market advanced in piecemeal fashion after 1929. American state and Canadian provincial governments continued with workmen's compensation programs. In 1946 the American federal government's Railroad Unemployment Insurance Act provided short-term disability benefits to certain classes of railway workers. During the 1940s the Rhode Island, California, New Jersey, and New York state governments introduced compulsory sickness insurance programs.[10] In 1971 the Canadian federal government's Unemployment Insurance Act allowed workers to claim unemployment benefits for reasons of temporary sickness or disability (after a two-week waiting period).[11]

The United States Unemployment Compensation Act of 1935 was the catalyst for the four state programs for compulsory disability insurance (Ilse, 1953: 190–217). The act levied an excise tax on employers to fund unemployment insurance. Ninety per cent of the sum collected in a state, however, could go to state unemployment compensation programs that met national standards. With this provision in play, state governments had incentive to offer benefits for persons who were unemployed because of disability.

The Rhode Island, California, New Jersey, and New York disability programs took effect in 1943, 1946, 1949, and 1950 respectively. Like the American federal government's program for railway trades, the Rhode Island program provided for a state monopoly. Thus commercial group plans vanished from the state in 1943. In contrast, the programs in the three other states gave employers the option of arranging coverage through private plans that met the government standard. By 1952 private plans included 45 per cent of the persons covered under the California law and 73 per cent of the persons covered under the New Jersey law.

The introduction of the four state programs boosted sales of group plans (Ilse, 1953: 217). Employers who had to provide for their employees tended to extend their group plan coverage to their employees in other states. Meanwhile employers in other states bought group plans in anticipation of state laws for compulsory sickness insurance.

The state programs had no effect on trends for IOOF benefit statistics in Rhode Island and New Jersey, but in California the IOOF's sick claim rate fell by 20 per cent between 1946 and 1950. The implementation of New York's program in 1950 had no immediate effect on IOOF benefit statistics for the state, but between 1952 and 1953 the IOOF's sick claim rate dropped by 54 per cent.

*Group Disability Plans* Sales of group disability plans grew steadily after 1929. In 1934, the first year for which statistics are available, 1.7 million Americans had coverage in group disability plans. The number reached 15.1 million in 1950 and 22.3 million in 1962. The number in group plans per 1,000 population in the United States registered a 7.6 fold increase between 1934 and 1950 and a 9.1 fold increase between 1934 and 1962.[12]

Various influences fed the popularity of group plans. One was the spread of employee benefit plans in collective bargaining agreements during the Second World War. The entry of casualty insurers into the group disability marketplace was another development. This was a natural extension of their long-established business in accident insurance. By the years 1947–51 casualty insurers collected 38 per cent of group plan premiums, and life insurance companies collected 62 per cent. The broadening of the definition for "group" also helped sales. During the 1920s, self-employed persons and small firms were ineligible for the purchase of group plans, but by the 1950s eligible groups included employees in different firms of a common employer, members of trade unions, and associations of self-employed persons or professional groups.

The flexibility of group plans was another reason for their popularity. The employer could choose the amount of the benefit, gear the amount to the employee's position or income, and determine the period for which coverage applied. In addition, disability insurance was one of several types of coverage that the employer might select from an insurance company's group insurance department. The employer might buy a group plan on its own, or add it to a package that might include group life, group annuity, group accidental death and dismemberment coverage, and group hospital, surgical, and medical expense insurance.

Finally the success of group insurance mitigated its one great disadvantage from the employee's viewpoint: that its coverage was temporary and ended when he left the firm. As group plans became widespread in collective bargaining agreements, the worker was likely to obtain benefits from his/her new employer that compensated for his/her loss of benefits at the old firm.

To summarize, commercial group plans displaced the friendly societies as the dominant source of market insurance for disability. Friendly societies were withdrawing from the traditional market for sickness insurance as commercial group insurers were developing a new mass market that friendly societies had never touched.[13]

APPENDIX A

# The Roman Catholic Church and Secret Societies

Official Roman Catholic opposition to secret societies developed gradually as the numbers and memberships of these societies proliferated. In 1738 a papal bull condemned Freemasonry as being subversive of religion and the social order. By the mid-nineteenth century, American bishops had misgivings about other secret societies, Catholic and non-Catholic (Macdonald, 1946; Preuss, 1924). At various times, bishops linked Irish-Catholic societies, such as the Ancient Order of Hibernians, to subversive activities in Irish politics and the American labour movement. They worried that non-Catholic societies, such as the Odd Fellows and Knights of Pythias, were like Freemasonry and had social links to it. Their concerns increased after the American Civil War, when these orders experienced an explosive growth of membership and recruited numbers of Roman Catholics.

For some years, the American-Catholic hierarchy was unable to give clear direction to church members. By agreement among American bishops in 1866, a bishop could speak generally against secret societies, but could not name names. Even collectively, the bishops could not agree on whether any particular society merited condemnation. Rome resolved the impasse in 1894, when the Holy See barred Roman Catholics from joining the Odd Fellows, the Knights of Pythias, or the Sons of Temperance, under pain of excommunication. In 1896 the Holy See softened its position slightly. Roman Catholics who had joined one of the banned societies before 1894 could continue in passive membership. Subject to approval by the Apostolic Delegate, they could keep their dues paid up to retain benefits, but were not to attend lodge meetings (Preuss, 1924: 224–8).

Thus Roman Catholics could not join the IOOF after 1894, under pain of ex-communication, but existing members could retain passive membership. Well before 1894, however, some bishops aggressively counselled parishioners against joining the Odd Fellows or remaining Odd Fellows, in some cases to the point of withholding the sacraments from them.

APPENDIX B

# Arrears for Dues and Suspensions of Membership

An Odd Fellow paid annual dues to his lodge in four quarterly instalments. He became ineligible for benefits (non-beneficial) if he fell into arrears for dues, according to the definition of arrears in his grand lodge jurisdiction. An Alberta, British Columbia, Manitoba, or Saskatchewan Odd Fellow became non-beneficial if he fell thirteen weeks in arrears. An Ontario member became non-beneficial by not paying his dues within thirty days of the date specified; he remained ineligible for benefits until four weeks after paying his arrears. Michigan allowed its lodges to decide the matter by passing bylaws for the purpose.

If a member fell one year behind in his dues, then his lodge could suspend him, after giving him written notice. Under IOOF law, suspension did not conclude membership. Thus the lodge continued to add unpaid dues, fines, and assessments to a suspended member's account and classed the amount owing under "assets." A suspended member had to pay his lodge the full amount of his arrearage (or a maximum sum, if the grand lodge set one) to become reinstated, resign from membership, or hold membership in another lodge.[1] The lodge could decline to reinstate a suspended member, even if he tendered the amount of his arrearage. The IOOF obliged the lodge to refuse him if he could not meet the medical standard for new members.

Rather than suspending a member who was in arrears for one year, the lodge could declare him "ceased" (dropped from membership). It also could take no action.[2] For each unsuspended member, however, a lodge paid its grand lodge one or two capitation taxes, depending on the jurisdiction. One tax went towards the overhead of the grand lodge and the SGL. The other, levied in most jurisdictions, supported the IOOF home program. In 1925, for example, the Michigan grand lodge levied capitation taxes of 40 cents for overhead and 10 cents for its IOOF home. Other grand lodges commonly charged $1 to $3 for the home tax. In Manitoba, an exceptional case, the home tax was $5.

The IOOF compiled statistics for members in good standing and suspended members. It did not, however, report subtotals for members in good standing who were in arrears. Thus IOOF statistics for benefits ("number of brothers relieved," "number of weeks benefits were paid," and "amount paid for the relief of brothers") have little value for measuring Odd Fellow sick-claim rates and rising-cost pressures on the sick benefit. One can calculate the proportion of members who made sick claims, but not the proportion of paid-up members who made sick claims.

*Statistics for Arrearage* Three of the six grand lodge head offices that we visited had information about arrearage. The Ontario information was in the semi-annual returns from the lodges. The form for the returns asked the lodge to state the number of members in arrears, the number in arrears for more than one year, and the amount of arrearage owing. The *Proceedings* for the grand lodge annual meetings report the year-end amounts owing for Saskatchewan (1917–29) and British Columbia (1926–9).

*The Evidence for Ontario* Table B.1 summarizes information from the semi-annual returns for 383 lodges (over 90 per cent of all lodges for the years 1919–50). On average 85 per cent of the lodges answered the question about arrears on one or both semi-annual returns. We used the higher of the semi-annual totals to calculate the proportion of members in arrears for the reporting lodges. In a few cases, the semi-annual totals differed considerably (for example, 103 and 64 for one lodge in 1923).

Between 1919 and 1929, as the table data show, the percentage of members in arrears rose from 21 to 33.[3] The proportion was consistently higher for recently-founded lodges than for long-established lodges. The explanation, established by grand lodge statistics for the 1895–1914 period, was that the recently-established lodges had younger memberships. As discussed in chapter 2, the mean age of suspended members was below average for their lodges.

On average, suspended members were 13 per cent of the members in arrears for the year preceding. Moreover, this proportion was stable through to 1929. This indicated that one could estimate the arrearage

Table B.1
The Percentage of Ontario Members in Arrears for Dues, 1919–29

| | *Total no. lodges* | *92 lodges estab. before 1875* | *80 lodges estab. after 1907* | *% Arrears for all lodges* | *Suspension rate* | *Susp. as % of no. in arrears* |
|---|---|---|---|---|---|---|
| 1919 | 399 | .15 | .27 | .21 | .023 | .12 |
| 1920 | 403 | .17 | .31 | .23 | .025 | .14 |
| 1921 | 404 | .19 | .35 | .26 | .033 | .14 |
| 1922 | 405 | .20 | .37 | .26 | .036 | .14 |
| 1923 | 408 | .20 | .35 | .26 | .037 | .12 |
| 1924 | 410 | .22 | .44 | .28 | .031 | .11 |
| 1925 | 410 | .24 | .44 | .29 | .031 | .11 |
| 1926 | 409 | .25 | .43 | .31 | .031 | .12 |
| 1927 | 409 | .25 | .47 | .32 | .037 | .13 |
| 1928 | 409 | .26 | .47 | .32 | .041 | .14 |
| 1929 | 408 | .26 | .47 | .33 | .044 | .13 |

rates for other jurisdictions from their statistics for suspensions, plus the assumption of the stable Ontario ratio of suspensions to arrearage.

*Estimates of the Arrearage Rates for Saskatchewan and British Columbia* Both jurisdictions reported their year-end amounts of arrearage. The Saskatchewan grand lodge issued lodge totals for the amounts, the amount of the annual dues in each lodge for 1917, and grand lodge subtotals for "overpaid dues" (paid in advance) in its statistics for "dues received." The Saskatchewan documents also gave the statistical definition for arrearage: the amounts owing for periods up to one year. Conversely, the statistical definition excluded amounts for periods after one year, such as the ongoing accumulations for suspended members.

Ideally one could estimate the number in arrears by dividing each lodge's year-end amount owing by the 1917 amount of its annual dues. Alternatively, one could calculate arrearage as a proportion of all dues to identify the trend for arrears.

The statistics present several problems for estimation, however. First, the grand lodge totals (the only statistics for British Columbia) are incomplete. In 1924, for example, the returns for 11 per cent of the Saskatchewan lodges did not answer the question about arrearage. Second, the year-end amount owing divided by the amount of the annual dues is ambiguous for interpretation. A product of ten, for example, could represent ten members, each in arrears for one year, or forty members, each in arrears for one quarter's dues.

Statistics for arrearage as a proportion of dues received also mislead. First, the arrearage statistics for some lodges include amounts that were owing for more than one year. In 1925, for example, the year-end amount owing for the thirty-seven members of Redvers Lodge No. 37 is equal to the annual dues of ninety-four members. Second, the statistics for dues received include overpaid dues. In hard times, moreover, overpaid dues follow a declining trend while amounts owing more than a year follow a rising trend. Thus the corrupting influences work in opposite directions on the numerator and denominator for calculation.

If none of the problems discussed above mattered, then the membership for a jurisdiction would have equalled the sum of its dues owed (dues received plus arrearage less overpaid dues) divided by the average amount of the annual dues for its lodges.[4] Yet the product of these calculations for British Columbia and Saskatchewan during the 1920s was between 1.20 and 1.34 instead of the expected unity. The sources of the excess were overpaid dues for British Columbia (not reported) and dues owing for more than one year for both jurisdictions.

We exploited the biases in the data to estimate the proportions of members in arrears for British Columbia and Saskatchewan. First, we calculated a high estimate of the number in arrears for dues: the year-end amount owing divided by the average amount of annual dues for lodges in the jurisdiction concerned. Second, we calculated a high estimate for membership: all dues (dues received plus arrearage less overpaid dues) divided by the average amount of dues for lodges in the jurisdiction concerned. Third, we took the excess predicted by the high estimate (the high estimate for membership less the known membership) as showing the amount of arrearage that was on the books for more than one year for Saskatchewan. Unreported overpaid dues also contributed to the excess of the prediction for British Columbia. To allow for this we estimated that overpaid dues produced 20 per cent of the excess (the known proportion for Saskatchewan).

Fourth, we subtracted the excess of the high estimate prediction for membership from the high estimate for number of members in arrears for dues. This calculation produced our minimum estimate of the number who were in arrears for periods up to one year. It makes the extreme assumption that each member in arrears owed his lodge exactly

Table B.2
Percentage of Members in Arrears in Ontario, British Columbia, and Saskatchewan

| | *British Columbia* | | | *Ontario* | *Saskatchewan* | | |
|---|---|---|---|---|---|---|---|
| | *Minimum* | *Final* | *Suspension rate estimate* | *(Known)* | *Minimum* | *Final* | *Suspension rate estimate* |
| 1924 | – | – | .26 | .28 | .21 | .53 | .51 |
| 1925 | – | – | .27 | .29 | .18 | .44 | .43 |
| 1926 | – | – | .17 | .31 | .21 | .53 | .42 |
| 1927 | .10 | .26 | .27 | .32 | .24 | .61 | .34 |
| 1928 | .11 | .27 | .36 | .32 | .21 | .52 | .46 |
| 1929 | .12 | .29 | .28 | .33 | .27 | .68 | .53 |
| 1930 | .15 | .37 | .38 | .34 | .34 | .84 | .73 |
| 1931 | .20 | .51 | .42 | .37 | .44 | 1.11 | .53 |
| 1932 | .27 | .66 | .37 | .44 | .48 | 1.19 | .68 |
| 1933 | .28 | .70 | .50 | .47 | .60 | 1.49 | .54 |
| 1934 | .26 | .65 | .57 | .46 | .50 | 1.25 | .36 |
| 1935 | .26 | .65 | .50 | .43 | .52 | 1.30 | .43 |

one year's dues. Our maximum estimate was four times the amount of the minimum estimate. It makes the extreme assumption that each member in arrears owed his lodge exactly one quarter's dues.

Fifth, we calculated our final estimate as 2.5 times the minimum estimate. This assumes that each member in arrears owed dues for 2.5 quarters (the mean between one and four).

Table B.2 presents the arrearage estimates for British Columbia and Saskatchewan. For comparison, it presents suspension rate estimates. These assume the stable Ontario ratio of suspended members to number of members in arrears. The final arrearage and suspension rate estimates are plausible for the 1920s because they are similar.

APPENDIX C

# IOOF Financial Statistics

As Table C.1 shows for 1924, the SGL compiled three different tables of summary statistics for revenues and expenses. To elaborate the contents of categories in these tables, we compared the SGL statistics for Ontario in 1929 with the more detailed statistics that the Ontario grand lodge issued for the same year.

In the first table, "current expenses" included "working expenses" and "other expenses, not enumerated," but not "furniture and regalia" and "invested funds." In the second table (Benefits), the "relief of brothers" included the weekly benefits (86 per cent), but also physicians' fees (10 per cent) and the hire of nurses (4 per cent). The "relief of widowed families" included the burials of deceased wives of Odd Fellows; thus "burying the dead" included the burials of deceased Odd Fellows only.

In a few jurisdictions, such as New York, the grand lodge did not report subtotals for the table on lodge receipts. Consequently the all-jurisdictions statistic for total receipts is greater than the sum of the all-jurisdiction statistics for the four subtotals. For calculation of per-capita statistics, therefore, one must remove the memberships of non-reporting jurisdictions from the data for the denominator.

The chief problem with the SGL statistics is the way in which they report contributions to IOOF homes for orphans and aged, indigent members. In 1931 the SGL introduced two special categories, "operating homes for orphans" and "operating homes for the aged" to its table on benefits. For earlier years, however, lodge contributions to IOOF homes were reported partly under "current expenses" and partly under

Table C.1
Summary Statistics for Revenues and Expenses in 1924 Tables

| | *Amount* | *Grand lodges reporting* |
|---|---|---|
| *i) Lodge Receipts, Current Expenses, and Invested Funds* | | |
| RECEIPTS | | |
| Dues | $10,556,512.00 | 53 |
| Joining fees | 1,520,475.13 | 53 |
| Rents and invested funds | 4,299,874.97 | 47 |
| Other sources | 6,081,063.22 | 55 |
| Total receipts | 22,457,924.82 | 56 |
| Current expenses | 12,538,442.13 | 56 |
| Invested funds | 82,105,931.05 | 54 |
| *ii) Expenses on Relief (Benefits)* | | |
| Relief of brothers | 3,518,015.87 | 56 |
| Relief of widowed families | 190,184.91 | 55 |
| Relief of orphans | 349,680.65 | 24 |
| Education of orphans | 333,894.17 | 14 |
| Burying the dead | 1,482,878.51 | 56 |
| Special relief | 694,445.97 | 53 |
| Total relief | 6,569,099.78 | 56 |
| *iii) Orphan and Other Homes Owned by the Order* | | |
| Cost of maintenance | 1,724,889.87 | 47 |

"relief expenses." For forty-nine of the sixty-three homes in 1929, the lodges contributed through per-capita taxes paid to the grand lodge. In these cases, the grand lodge reported the lodge contributions under "current expenses." For the other fourteen homes, the lodges contributed under the categories of "the education of orphans" and "special relief."

To sort out lodge contributions to homes, we compared the relief statistics for 1930 with those for 1931, when the new special categories

Table C.2
Per-Capita Expenses on Relief, 1930–1

| | *1930* | *1931* | *Change* |
|---|---|---|---|
| Total relief | $3.82 | $4.71 | + $0.89 |
| Education of orphans | .25 | .20 | − .05 |
| Special relief | .54 | .26 | − .29 |
| Net change in two subtotals | | | − .34 |
| Net change in all other relief categories | | | + .05 |
| Homes for orphans | – | .48 | |
| Homes for the aged | – | .70 | |
| Total for homes | | 1.18 | + 1.18 |

for homes came into play (see Table C.2). In 1931 the per-capita contribution under the new "Homes" categories was $1.18. Yet the total increase in the statistic for all relief was just $0.89, or $0.29 less. This corresponds exactly with the net change in the categories used in 1930: − 0.05 (education of orphans) − 0.29 (special relief) +0.05 (net change in other categories) = − $0.29.[5]

Thus 75.4 per cent ($0.89) of the $1.18 statistic for homes comes from monies hitherto unreported in the table for relief expenses, and 24.6 per cent ($0.29) comes from monies hitherto reported under "the education of orphans" and "special relief." In 1931 the reported lodge contributions paid 80.9 per cent of the reported home maintenance costs. Thus the former "current expenses" portion of the lodge contributions was equal to 61 per cent (.754*.809) of the reported home maintenance costs.

APPENDIX D

# Grand Lodge Jurisdictions by Classification Group

Table D.1 reports the jurisdictions by classification group, the sick weeks statistics that we used for classification, and changes in the legislative status of the sick benefit. For comparison, it also reports the classification group for thirty-two grand encampments. A description of the procedure for classing the grand encampments precedes and follows Table D.1.

*Classing the Grand Encampments* We lacked information about grand encampment legislation for the sick benefit after 1896, when the SGL made the encampment benefit optional. Thus we used statistics for benefits to class the grand encampments. For each jurisdiction, we calculated the grand encampment's sick weeks statistic (the number of sick weeks per patriarch) as a proportion of the comparable statistic for the grand lodge. We then compared the statistic for 1924 (when the sick benefit was optional for encampments but mandatory for lodges) with the statistics for 1890 and 1895 (when the benefit was mandatory for both branches). A steep drop in the ratio statistic between 1895 and 1924 would indicate a widespread abolition of the sick benefit in the grand encampment. A ratio statistic of zero for 1924 would indicate the total abolition of the encampment benefit.

We interpreted the ratio statistics with caution. Compared to lodge members, members of encampments were older, had higher sick claim rates, and had higher rates for suspension and arrearage. Thus even in jurisdictions where all encampments retained the sick benefit, the ratio statistic was likely to be less than 1.

Table D.1
IOOF Grand Lodge Jurisdictions by Classification Group

| *1924 Encampment class* | | *1925–9 Legislative change* | *1924* | *1925* | *1926* | *1927* | *1928* | *1929* | *1930* | *1931* |
|---|---|---|---|---|---|---|---|---|---|---|
| | | | ABOLITION GROUP | | | | | | | |
| | Arizona | O27 | 0.36 | 0.42 | 0.46 | 0.24 | 0.10 | 0.10 | 0.17 | 0.17 |
| A | Arkansas | O25/A26 | 0.16 | 0.15 | 0.08 | 0.03 | 0.00 | 0.00 | 0.00 | 0.00 |
| | Georgia | O26 | 0.32 | 0.34 | 0.27 | 0.22 | 0.21 | 0.12 | 0.13 | 0.09 |
| A | Idaho | A26 | 0.55 | 0.54 | 0.00 | 0.00 | 0.00 | 0.00 | 0.00 | 0.00 |
| | Kansas | A29 | 0.53 | 0.50 | 0.49 | 0.43 | 0.40 | 0.40 | 0.00 | 0.00 |
| A | Louisiana | O26 | 0.12 | 0.11 | 0.03 | 0.03 | 0.02 | 0.03 | 0.01 | 0.03 |
| R | Michigan | A25/O30 | 0.31 | 0.00 | 0.00 | 0.00 | 0.00 | 0.00 | 0.00 | 0.00 |
| | Minnesota | A27/O28 | 0.39 | 0.36 | 0.40 | 0.04 | 0.13 | 0.24 | 0.20 | 0.20 |
| | Missouri | A27 | 0.40 | 0.40 | 0.39 | 0.22 | 0.00 | 0.00 | 0.00 | 0.00 |
| | Nebraska | O26 | 0.32 | 0.31 | 0.23 | 0.22 | 0.16 | 0.13 | 0.12 | 0.12 |
| | New Mexico | O25/A30 | 0.25 | 0.26 | 0.28 | 0.07 | 0.02 | 0.01 | 0.00 | 0.00 |
| R | N.Carolina | A27/O29 | 0.30 | 0.26 | 0.41 | 0.00 | 0.00 | 0.16 | 0.07 | 0.00 |
| A | N.Dakota | A27 | 0.22 | 0.19 | 0.22 | 0.13 | 0.04 | 0.01 | 0.02 | 0.00 |
| A | S.Dakota | A26 | 0.22 | 0.31 | 0.17 | 0.00 | 0.00 | 0.00 | 0.00 | 0.00 |
| A | Wisconsin | A27 | 0.31 | 0.27 | 0.27 | 0.14 | 0.00 | 0.00 | 0.00 | 0.00 |
| A | Wyoming | A27 | 0.40 | 0.45 | 0.46 | 0.32 | 0.00 | 0.00 | 0.00 | 0.00 |
| | | | 1924 | 1925 | 1926 | 1927 | 1928 | 1929 | 1930 | 1931 |
| All jurisdictions: | | | 0.59 | 0.57 | 0.60 | 0.55 | 0.54 | 0.55 | 0.53 | 0.51 |
| | | | MIDDLE GROUP | | | | | | | |
| | | | 1924 | 1925 | 1926 | 1927 | 1928 | 1929 | 1930 | 1931 |
| A | Alabama | O30 | 0.26 | 0.30 | 0.34 | 0.21 | 0.29 | 0.30 | 0.18 | 0.10 |
| | Maine | O26 | 0.83 | 0.82 | 0.89 | 0.77 | 0.49 | 0.59 | 0.58 | 0.55 |
| R | N.Hampshire | O26 | 0.78 | 0.75 | 0.74 | 0.64 | 0.55 | 0.45 | 0.42 | 0.38 |
| | Sask. | O27 | 0.26 | 0.27 | 0.24 | 0.25 | 0.22 | 0.15 | 0.10 | 0.09 |
| A | S.Carolina | O30 | 0.32 | 0.27 | 0.17 | 0.19 | 0.15 | 0.14 | 0.11 | 0.11 |
| R | Tennessee | O25 | 0.34 | 0.36 | 0.35 | 0.20 | 0.23 | 0.19 | 0.19 | 0.13 |
| | Texas | O26 | 0.26 | 0.27 | 0.25 | 0.18 | 0.16 | 0.15 | 0.08 | 0.07 |
| A | Utah | O30 | 0.60 | 0.80 | 1.02 | 0.95 | 0.71 | 0.52 | 0.58 | 0.00 |
| | | | 1924 | 1925 | 1926 | 1927 | 1928 | 1929 | 1930 | 1931 |
| All jurisdictions: | | | 0.59 | 0.57 | 0.60 | 0.55 | 0.54 | 0.55 | 0.53 | 0.51 |

Table D.1 (*continued*)

| *1924 Encampment class* | | *1925–9 Legislative change* | *1924* | *1925* | *1926* | *1927* | *1928* | *1929* | *1930* | *1931* |
|---|---|---|---|---|---|---|---|---|---|---|
| | | | RETENTION GROUP | | | | | | | |
| | Alberta | O28 | 0.34 | 0.34 | 0.23 | 0.28 | 0.26 | 0.28 | 0.22 | 0.22 |
| | B.C. | O31 | 0.98 | 0.97 | 0.93 | 0.93 | 0.91 | 0.97 | 0.92 | 0.87 |
| R | California | O30 | 0.79 | 0.85 | 0.84 | 0.84 | 0.86 | 0.90 | 0.91 | 0.95 |
| | Colorado | O26 | 0.52 | 0.50 | 0.49 | 0.53 | 0.47 | 0.51 | 0.43 | 0.39 |
| R | Connecticut | NC | 0.94 | 0.99 | 0.97 | 0.91 | 0.92 | 1.00 | 1.05 | 0.49 |
| | Delaware | NC | 0.72 | 0.85 | 0.91 | 0.79 | 0.81 | 0.81 | 0.95 | 1.05 |
| | Dist.Col. | NC | 1.00 | 0.96 | 1.02 | 0.74 | 0.73 | 0.74 | 0.97 | 0.94 |
| | Florida | O30 | 0.21 | 0.24 | 0.18 | 0.19 | 0.22 | 0.19 | 0.25 | 0.11 |
| R | Illinois | O25 | 0.44 | 0.44 | 0.51 | 0.37 | 0.35 | 0.37 | 0.31 | 0.25 |
| R | Indiana | O30 | 0.72 | 0.74 | 0.73 | 0.73 | 0.71 | 0.68 | 0.61 | 0.62 |
| R | Iowa | O26 | 0.39 | 0.40 | 0.40 | 0.33 | 0.30 | 0.29 | 0.25 | 0.23 |
| R | Kentucky | O25 | 0.43 | 0.45 | 0.52 | 0.45 | 0.47 | 0.47 | 0.50 | 0.50 |
| R | Manitoba | NC | 0.69 | 0.67 | 0.64 | 0.69 | 0.63 | 0.57 | 0.60 | 0.55 |
| | Maritimes | O30 | 0.78 | 0.72 | 0.70 | 0.71 | 0.73 | 0.71 | 0.61 | 0.58 |
| A | Maryland | O27 | 0.51 | 0.50 | 0.60 | 0.56 | 0.63 | 0.63 | 0.96 | 0.69 |
| | Mass. | NC | 1.05 | 0.79 | 1.07 | 1.07 | 1.05 | 1.08 | 1.05 | 1.13 |
| A | Mississippi | O31 | 0.42 | 0.39 | 0.33 | 0.30 | 0.35 | 0.40 | 0.27 | 0.39 |
| | Montana | A26/O30 | 0.40 | 0.47 | 0.46 | 0.42 | 0.42 | 0.38 | 0.38 | 0.37 |
| A | Nevada | NC | 0.71 | 0.64 | 0.60 | 0.62 | 0.47 | 0.50 | 0.67 | 0.65 |
| | New Jersey | NC | 0.77 | 0.78 | 0.84 | 0.79 | 0.83 | 0.68 | 0.90 | 0.91 |
| R | New York | NC | 0.65 | 0.64 | 0.63 | 0.56 | 0.54 | 0.55 | 0.55 | 0.53 |
| R | Ohio | A30 | 0.74 | 0.72 | 0.72 | 0.73 | 0.68 | 0.67 | 0.56 | 0.16 |
| A | Oklahoma | O26 | 0.25 | 0.26 | 0.22 | 0.22 | 0.16 | 0.22 | 0.21 | 0.18 |
| | Ontario | NC | 0.74 | 0.74 | 0.76 | 0.69 | 0.66 | 0.68 | 0.62 | 0.60 |
| R | Oregon | O27 | 0.56 | 0.59 | 0.63 | 0.63 | 0.51 | 0.54 | 0.47 | 0.42 |
| R | Penn. | O30 | 0.90 | 0.98 | 1.07 | 1.08 | 1.12 | 1.21 | 1.21 | 1.32 |
| A | Quebec | O30 | 0.49 | 0.56 | 0.57 | 0.60 | 0.59 | 0.63 | 0.63 | 0.77 |
| | Rhode I. | NC | 0.82 | 0.84 | 1.06 | 1.22 | 1.23 | 1.34 | 1.24 | 1.17 |
| | Vermont | NC | 0.49 | 0.40 | 0.46 | 0.50 | 0.43 | 0.28 | 0.46 | 0.49 |
| R | Virginia | O27 | 0.63 | 0.65 | 0.69 | 0.69 | 0.68 | 0.64 | 0.55 | 0.56 |
| | Washington | NC | 0.59 | 0.61 | 0.55 | 0.57 | 0.56 | 0.55 | 0.57 | 0.52 |
| R | W.Virginia | O30 | 0.18 | 0.18 | 0.17 | 0.19 | 0.19 | 0.20 | 0.19 | 0.28 |

Table D.1 (*continued*)

| *1924 Encampment class* | *1925–9 Legislative change* | *1924* | *1925* | *1926* | *1927* | *1928* | *1929* | *1930* | *1931* |
|---|---|---|---|---|---|---|---|---|---|
| All jurisdictions: | | 0.59 | 0.57 | 0.60 | 0.55 | 0.54 | 0.55 | 0.53 | 0.51 |

*Legend for 1924 Grand Encampment Classification*:
A = Abolition; R = Retention
*Legend for Legislative Change*:
O = Optional for Lodges (O29 = made optional for lodges in or by 1929); A = Abolition;
NC = No Change

We declined to class twenty-four of the fifty-six grand encampments. Seven jurisdictions did not have an encampment branch before 1896; thus we had no base-year statistic for comparison with 1924. In some cases, the ratio statistics fluctuated randomly due to small numbers in the encampment branch. Thus the ratio statistics for 1890, one of our two base years, ranged from 0.20 for Arkansas to 1.89 for North Dakota. In other cases, it dropped moderately between the 1895 base year and 1924. This indicated a mixed pattern for abolition in the encampment branch. Hence we declined to class it in the abolition or retention groups.

For each of the fifteen abolition group grand encampments, the ratio statistic for 1924 was less than 0.10 and decidedly below its 1895 base-year statistic. In our judgment, each of the seventeen retention group grand encampments had similar ratio statistics for 1924 and 1895.

APPENDIX E

# Technical Details for the Risk-Loading and Probability-of-Ruin Measures

THE AGGREGATE CLAIMS DISTRIBUTION The risk-loading and probability-of-ruin measures require estimates of the claim size distribution, F(Z). The nature of our data requires a collective approach to the task.[6] We treat the distribution of the aggregate sickness claim, F(Z), as a compound process that expresses stochastic variation in claim numbers and sizes.[7] For example, a lodge's aggregate sick claim payment for a given year may represent one member's claim or the sum of two or more individual claims. Given the variable decomposition of an aggregate claim, our approximation of the claims distribution allows for the probabilities of different numbers of claims and the probability that a given number of claims would generate the observed aggregate claim size.

For a lodge membership of size M, the probability distribution of the aggregate claim incurred during a one year time interval

$$Z = \sum_{i=1}^{M} z_i,\ z_i \geq 0\ \forall i,$$

is expressible as

$$F(Z) = \sum_{k=0}^{K} p(k) S^k(Z). \tag{1}$$

The function p(k) gives the probability that the number of claims in one year is equal to k, and $s^k(z)$ is the distribution function for the sum of k claim amounts.

The claim-number process, p(k), reflects two influences: the number of lodge members and the chance that a particular member will make a claim. If the claim numbers are non-negative, random integers that meet the requirements for the Poisson distribution,[8] then the claim-number process, p(k), is expressible as

$$p(k) = Pr[\ \#\ of\ Claims = k] = \frac{\delta^k \cdot e^{-\delta}}{k!},\ \delta \geq 0, \tag{2}$$

For the Poisson process the expected number of claims and its variance in a given time unit are

$$E[k] = \delta = Var[k]. \tag{3}$$

The claim-size process, $s^k(z)$, is the second component of the compound distribution. Here $z_i \geq 0$ represents an individual member's claim against the lodge's funds. $z_i$ is a random variable, and one assumes that individual claim sizes are mutually independent and identically distributed with the distribution function $s_i(z_i)$. If the distribution function for an individual claim is known and identical for all individuals, then $s_i(\cdot)=s(\cdot)$ for all i=1, ... M members. Since the individual claims (the $z_i$) are mutually independent, the sum of the k claim amounts has the distribution function $s^k(z)$, where $s^k(z)$ is the kth convolution of the distribution function $s(\cdot)$.

Implicitly $z_i=0$ if member i does not make a claim, and $z_i>0$ if member i makes a claim and receives a benefit. If we assume that the claim sizes of the claiming members are distributed exponentially,[9] then

$$S(z_i) = 1 - e^{-\beta z_i} \tag{4}$$

Thus the expected claim size for an individual claimer is

$$E[z_i] = \int_0^\infty z_i ds(z_i) = \frac{1}{\beta} \tag{5}$$

When the individual claim sizes have independent and identical exponential distributions, the sum of k claims has a Gamma distribution.[10] Thus for a given number of claims, k,

$$S^k(Z) = \int_0^z \frac{(u\beta)^{k-1}\beta e^{-u\beta}}{\Gamma(k)} du \qquad (6)$$

with the expected total claim

$$E\left[\sum_{i=1}^{M} z_i\right] = \frac{k}{\beta}. \qquad (7)$$

For the compound-Poisson distribution, the expected aggregate claim for a lodge is the product of the expected number of claims given in (3) and the expected individual claim size defined in (5):

$$E[Z] = \int^{\infty} Z dF(Z) = \frac{\delta}{\beta}. \qquad (8)$$

The variance of the aggregate claim is

$$Var[Z] = \frac{\delta}{\beta^2}. \qquad (9)$$

To estimate the moments of F(Z) and to evaluate F(Z) for probabilities of ruin, one needs estimates for δ and β. If for l=1, … , n lodges we observe pairs of numbers of claims, k, and the total value of claims paid, z, then for each observation, l, we observe $\{k_l, z_l\}$. Note that if $k_l=0$, then $z_l=0$ with probability one. If $k_l>0$, then $z_l>0$ since a minimum claim size obtains for any claim. Thus one can conceptualize F(Z) as having a mass point at a claim size of zero and a continuous density for all $z>0$. When the claim number process is Poisson, the likelihood of observing an aggregate claim of zero dollars is

$$F(0) = Pr[k = 0] = e^{-\delta}. \qquad (10)$$

When $k_l>0$ the likelihood of observing a $\{k_l, z_l\}$ combination is given by the density,

$$f(Z) = \frac{\delta^k e^{-\delta}}{k!} \cdot \frac{(Z\beta)^{k-1}\beta e^{Z\beta}}{\Gamma(k)}. \qquad (11)$$

Define $D_l=0$ if $z_l=0$, and $D_l=1$ if $z_l>0$. The contribution of the lth observation to the likelihood function is

$$l_1 = (e^{-\delta})^{1-D_l} \cdot \left( \frac{\delta^{k_l} e^{-\delta}}{k_l!} \cdot \frac{(Z_1\beta)^{k_l - 1} \beta e^{-Z_l\beta}}{\Gamma(k_l)} \right)^{D_l} \tag{12}$$

The Log of the likelihood function for n observations is

$$LLF = \log(L) = \sum_{l=1}^{n} \log(l_l). \tag{13}$$

We introduce time-invariant covariates (denoted by X) to control for differences in the extent and intensity of a lodge's exposure to risk. Thus

$$\delta(X) = \exp(X\theta), \text{ and, } \beta(X) = \exp(X\phi). \tag{14}$$

The maximum likelihood estimation of (13) yields estimates of $\delta(X)$ and $\beta(X)$.

Estimates of the aggregate claims distribution, $F(Z)$, treat each annual observation of claims for each lodge as an independent draw from the aggregate claim process.[11] Thus the aggregate claims of each lodge are independent of other lodges' aggregate claims. Similarly a lodge's aggregate claim in one year is independent of its aggregate claims for other years. Under these conditions we have 397 observations (lodge-years of operation) for the twenty-seven lodges in the period 1890–1929.

Based on the estimated aggregate claim distributions for the twenty-seven lodges during the period 1891–1929, we estimated the aggregate claims by:

$$E[Z] = \frac{\delta(X)}{\beta(X)}$$

When we plotted the observed total claims payments against the corresponding predicted claims, the data points were evenly distributed around the 45 Degree Line (Emery, 1996: Fig. 1). This indicated that the estimation provide an accurate representation of the mean of the claims distribution.

Estimates of the aggregate claims distribution capture the extent and intensity of a lodge's risk exposure. Perhaps membership size influenced the probability of claims. For example, membership size may capture an aging effect that the lodge-age variable misses. Alternatively, an increase of size may diminish the lodge's capacity to police the moral hazard.[12] To allow for these possibilities, we included the reported number of members, M, in the expected-number-of-claims parameter, $\delta$ (x).

The reported totals for membership may inflate a lodge's exposure to claims. At any point in time, some members ineligible for the benefit because they were in arrears for dues or unemployed. For experimentation, we replaced the reported membership, M, with a proxy for eligible members, EM, in the expected-number-of-claims parameter, $\delta$ (x). Our estimate of the eligible members was the receipts from dues divided by $12; the proxy, EM, was a ratio of eligible to reported members. We discarded the proxy because it little difference to the risk-loading and probability-of-ruin estimates.

Over time the mean age of a lodge's members tended to rise. Thus a lodge's exposure to the risk of claims tended to increase the longer it was in operation. To capture the influence of membership aging on a lodge's exposure to risk, we incorporated a proxy variable, lodge-age (its number of years of operation by a given year), into the expected-number-of-claims parameter $\delta$ and the claim-size parameter $\beta$. The specifications included lodge-age and lodge-age squared. To control for the possibility that a newly-instituted lodge required some time to become fully operational, we also included a variable, $D_{Open}$. $D_{Open}$ equalled 1 if the lodge's age was less than 2 and 0 otherwise.

Lodges in cities possibly had above-average amounts for the weekly benefit. Odd Fellows in cities faced an above-average cost of living. Their lodges also faced above-average competition from other insurers. In case rural-urban differences mattered, we gave a variable, $D_{Urb}$, in both the expected-number-of-claims parameter $\delta$ and the claim-size parameter $\beta$.[13] $D_{Urb}$ equalled 1 for lodges in Victoria, Vancouver, New Westminster, and Nanaimo and 0 otherwise.

Using the known aggregate claims, numbers of claims, and the variables described above, we estimated the log of the likelihood function defined by (12) and (13) with the following parameter specifications of $\delta$ and $\beta$:

$$\begin{aligned} \delta(X) &= \exp(\theta_o + \theta_1 M + \theta_2 D_{OPEN} + \theta_3 Age + \theta_4 Age^2 + \theta_6 D_{Urb}) \\ \beta(X) &= \exp(\phi_o + \phi_1 D_{OPEN} + \phi_2 Age + \phi_3 Age^2 + \phi_4 D_{Urb}) \end{aligned} \tag{15}$$

THE IMPLICIT DEGREE OF RISK-LOADING ESTIMATES The risk-loading measure builds on the following decomposition of the price charged to an individual for insurance coverage (Borch, 1990):

$$P = c + E + R \tag{16}$$

The price, P, is set to cover E, the expected claims of the contract; C, a portion of the insurer's overhead costs in providing the coverage; and R, a risk-loading premium charged over and above the expected claims to reduce the insurer's risk of insolvency.

Suppose that an individual purchases sickness insurance from an insurer. Let $z_i \geq 0$ denote the dollars-per-year claim size for an insured person i. $z_i$ has the distribution function $S_i(z_i)$ with the mean

$$E[z_i] = \int_0^{\infty} z_i dS_i(z_i).$$

Assuming proportional risk loading, $R = \pi E[z_i]$[14], where $\pi$ is a parameter representing the degree of risk loading, then

$$P_i = C_i + E[z_i] + \pi E[z_i] \tag{17}$$

Here $c_i$ is the share of the insurer's overhead costs paid by individual i, and $\Sigma_i c_i = C$, the insurer's total overhead costs.

We can now impose a lodge's observed membership dues and sick benefit arrangements on the pricing equation. In a given year, a lodge of $i = 1, \dots, M$ members would experience total claims of

$$Z = \sum_{i=1}^{M} z_i$$

Here Z is the lodge's aggregate claim, the product of the total weeks of benefit claimed and the stipulated weekly benefit. If each member i, $i = 1, \dots, M$, faces a claim-size distribution $s_i(\cdot)$, and claim-size distributions are independent across all i members, then the expected aggregate claim against lodge funds is

$$E[Z] = E\left[\sum_{i=1}^{M} z_i\right] = \sum_{i=1}^{M} E[z_i]$$

Given the known lodge practice of charging a flat-rate price (membership dues) for all M members, the price expression given in (16) becomes

$$P = \frac{C}{M} + (1 + \pi)\frac{E[Z]}{M} \tag{18}$$

As (18) expresses, the members shared equally the lodge's total overhead costs, C, and their aggregate risk loaded liabilities. Note that the price in (17) represents an actuarial price because it reflects the risk characteristics of the individual purchaser. By contrast, the price in (18) is a non-actuarial price. It is based upon the total membership claims, Z, and is insensitive to risk factors such as age for individuals.

Within the pricing framework described above, one can interpret $\pi$ (the risk-loading parameter) as a measure of the adequacy of the price of membership, net of operating costs, for meeting expected sick claims.[15] A rearrangement of the pricing equation (18) expresses the degree of risk loading as

$$\pi = \frac{M \cdot P - C}{E[Z]} - 1 \qquad (19)$$

Positive risk loading, $\pi > 0$, implies that the prescribed membership dues are more than adequate, on average, for meeting annual operating expenses and expected claims. If $\pi = 0$, then the prescribed price is barely sufficient to cover claims and operating expenses. Negative risk loading, $\pi < 0$, indicates that the lodge would have to run down accumulated reserves (or assets) to meet expected claims and overhead costs. Finally, if $\pi < -1$, the price of membership will not even meet operating expenses.

British Columbia lodges rarely changed their prescribed dues and weekly sick benefits. Effectively the dues, P, were insensitive to change in the lodge's overhead costs and also to change in the membership's risk-factor composition. Thus a change of either type implied a compensating adjustment in the risk-loading parameter, $\pi$. Thus, the implicit degree of risk loading indicates whether pricing was a problem in the lodges and whether its adequacy deteriorated over time.

THE PROBABILITY OF RUIN This procedure estimates the probability that high claims in a given year could bankrupt a lodge. The probability of ruin incorporates assets and accumulated funds. In the process, it illuminates how lodge assets might have influenced the perceived adequacy of the price of membership and in turn, the financial viability of lodges.

A formal expression of the probability of ruin is

$$P^R = Pr[Z > TR - C + A] = 1 - \int_0^{TR - C + A} dF(Z) \qquad (20)$$

Here TR represents the annual total revenues, and A is the value of the lodge's assets at the beginning of the year. F(Z) is the distribution function of the aggregate claim. Clearly the degree of risk loading, $\pi$, influences the trend for $P^R$ over time. With a positive $\pi$ the lodge accumulates assets and the probability of ruin decreases; with negative $\pi$, the opposite obtains.

We estimated probabilities of ruin for the twenty-seven lodges from the estimated coefficients of the aggregate claims distribution in Table 4.7; the parameter specifications in equation 15; the Poisson specification in equation 2; the Gamma specification in equation 6; the reported value of assets from December of the previous year; and the addition to assets during the year (revenues net of operating expenses and other non-sickness relief expenditure).

For a given finite number of claims k, where k is a positive integer, if Z has a Gamma distribution with parameters k and $\beta$;

$$S^k(Z) = 1 - \sum_{j=1}^{k} \frac{(Z\beta)^{k-1} e^{-Z\beta}}{(k-1)!}$$

Thus, using the following recursion to evaluate the Standardized Gamma claim-size distribution;[16]

$$S^k(Z) = 1 - e^{-Z\beta}\left[1 + Z\beta + \frac{(Z\beta)^2}{2!} + \ldots + \frac{(Z\beta)^{k-1}}{(k-1)!}\right]$$

one can evaluate the probability of ruin numerically

$$Pr[Z_t > TR_t - C_t + A_t] = 1 - \sum_{k=1}^{\bar{k}} p(k) \cdot S^k(TR_t - C_t + A_t).$$

The estimation of the ruin probabilities requires some confidence in the statistics for lodge assets. In general this is warranted. In 1926, the first year for which we have detailed information, the reported total of assets for all British Columbia lodges was \$911,731. Most of this came from real estate (53 per cent), bonds and other investments (28 per cent), and cash held by lodge treasurers (8 per cent). Assets in these categories had substantial real value. During the years 1890–1929, they generated an average return of 3.3 per cent for the twenty-seven study lodges and 4.5 per cent for all British Columbia lodges.

The balance of the assets came from furniture and regalia (9 per cent) and dues in arrears (2 per cent). These items would not have been admissible as assets for liquidation under commercial accounting practices. On the other hand, the IOOF's reported assets excluded human capital. The Odd Fellows themselves generated returns through the recruitment of new members and the provision of low-cost or no-cost administrative services.

APPENDIX F

# Technical Details for the Calculation of the Hazard Rates

The hazard rate states a member's probability of exit for each year of membership between 1 and j (Kiefer, 1988). For each year of membership, (j), members in the population (N) draw an income and accumulate savings. The income and savings of individuals are unobserved, random variables. Based on their savings at a given moment, some members decline to pay their dues and renew their membership. After $j = 1, \ldots, T$ years in the membership, $n_j$ members quit. The hazard rate for the first year of membership is $H(1) = n_1/N$. At the end of the first year, the members who survive in the membership into the second year, hence are still at risk to exit, number $S(1) = N - n_1$. During the second year ($j = 2$), $n_2$ members exit. The hazard rate for the second year of membership is $H(2) = n_2/(N - n_1) = n_2/S(1)$. This is the number of exiting members divided by the number of members who are still around to exit after one year.

Generally the hazard rate for j years in the membership is $H(j) = n_j/S(j-1)$. A member's probability of quitting in year j is conditional on having remained in the membership up to year $j-1$. Thus the hazard rates, $H(1..t)$, are a sequence of probabilities of exit for the random variable $t_i$, the length of membership.

For convenience we describe the hazard function as a ratio of the exiting members to persisting members for a given length of spell, $t_i$. In technical language, the hazard function for $t_i$ is a ratio of the density function, $f(t)$, to the survivor function, $S(t) = (1 - F(t))$. This represents one minus the distribution function for spell length t:

$$h(t) = \frac{f(t)}{1 - F(t)}$$

To allow for right-censored spells, we give a dichotomous variable, $d_i$, the value of 1 for completed membership spells and 0 if the observed spell is censored at the duration length, $t_i$. Suppose that we have a sample of i = 1, ... ,n observations of $t_i$, the observed length of time individual i was a member in an Odd Fellows lodge, and $d_i$. We assume that the underlying parameters of the distribution for membership duration were stable over time. We estimate the underlying parameters, $\phi$, by maximizing the likelihood function:

$$L(t) = \prod_{i=1}^{n} f(t_i, \phi)^{d_i} [1 - F(t_i, \theta)]^{1-d_i}$$

The first term in the equation is the density function, which describes the lengths of completed spells. The second term is the survivor function, which accounts for censored, or uncompleted, spells.

Next we use two specifications of the functional form for the baseline hazard function: the Weibull density function and the Weibull-Gamma mixing density function.

The Weibull density function is given in (1).

$$f(t_i) = ba^b t_i^{b-1} \cdot \exp(-at_i^{\,b}) \qquad (1)$$

This specification allows us to test whether a hazard function is increasing or decreasing, but it also imposes a monotonic increasing or decreasing hazard function (the hazard function is either always non-increasing or always non-decreasing). If $b>1$ then the Weibull hazard function displays *positive-duration dependence*. Thus as the young man's insurance model predicts, the probability of exit increases with the length of the membership spell. If, however, $b<1$, then the Weibull hazard function displays *negative-duration dependence*. Thus as the old man's insurance model predicts, the probability of exit falls as the membership spell lengthens.

The Weibull distribution alone does not allow for the unobserved heterogeneity of demand for Good s (discussed above). To allow for this influence on the hazard rates, we combine a Gamma-mixing distribution with the Weibull density function, given in (1). This yields the mixing-density function, given in (2):

$$f(t_i) = \frac{ba^b t_i^{b-1}}{[1 + \delta(at_i)^b]^{\frac{1}{\delta}+1}} \qquad (2)$$

The mixing-density function is Log-Logistic. The parameter $\delta$, which is estimated directly, captures the unobserved heterogeneity.

We assume a proportional hazard model to incorporate covariates such as members' ages into the framework. Thus the covariates proportionally shift a baseline hazard function $h_o(\cdot)$ in the fashion of:

$$h(t) = h_o(t) \exp (Z'\phi)$$

Z is a vector of covariates; $\phi$ is a parameter vector.

Our estimations incorporate the following covariates: the member's age at initiation, ($A_i$); and time effects ($Y_i$) as represented by the individual's year of initiation minus 1856. We open with general estimations that pool observations from the six lodges. We then calculate hazard rates separately for the six lodges to capture lodge-specific influences. We introduce covariates into the parameters of the Weibull density function specifications (with and without Gamma mixing) as follows:

$$a(X) = \exp (\phi_o + \phi_1 A_i + \phi_2 Y_i)$$

# Notes

## PROLOGUE

1 The Canadian literature is limited to two studies of the Orange Order (Houston and Smyth, 1980; Senior, 1972).

2 *Gold Dust*, September 1927, London Life archives. (London Life introduced *Gold Dust* in 1927. It was a promotional newsletter for the employees in the company's group branch.) The Benevolent and Protective Order of Elks dated from 1867 and operated exclusively in the United States. The Benevolent and Protective Order of Elks of Canada was founded in Vancouver in 1912.

3 Policyholder's metal tag, presented to the writers by Richard Bywaters, London.

4 Fraternal assessment-method insurance was historically important in the United States and Canada. Friendly societies and insurance orders were the major source of sickness and accident insurance into the 1920s. Fraternal life-assessment insurance dated from 1869 and provided commercial insurance with strong competition through to the 1920s. By 1883 fraternal orders insured two American lives for every five in commercial insurance (Stalson, 1942). Their share of the market peaked in 1895 but remained substantial through to 1929. Their number of policies in force peaked in 1924.

## CHAPTER ONE

1 According to a United States National Health Survey for 1935–6, sickness caused 91 per cent of all disability, non-workplace accidents caused 7 per cent, and industrial accidents caused 2 per cent.

2 Janet Galley, a graduate student at the University of Western Ontario, drew the sample for us. Our random sample of 393 cases is accurate to within 5 per cent, 95 times out of 100. The categories overlap for the statistics cited here; hence the percentages total more than 100 per cent.

3 "That the sickness of the breadwinner brought financial difficulties to the family was manifest to our earliest brethren," noted Moffrey (Moffrey, 1910: 188).

4 *Statistical Abstract of the United States*, 1920–9; *Canada Year Books*, 1920–9. We cannot say if insurers did better in the smaller Canadian market because our premium statistics for the two countries are not comparable. The Canadian statistics are for the categories of "sickness" and "accident and sickness combined," but exclude the category of "accident." The American statistics are for "accident" and "health" categories.

5 The grand lodge of the Maritime provinces was an exceptional case. Its jurisdiction included three provinces (Nova Scotia, New Brunswick, and Prince Edward Island) and Newfoundland. The IOOF also expanded beyond North America. By 1890 it had lodges in Cuba, Mexico, Chile, Peru, Japan, the Sandwich Islands (Hawaii), the Netherlands, Sweden, and France. By 1907 it had chartered grand lodges for Australasia, Denmark, Germany, the Netherlands, Sweden, and Switzerland; the six had 543 lodges and 45,000 members. Through to 1929 it also chartered grand lodges for Norway (1920), Czechoslovakia (1924), Cuba (1925), and Poland (1925), With the exception of Cuba, the SGL gave these grand bodies the status of "quasi-independent jurisdictions" and reported statistics for them separately. In 1921 the offshore jurisdictions accounted for 3.6 per cent of the IOOF's world membership. Between 1920 and 1929, when membership in America and Canada showed a decline, the memberships of the offshore jurisdictions rose from 65,000 to 95,000.

6 We thank Joy Parr for this suggestion in response to a paper that we presented in 1997. The suggestion came from her research for the Ontario towns of Hanover and Paris (Parr, 1990).

7 Interview with Harvey Campbell, Toronto, August 1994.

8 Indirect evidence of the paternal influence is in the IOOF's 1911 directory for Toronto, which holds ninety-six cases of two or more members who had the same family name and residential address.

## CHAPTER TWO

1 Stillson, 1897: 126. The IOOF did not remove the race restriction until 1969.

2 In 1943 the SGL resolved that American Indians were of "white blood" for purposes of the order.

3 Non-whites were just 2 per cent of Canada's population in 1931. They were 10 per cent of population in the United States in 1930; the percentages for nine southern states of the old civil war confederacy ranged from 26 to 50.

4 With 60,000 members in 1907, Negro Masons had the largest fraternal membership in Georgia and ranked third in Florida and South Carolina. The negro Knights of Pythias had 40,000 members (Stevens, 1907).

5 Toronto, Manulife Insurance Company Archives, Manulife Medical Director's Scrapbook, Manulife Policy Department Scrapbook, 1915–32 memorandum dated 28 September 1927. Janet Galley, a graduate student in the MA program at the University of Western Ontario, kindly allowed us to cite this information.

6 The major Roman Catholic societies were the Ancient Order of Hibernians, founded in New York in 1836; the Union St Joseph du Canada, founded in Ottawa in 1863; the Catholic Mutual Benefit Association, founded in Niagara Falls, NY, in 1876; the Société des artisans Canadien-français, founded in Montreal in 1876; the Knights of Columbus, founded in New Haven, Connecticut, in 1882; and the Catholic Order of Foresters, founded in Chicago in 1883. Appendix A describes the evolution of church policy on secret societies. Although acting as a counter-institution, the Hibernians faced opposition from the church.

7 Gist, 1940: 47. In 1952 the IOF rekindled its ties with Roman Catholics by absorbing the Catholic Mutual Benefit Association (Schmidt, 1980: 117).

8 In a trailing statement, issued in 1896, the Holy See allowed Roman Catholics who had joined one of the banned societies before 1894 to continue in passive membership. Subject to approval by the apostolic delegate, they could pay their dues to retain benefits, but were not to attend lodge meetings. Effectively, they could remain Odd Fellows "just for the insurance" (see Appendix A).

9 IOOF, Michigan grand lodge, *Proceedings*, 1912: 146–50.

10 In the end, the IOOF's grand sire barred lodges from subscribing to the journal and cancelled the charter of the editor's lodge, after it declined to expel him from the order. See ibid., 1914: 273, 356–74.

11 Roman Catholics were 20 per cent of Ontario males and 86 per cent of Quebec males in 1921.

In Canada Roman Catholics were 37 per cent of population in 1901 and 41 per cent in 1921. With Quebec excluded, the proportions were 18 and 24 per cent. In the United States, the Roman Catholic Church had more communicants than any other denomination in 1906. State populations with the highest proportions of Roman Catholics were those of New Mexico, Rhode Island, Massachusetts, Louisiana, and Connecticut. State populations with the lowest proportions were those of southern states that had supported the civil war confederacy, exclusive of Louisiana. In 1916 Roman Catholic communicants were 36 per cent of all church members and 15 per cent of population. The comparable statistics for 1926 were 34 and 16 per cent. See United States, Bureau of the Census, *Statistical Atlas of the United States* (1914): 88–90, plates 479–92; *Statistical History of the United States*, series H788–805; *Statistical Abstract of the United States*, 1942: 65–6.

The United States census bureau did not collect comprehensive population statistics for denominational affiliation. It did, however, compile statistics for church communicants (members), as reported by the churches, for 1906, 1916, and 1926. A problem with these statistics is the huge proportion of "unchurched": 58 per cent in 1916 and 54 per cent in 1926. Although the category of "unchurched" included persons that did not have a denominational affiliation, it also included children who were too young to qualify for membership in their respective denominations.

12 Sources: membership registers for Ingersoll, Samaritan Lodge No. 35 (1856–1929); Ingersoll, Oxford Lodge No. 77 (1871–1902); Harrietsville, Hope Lodge No. 69 (1870–1929); and the 1881 and 1901 censuses for Ingersoll and the two townships.

Our case studies provide soft tests for Roman Catholic joiners in IOOF lodges. By 1897 Ingersoll had branches of two Roman Catholic counter institutions. A case study locality without counter institutions would have provided a stiffer test. Few Roman Catholics lived in North Dorchester and South Dorchester townships (e.g., fifty-seven in 1881). In addition, North Dorchester included the territories of two other IOOF lodges: Lilly Lodge No. 211 (1878– ) in Dorchester village and Star Lodge No. 304 (1894– ) in the hamlet of Crampton.

13 In 1926 American-Jewish church members were 7 per cent of all American church members and 3 per cent of the national population. In 1921 Jews were 1 per cent of the Canadian population, but 7 per cent of the Montreal, Toronto, and Winnipeg city populations.

14 Jewish men were section workers in a ready-made clothing industry that was undermining the custom work of Anglo-Canadian tailors. Anglo-Canadian tailors shunned the Jewish garment workers out of anti-semitism, dislike of the radical Jewish politics, and resentment of Jews as economic competitors.

15 Ontario, Report of the Insurance Superintendent, 1921.

16 Greene, *Who's Who and Why, 1919–20*, 249.

17 Sunnyside Lodge had an all-Jewish membership when it surrendered its charter, a few years ago. Source: interview with Don Wright, grand secretary, 22–24 February 1994; inference of Jewish ethnicity from family names in the lodge's semi-annual reports, Toronto, and Ontario grand lodge, *Journal of Proceedings*. Given the social cleavage between Jews and Anglo-Canadians before 1960, a mixed Jewish-Protestant membership is unlikely for the interwar years. Like the city's Jewish population, the lodge's membership grew during the 1920s (a 25 per cent increase between 1921 and 1929); in contrast, the combined membership for all city lodges fell by 38 per cent.

18 These statistics include the "foreign-born" and "native white of foreign or mixed parentage": effectively, immigrants and the children of immigrants.

The figures for northwestern Europe exclude Great Britain and Ireland. Blacks were 4 per cent of population for the nineteen cities. Asians were less than 1 per cent. Persons of Irish stock (Roman Catholic and Protestant) were 12 per cent, British stock 5 per cent, and Canadian stock (French and English) 3 per cent.

19 For nativism in the United States, see Bennett, 1988; Clawson, 1989: 131. In Canada the Presbyterian and Anglican churches opened missions among the rapidly-growing Jewish populations of Montreal, Toronto, and Winnipeg.

20 Data from Orr and McNall, 1991; Clawson, 1989: 97 (data from John S. Gilkeson); Cumbler, 1979: 46; and Thelen, 1986: ch. 9.

21 We leave the offending authors nameless. Three of them refer to the IOOF as the "*International* Order of Odd Fellows." Another author has the IOOF organizing state-wide beneficial associations that paid "premiums" up to $4,000; apart from the author's misuse of the word premium, the IOOF's constitution barred grand lodges from providing centrally-funded life insurance or annuity benefits. Still another study describes the moral hazard in sickness insurance in terms that apply to adverse selection, a different problem.

22 The *IOOF Directory* was issued sometime in 1910; the *Toronto City Directory* was issued in January 1911. Between these dates, Toronto annexed the City of West Toronto, the suburbs of Bracandale and Norway, North Dovercourt, and Earlscourt. This caused a change in the names of several streets and complicated the work of record linkage. We were unable to trace most Odd Fellows who changed their street address or died between the two dates of issuance.

23 Where our random number selected a woman or a male with no occupation, we moved forward to the first male whose occupation was listed. For a sample of 386 cases, the confidence-interval statistic is .10 and the confidence-level statistic is .05; that is, one can be 95 per cent certain that the sample's distribution for a given attribute is within 5 per cent of the distribution for the entire directory population.

24 Evidence of lodge practice comes from efforts by physicians to eliminate it. See Naylor, 1986: 31–2; Rosen, 1977. For Toronto evidence, see *Canada Lancet*, November 1895, 100–1, and *Canadian Medical Review*, January 1896, 24. These two journals also hold evidence for the Ontario centres of London, Trenton, and Forest.

25 Thirty-three of forty-six claimants had reported farmer as their occupation at joining. The stated causes of their disabilities included farm accidents and the usual variety of acute and chronic illnesses. One farmer, an extreme case, was "on the lodge" for 665 days during the years 1897–1920, from the age of fifty-four to eighty-seven. Source: Sick Claim Forms, Hope Lodge No. 69, Harrietsville.

26 One man reported the profession of farm labourer in the membership register. The 1901 census manuscript listed four other joiners as farm labourers. In both sources, the totals for farm labourer exclude farmers' sons.

27 IOOF, Lodge Bylaws, Oxford No. 77 (1871–1902) and Samaritan No. 35 (1856– ); Masonic, King Hiram No. 37 (1803– ) and St John's No. 68 (1856– ).

28 The Canadian grand lodges led the campaign for the change. In 1869 the IOOFMU's minimum age was eighteen (Moffrey, 1910: 83).

29 The risk was greater for housewives and unemployed women than for women in the labour force (Hailman, 1941). During the 1930s, men lost seven to nine days of work per year due to sickness, compared to eight to twelve for women (Millis, 1937: ch. 1).

30 "Oddfellowship: What It Is, What It Does, Why You Should Join It," IOOF promotional pamphlet, Grand Lodge of Ontario, 1896.

31 Minute Books, Samaritan Lodge No. 35, Ingersoll.

## CHAPTER THREE

1 SGL, *Proceedings*, 1923: 16.

2 IOOF, grand lodge constitutions: Alberta (1913, 1927), British Columbia (1897, 1906, 1928), Manitoba (1896), Michigan (1893, 1914), and Ontario (1900, 1912). The British Columbia and Michigan grand lodges set the minimum funeral benefit at $30. The Ontario grand lodge set the maximum funeral benefit and maximum widows' and orphans' benefit at $100.

3 Ontario, *Statutes*, 1912, chap. 33; 1924, chap. 50. The grand lodge was also subject to Ontario's Companies Act and the 1929 Odd Fellows Act of Incorporation (chap. 131).

4 One capitation tax went towards the overhead of the grand lodge and the SGL; a second tax, levied in most jurisdictions, went to the support of homes for orphans, widows, and aged, indigent members. In 1925, for example, the Michigan grand lodge levied capitation taxes of 40 cents for overhead and 10 cents for its IOOF home. Other grand lodges commonly charged $1 to $3 for the home tax. In Manitoba, an exceptional case, the home tax was $5.

5 On average in Ontario during the years 1919–29, suspended members were 13 per cent of the members in arrears for the year preceding. Thus 87 per cent paid their arrears before reaching the stage of suspension.

6 Reinstatements of suspensions for all fifty-six jurisdictions ranged from 32 per cent in 1921 to 7 per cent in 1929.

7 Bourbeau et Légaré, 1982: 80–7, tables de mortalité du moment. The statistics for both sexes are means for the s(15) statistics for males and females.

8 Kingston area Odd Fellows founded this association in 1874. Under its 1890 agreement with the Ontario grand lodge, the latter appointed three directors who advised the association on insurance matters.

9 The laws and regulations for homes in some jurisdictions, grand sire Thompson noted in 1925, "prevent the admission of half orphans and children where both parents were living, [but have] flexible provisions permitting the Grand Body to waive some of these requirements in extreme cases." The IOOF home could train orphans adequately for life. Only adoptive parents, however, could give the orphans someone to turn to if they met adversity "during early manhood or womanhood" after going into the world on their own (SGL, *Proceedings*, 1925: 41–2).

10 Ibid., 1929.

11 Michigan grand lodge, *Proceedings*, 1930, report of the special committee on benefits, 28–35.

12 SGL, *Proceedings*, 1882: 8974.

13 Ontario Grand Lodge, *Proceedings*, 1887: 4084–5.

14 SGL, *Proceedings*, 1923: 14–18; 1925: 37–42.

15 An Odd Fellow in Alberta, British Columbia, Manitoba, or Saskatchewan became non-beneficial when he fell thirteen weeks in arrears for dues. An Ontario member became non-beneficial within thirty days of the date specified and remained ineligible for benefits until four weeks after paying his arrears. Michigan allowed its lodges to decide the matter by passing bylaws for the purpose.

16 In such a case, sickness did not prevent the member from following his usual occupation, which was "enforced idleness." Ontario Grand Lodge, *Proceedings*, 1939: 53.

17 Saskatchewan Grand Lodge, *Proceedings*, 1918.

18 Campbell was a homeopathic physician from London, Ontario, and a future grand sire (1890–2). Sheppard was a future sovereign grand treasurer (1885–95).

19 In 1936 29 per cent of 367 Ontario lodges charged dues on a sliding scale. The proportion was 46 per cent for lodges instituted in 1872 or earlier (see semi-annual returns from the lodges for 1936). According to information in the bylaws for thirty-six Ontario lodges, five (14 per cent) used a sliding scale for initiation fees and dues; eleven (31 per cent) used one for dues only; eleven used one for initiation fees only; and nine (25 per cent) had flat rates for both the initiation fee and dues. Their initiation fees varied markedly. One lodge levied a flat rate of $10; another scaled its fee from $10 at age twenty-one to $45 at age fifty and $2 for each additional year of age.

20 *Ceteris paribus*, we expected a ratio statistic of unity (1.0) in 1890 and 1895, when the sick benefit was mandatory for lodges and encampments. Yet other things were not equal. On the one hand, encampments had older members and higher claim rates. On the other hand, they had proportionately more members who were in arrears for dues and ineligible for benefits. As Table 3.3 shows, the rate of membership suspensions for non-payment of dues was consistently higher in the encampment branch. Effectively, the differential arrearage rates deflated the ratio statistic that we used for classing, while

differential age profiles inflated the statistic. Arrearage clearly was the greater of the contaminating influences. As Table 3.3 reports, the ratio statistics for 1890 and 1895 were 0.96 instead of the expected 1.0.

21 The right-hand column shows the encampment suspension rate as a percentage of the lodge branch rate. As the data in the right-hand column show, the encampment rate was consistently higher than the lodge rate. The difference between the rates, however, was stable, except for 1921.

22 SGL, *Proceedings*, 1925: 210.

23 To convert nominal dollars into constant dollars, we used the following cost-of-living indexes: *Historical Statistics of the United States* (1975), Burgess series, E-184, 1841–1920; Douglas series, E-185, 1890–1926); and *Historical Statistics of Canada* (1983), series K-1, 1913–52. The table data are from the Burgess series to 1920, the Douglas series for 1925, and the Canada series for 1929. For their periods of overlap, the three series made small differences to the statistics and no differences to the trends.

24 IOOF statistics for all benefits are incomplete for 1900 and later years (see Appendix C). In 1892 the SGL permitted grand lodges to levy a capitation tax on lodge members for the support of IOOF homes for orphans and aged, indigent Odd Fellows. For the years 1892–1930, the IOOF's statistics for the "education of orphans" and "special relief" included special grants to homes, but not capitation tax contributions from the lodges. We estimated the amounts of those contributions to calculate the table data for the years 1921, 1924, and 1929. We lacked information to estimate the amounts for earlier years.

25 SGL, *Proceedings*, 1923, grand sire's report. Trends for the IOOF's benefit program were part of larger developments. Other friendly societies, for example, made their sick benefit optional. The Knights of Pythias did so in 1894, and the Fraternal Order of Eagles followed suit in 1927. Conversely, institutional homes became increasingly popular. In 1912 the Loyal Order of Moose built a great orphanage in Mooseheart, Illinois, to serve as its showcase attraction. It followed with "Moosehaven" in Florida, a home for its aged, indigent members. During the 1920s, as a recent study notes, "private homes for the care of the poor and other elderly sprouted up throughout the country. In 1929 the Bureau of Labor Statistics located 1,200 such homes, housing 63,000 persons and having capacity for 17,000 more" (Weaver, 1982: 31).

26 IOOF, Saskatchewan grand lodge, *Proceedings*, 1926, report of the grand representatives.

27 In 1927 the SGL rejected a North Carolina bill that would have abolished stipulated benefits. SGL, *Proceedings*, 1927: 236.

28 Ibid., 1925: i-viii, 407. We classed the grand lodges into abolition group and retention group jurisdictions according to their action on the abolition question between 1925 and 1929 (see chapter 4). The fourteen nay votes on

the 1925 legislation came from delegates of both abolition group and retention group jurisdictions. Apparently a few delegates from the opposite extremes of opinion question united to oppose the middle ground.

29 In 1924 the SGL had lowered the minimum age for admission to membership from twenty-one to eighteen. IOOF, Ontario grand lodge, *Proceedings*, 1925: 249.

30 SGL, *Code of Laws*, 1944, chap. 4; Ontario grand lodge, *Proceedings*, 1925: 247–8; 1931: 317–18; 1932: 162.

31 IOOF, Ontario grand lodge, *Proceedings*, 1932: 417–19, Report of Special Committee on Stipulated Sick Benefits; 1933: 221–3; Michigan grand lodge, *Proceedings*, 1930: 24–37.

## CHAPTER FOUR

1 Kip, 1953: 105. The fraternal reserve fund, however, was for contingencies, not deferred liabilities. Unlike the liability reserves of commercial insurers, the contingency reserve was not computed according to actuarial principles.

2 Examples include the endowment branch of Knights of Pythias (1930), the Maccabees (1958), and several state branches of the Ancient Order of United Workmen (Schmidt, 1980: 185, 212, 219, 358).

3 The IOOFMU was the major pioneer. In the United States, the introduction of group insurance was the major contribution from commercial insurance. Even so, the commercial insurers used IOOFMU experience tables for 1893–7 to calculate their premiums for group disability contracts (Ilse, 1953: 179–80).

4 Cited in Starr, 1982: 242. British industrial life companies began to offer sickness insurance in 1911, when government allowed them to qualify as approved societies under the National Health Act. Their motive was not to write sickness insurance, but to protect their interest in burial insurance against the friendly society funeral benefit. See Beveridge, 1948: 81; Gilbert, 1966: 323.

5 *Gold Dust*, February, 1928, archives of the London Life Insurance Company, London. If persons over sixty years of age constituted 10 per cent or more of the insured group, London Life levied premium surcharges. These were scaled by the proportion of such persons in the group.

6 SGL, *Proceedings*, 1925: 28–9.

7 Thompson failed to explain how he and Bruner could report on all fifty-six jurisdictions when they lacked information for three. In 1924, for example, the grand lodges of Florida, Mississippi, and New York, did not report subtotals for dues and joining fees.

The SGL's committee on homes also showed a misunderstanding of IOOF statistics in its report for 1925. Like Brunner, it disregarded lodge income from "rent and investment" and "other sources." On the expense side the ledger, it excluded disbursements on benefits in the mistaken belief that "current expenses" included them. Also mistakenly, it credited the lodges with paying the entire reported "cost of maintenance" for the homes. In fact, the homes also drew revenues from endowment funds, farming operations, Rebekah lodges, and new residents, who had to sign over assets, including pensions, to gain admission. Finally, the committee double-counted lodge contributions to homes in the form of special grants. IOOF benefit statistics already included these in subtotals for the education to orphans and special relief.

8 This was slightly higher than the totals for earlier years. Grand lodge with net lodge losses numbered seven in 1901, nine in 1910, and eight in 1920. The total was fourteen for 1929, by which time the sick benefit was optional for grand lodges.

9 See chapter 3, note 23, for information about the inflation indexes used. For consistency with the information available for 1901 and 1910, the statistics for 1921, 1924, and 1929 include per capita lodge contributions to homes under lodge overhead rather than benefits, as in Table 3.4. Thus the Table 4.1 statistic for benefits in 1924 differs slightly from the comparable statistic in Table 3.4.

10 Moffrey, 1910: 104. The actuary assumed a universal rate of 3 per cent for the first valuation. He assumed a 4 per cent rate for 46 per cent of the lodges to calculate the second valuation. Scholarly critics of fraternal insurance commonly do not use known interest rates to calculate their own valuations. Rather they accept the IOOFMU's *ex ante* valuations.

11 Ontario grand lodge, *Proceedings*, 1932: 417–19, Report of Special Committee on Stipulated Sick Benefits; ibid., 1933: 221–3.

12 SGL, *Proceedings*, 1927, grand sire's report, 16–25; Ontario Grand Lodge, *Proceedings*, 1932, 417–19, Report of Special Committee on Stipulated Sick Benefits; ibid., 1933, 221–3; Michigan Grand Lodge, *Proceedings*, 1930, Report of the Special Committee on Stipulated Benefits, 24–37, esp. the report's Appendix A.

13 IOOF, Ontario Grand Lodge, *Proceedings*, 1932: 417–19; ibid., 1933: 221–3. Reverse-direction change poses another complication. The grand lodges of Michigan, Minnesota, Montana, and North Carolina each abolished the benefit, but subsequently made it optional. Many lodges that had "abolished stipulated benefits under the optional plan" were "returning to the old law" by 1931.

14 In 1927 the grand lodge of Washington reportedly abolished the benefit. The legislation, however, merely "repealed the provision" for the mandatory benefit in the grand lodge constitution. It neither abolished the benefit nor made the benefit optional for lodges. After controversy, it was nullified on constitutional grounds.

15 In principle, a rise in the proportion of members who were in arrears and ineligible for benefits could cause a decline in the sick weeks statistic. We assume that the influence of the arrearage trend was small for three-year intervals.

In some cases, a decline in the sick weeks statistic understates the decline for the stipulated benefit. The grand lodge of Michigan, for example, abolished the stipulated benefit in 1925. During the first four years of abolition (1926–9), however, the Michigan lodges paid a discretionary sick benefit to 1.6 per cent of their members. This was 38 per cent of the proportion of brothers who had received the stipulated benefit in 1924. Thus the inclusion of discretionary-benefit recipients in the statistics masked 38 per cent of the 100 per cent decline of the stipulated benefit in the Michigan lodges.

At an earlier stage in our investigation, we classed by legislation alone (Emery and Emery, 1997). Our findings for the legislation-based classification were similar to those for the more complex classification used here.

16 The old south region includes Kentucky and the eleven states that had supported the confederacy during the American civil war. In Ayers (1995), the south includes West Virginia. Grantham (1988) excludes West Virginia, but adds Oklahoma, based on "solid-south" support for the Democratic Party during the early twentieth century. Our old south excludes both states. The northeast region includes thirteen states that lay north of the old south region and east of the Appalachian mountains. The far west region includes the three west coast states, and Nevada. The middle west region includes all other American states.

17 For convenience we use quit and suspension interchangeably. Suspension was the principal means of exit from membership, but others existed. Lodges could expel members without a preliminary stage of suspension. A paid-up member could withdraw or resign from his lodge. This protected his rank and standing if he later applied to become a charter member of a new lodge or a member of an existing lodge. A paid-up member who moved to another lodge's territory could transfer his membership, subject to the receiving lodge's approval. Some transfers were between grand lodge jurisdictions.

18 The chi square statistics for the three time periods were 0.067. 0.379, and 1.054(DF = 1). Appendix D reports the classifications for thirty-two grand encampments.

19 The chi square statistics for membership growth (above average, below average) by net grand lodge profit (above average, below average) were respectively 0.930, 0.074, and 0.386 (DF = 1). None of the statistics were significant at the 0.05 level.

20 For convenience, operating costs are a residual category that includes all disbursements except those for sick claims.

21 Nevertheless, Cloverdale Lodge No. 15 was ruined in 1894 when fire destroyed its uninsured lodge hall. In this case, donations from members of a nearby lodge allowed the Cloverdale members to rebuild. In 1904 the members lost their hall to fire again, but this time fire insurance covered part of the loss. The lodge's estimated probability of ruin for that year was 1. Its statistical ruin, however, was a function of the lodge's accounting practice, which counted the cost of a new hall as a current expense rather than an addition to assets. For reasons unknown to us, Duncan Lodge No. 17 also had a probability of ruin of 1 in 1894.

22 See Table 4.7. Six lodges closed because mining activity declined and the members left town. Ten closed by merging with a nearby lodge. Two lodges closed for want of enough members to hold regular lodge meetings. The lodge at Mission closed when most members left the area due to an agricultural depression. The lodge at North Bend closed in 1906 because many of its members were in the railway-running trades and frequently out on the line.

## CHAPTER FIVE

1 See Osborn, 1958: ch. 3; Beveridge, 1948. Under the German plan, employers paid one-third of the cost, and mutual benefit associations provided the administration. By the 1920s this plan covered two-thirds of gainfully-employed Germans. Britain administered its plan through friendly societies and commercial insurers. The British plan covered some 80 per cent of the employed and provided for flat-rate dues and a weekly benefit that was less than the wages of low-paid workers. Because the benefit was low, the British plan created a market for supplementary benefits from commercial and friendly society insurers.

2 In 1921 Metropolitan Life introduced non-cancellable policies, supported by premiums scales by age of issue. Three years later it withdrew this type of policy due to lack of demand.

3 Estimated from data in Canada, Insurance Department, *Annual Reports*, and *Canada Yearbooks*.

4 Ilse (1953) gives a general information about the group disability business in the United States during the 1920s. Records of the London Life Insurance Company provide more detailed information for Canada (Campbell, 1965, 1966; *Gold Dust*, 1927–9).

5 Thereafter a life company could sell group-disability insurance by establishing a sickness and accident branch, essentially a requirement for bookkeeping. To satisfy requirements of the statute, the insurer wrote group disability plans in separate contracts. Salesmen in its group branch, however, sold them with group plans for other risks.

6 The London Life Insurance Company, and other companies that were members of a "group association," would not sell renewable term group insur-

ance to "lodges, unions, mutual benefit associations or similar associations." Adverse selection was the problem. Those who wished to be insured tended to be older men with above-average risk.

7 The 1928 total was due largely to one contract that covered 180,682 employees of General Motors (James, 1947, 262–6; Ilse, 1953, ch. 7). In 1934, the first year for which industry-wide statistics are available, group policies covered 1.7 million Americans (Ilse, 1953).

8 To estimate the coverage for 1929 we divided $10 into the amount of premiums that life companies received for "sickness and accident" insurance. The cost of group plans varied according to details of the contract. Ten dollars is our approximation of the cost per individual in an average plan. As estimated, Metropolitan Life insured 90 per cent of the Canadians in group disability plans, and London Life insured 10 per cent. The London Life Company sold its first six group disability contracts in 1928 and fifty-six group contracts in 1929. Despite this modest growth, the company correctly noted an absence of competition in the field (*Gold Dust*, 1929: 182).

9 Lorwin, 1972: 316–17. According to Millis, the United States Labor Bureau found just eleven unions that paid sick benefits in a "comprehensive" survey of trade union beneficial activities for 1927–8 (Millis, 1937: ch. 1). If Lorwin's AFL statistics for 1930 are reliable, then the 1927–8 survey was less comprehensive than Millis believed.

10 Ontario, Bureau of Labour, *Annual Report*, 1912, 1916.

11 Methodist and Presbyterian Churches, "Report of a Preliminary and General Social Survey of Hamilton, April, 1913" (Toronto: United Church Archives, Toronto, 16). The union locals with a sick benefit held 1,819 members.

12 The data are from Wolman, 1936: 16, 239; Leacy, 1983: series E175; and Lipset, 1986: ch. 4. By 1931 just 10 per cent of non-agricultural workers in the United States were unionized, down from 19 per cent in 1919 (Bernstein, 1960: ch. 2). AFL unions accounted for 80 per cent of American union members (Wolman, 1936: 7). Its reported membership statistics are high. The affiliated unions paid the per-capita tax on more than their paid-up memberships for prestige and to maintain their voting strength at AFL meetings. In 1929 the United Mine Workers, an extreme case, reported 400,000 members, but probably had just 262,000 members, including 93,000 "exonerated" members (kept on the books because they were unemployed or on strike).

Lipset reports statistics for union density – that is, union members as a proportion of the non-agricultural labour force (Lipset, 1986: chs. 3–4). If the 1921 density statistics are set at 1.00, then for 1927 they are 62 per cent for the United States and 76 per cent for Canada.

13 See Ontario, Insurance Department, *Annual Reports*, 1921, 1925, 1929. The membership totals for 1921, 1925, and 1929 were 6,620, 5,188, and

5,614 respectively. Two societies sponsored by the Toronto and Hamilton locals of the Cigarmakers' International Union had ceased operations by 1929. The Toronto and Ottawa locals of the Typographical International Union, the Canadian executive board of the Amalgamated Society of Carpenters and Joiners, and the Toronto Railway Employees Union were the union sponsors of the four surviving societies.

Like IOOF lodges, unions faced rising-cost pressures for their sick benefit during the 1920s. As their memberships fell, their members aged and their rates of sick claim rose. At the same time, inflation pressed them to raise the nominal amount of the benefit (Lorwin, 1972: 318).

14 In Britain some of the larger employers had compelled their employees to join the company society or withdraw from other societies. The Compulsory Shop Clubs' Act of 1902 outlawed these practices.

15 Canada, Superintendent of Insurance, *Annual Report*, 1925: 644, 678; Independent Order of Foresters, *Minutes*, Supreme Court, 1902: 42–8; Canadian Order of Oddfellows, 1911 *Constitution*, 38–42.

16 *History of the Maccabees*, 1896: 149–54; Independent Order of Foresters, *Minutes*, Supreme Court, 1902: 42–8; Canadian Order of Foresters, 1911 Constitution, 38–42.

17 Ingersoll, *Directory*, 1897. The town also had two Masonic lodges and a lodge of the Catholic Order of Foresters, a Catholic life insurance order.

18 *World Almanac and Book of Facts* (New York: New York World, issued annually); Stevens, 1907; Preuss, 1924; Canada, Insurance Department, *Annual Reports*, 1920–30; *Statistics Fraternal Societies*, 1909; *Proceedings*, Knights of Pythias, Grand Lodge of Ontario, 1928; Gist, 1940: 42–3.

19 *Proceedings*, Ontario Grand Lodge, Knights of Pythias, 1880–4, 1894: 423–30.

20 *Proceedings*, Knights of Pythias, Grand Lodge of British Columbia, 1903: 26; 1914: 25.

21 Ontario, *Annual Reports* of the Insurance Superintendent and Registrar of Friendly Societies; Canada, *Annual Reports* of the Insurance Department.

22 Starr, 1982: 257–66. The cost of physicians' services rose through a tightening of licensing restrictions and an increase in the quality of the physicians' care. In 1914, for example, a Buffalo physician noted "the rapid development of surgery, the startling growth of specialties, the immense and scientific equipment required, the great cost of medical education, the pharmacist, and the nurse" (cited in Rosen, 1977: 377). Between 1918 and 1929 hospital costs rose from 8 to 13 per cent of the medical bill (Starr, 1982; Gagan, 1989). Between 1917–20 and 1932, medical costs rose from 27 to 42 per cent of workmen's compensation claims (Weis, 1935).

23 For discussion of the moral hazard, see Starr, 1982: 290–1; McIntyre, 1962. For information about market insurance for health care, see Derickson, 1988: ch. 8; McIntyre, 1962: 37–49; James, 1947. During the years

1891–1918 union locals of the Western Federation of Miners founded seven hospitals and staffed them with union doctors. By the 1920s, however, these hospitals were closing or passing into employers' hands. Private non-profit and commercial group insurance was unavailable until the 1930s. Multiple-hospital private pre-payment plans dated from 1932. Commercial group hospital insurance dated from 1934. Group surgical and family dependants' insurance dated from 1938.

## CHAPTER SIX

1 Grand Lodge of Saskatchewan, *Proceedings*, 1926.
2 For discussion of the theory, see Ehrlich and Becker, 1972; Mayers and Smith, 1983.
3 Ontario Grand Lodge, *Proceedings*, 1895–1914. The grand secretary compiled the statistics for these years only.
4 The average spell was five weeks in the survey undertaken by the 1917 California Social Insurance Commission and 7.3 weeks in the US National Health Survey for 1935–6.
5 The statistics ranged from 1.2 weeks for households in the lowest-income quartile to 4.4 weeks for households in the highest quartile (Costa, 1995: 10). The occupational profile and the life-course trend for wages places young Odd Fellows somewhere in the middle.
6 The literature for bundled goods focuses on whether, and under what conditions, a firm would find bundling profitable (Adams and Yellen, 1976; McAfee, McMillan, and Whinston, 1989; Salinger, 1995). Our concern, in contrast, is how bundling affected the demand for the IOOF's sickness insurance.
7 Our data miss the men who joined Cloverdale Lodge before 1904 when fire destroyed the lodge and its records.
8 Samaritan Lodge, for example, initiated Edward Boles in 1889 and then suspended and reinstated him three times between 1891 and 1901. In our study, his spell of membership ends in 1891, the year of his first suspension.
9 The records omit the initiate's age in 101 other cases (8 per cent of all cases in the file).
10 His probability of exit in year *n* is conditional on having been a member for *n-1* years.
11 This strategy builds on the framework of Adams and Yellen (1976).
12 Marginal utility refers to the extra satisfaction that an individual obtains from purchasing an extra unit of a good.
13 Along with the lodge's annual dues ($p_B$), the joiner had to pay one-time fees for each of the IOOF's four degrees of membership. Thus the joiner's reservation price ($r_B$) had to match or exceed the combined amount of the entry tariff and annual dues (Oi, 1971). Here we assume that joiners were for-

ward-looking agents whose reservation values could incorporate an expected lifetime benefit from the consumption of the good.

14 The estimated Weibull-Gamma mixing parameter δ (8.9) is significantly different from zero.

15 We use the estimated coefficients in Table 6.3 (column II) and the mixing distribution to generate the hazard functions and survival functions.

16 The negative influence for age-at-joining also is consistent with the old man's model. Possibly older joiners were less likely to quit because they were closer to the ages where the benefit was available at the subsidized old man's price.

17 We thank Richard Sutch, University of California at Berkeley, for this observation in his commentary on the paper that we presented in New Orleans (Emery and Emery, 1997).

## CHAPTER SEVEN

1 The lodges whose representatives supported abolition included 92.4 per cent of Michigan's past grand masters and 88.8 per cent of its members. See *Proceedings*, Grand Lodge of Michigan, 1930: 28.

2 Grand Lodge Head Office, Litchfield, Michigan.

3 Ontario Grand Lodge, *Proceedings*, 1938: 42; see also 1936: 48. Similarly in 1941 the grand master warned against "stressing too exclusively the younger generation in our campaigns for new members ... our non-beneficial class of membership opens up an avenue whereby men of a mature age might be attracted to our Order, and because of their more mature age, better financial stability and a greater desire for fraternal fellowship, their ardor would be less apt to cool after the novelty of the initiation ceremony had passed." See Ontario Grand Lodge, *Proceedings*, 1941: 38.

4 Toronto, Ontario Grand Lodge Head office, semi-annual returns for 329 of the 339 lodges listed for 1943.

5 Interview with Lloyd Shelvy, Manitoba grand secretary, 8 June 1994. Shelvy is a past grand master and Manitoba's only past sovereign grand master.

6 The Manitoba grand secretary last reported statistics for "brothers relieved" in 1964.

7 Neither yearbook reports the numbers of persons who bought sickness insurance.

8 *Canada Year Books*, 1920–50; *Statistical Abstract of the United States*, 1920–50. The Canadian statistics are for the categories of "sickness" and "accident and sickness combined," but not the category of "accident." The American statistics are for "accident and health" categories. We did not calculate premium statistics for 1948 and later years because of change in the way our sources reported the information. The *Canada Year Book* ceased

reporting premium totals by category of insurance in 1948. The *Statistical Abstract of the United States* apparently changed its reporting procedures in 1947; thus the ratio statistic jumped from 1.7 to 7.1 between 1946 and 1947.

9 *Statistical Abstract of the United States*, 1920–48.

10 Like workmen's compensation laws, the state disability insurance laws excluded certain classes of workers. Coverage under the Rhode Island law, for example, excluded farm labourers, domestic servants, employees of non-profit organizations, railway and government employees, and persons who had earned less than $100 during the calendar year preceding their claim.

11 One earlier measure, Canada's Disabled Person's Act of 1954, provided means-tested allowances for severely disabled persons (Guest, 1985: 144–5, 166).

12 See Ilse, 1953: 188–9; Follmann, 1965. Ilse warns that the statistics include some certificates for health insurance; hence they inflate the totals for disability insurance.

13 Ilse celebrates group insurance as an American private enterprise solution to the problem of social security (Ilse, 1953: 442–5, 450). "By opening the channels of insurance to all industrial workers, regardless of age, sex, physical condition, or character of employment," she judged, "group insurance has performed an outstanding service." One must qualify her rhapsodic judgment. As chapter 4 notes, group insurers levied premium surcharges when more than 10 per cent of the insured group were women, persons of colour, or persons over sixty-five years of age.

"From a social standpoint," she continues, "the effect of receiving benefits as a contractual right, rather than charity through the 'pass the hat' method, is undeniable in terms of enhanced human dignity." That, of course, was the achievement of nineteenth-century Odd Fellows, not twentieth-century group insurers.

## APPENDICES

1 The suspended member could obtain a dismissal certificate from his lodge, on payment of one dollar. The certificate certified that the member had been suspended for non-payment of dues. It entitled the suspended member to apply for membership in any lodge (conditional on payment of his arrears) and to hold his rank if elected to membership. A member in good standing could apply for a withdrawal card to show that he had no arrears. The withdrawal card removed him from membership of the lodge, but preserved his membership and rank in the order for one year. During this time, he could apply for admission in another lodge, and keep his rank if admitted.

2 The 1890 bylaws for Samaritan Lodge No. 35 in Ingersoll, Ontario, required the noble grand to suspend a brother who was twelve months in ar-

rears, unless the lodge voted to delay suspension for a period not to exceed six months. The noble grand was to declare any member eighteen months in arrears "ceased from membership" unless the lodge voted to give the member up to three months more to pay his arrears.

3 The proportion peaked at 47 per cent in 1933 and then fell to 28 per cent in 1945.

4 The mean amount of dues for Saskatchewan lodges in 1917 was $7.80. The universal amount for lodges in British Columbia was $12.00. Sources: IOOF, Saskatchewan, *Proceedings*, 1917; lodge bylaw collection, head office, Grand Lodge of British Columbia.

5 The statistics for relief of brothers, relief of widowed families, and burying the dead did not change, while that for relief to orphans rose by $0.05. A deterioration in economic conditions between 1927 and 1929 explained this pattern in Ontario. The demand for places in the grand lodge home surpassed its supply of places; the grand lodge's solution was to increase assistance to children who were in the care of a surviving parent. Ontario Grand Lodge, *Proceedings*, 1930: 104.

6 See Beard, et al., 1984: 18–19. The collective method ignores the structures of individual policies and considers the portfolio as a whole. The alternative individual method considers the lodge as a portfolio of individual policies, each with its own probability of a claim (e.g., the probability that a member of age $a$ claims at least a week of sickness benefit is $p(a)$). The total lodge claim is the sum of the claims from the individual policies and their associated probabilities. This individual method is ideal, but it is not feasible with our data.

7 Beard et al. suggest assuming a normal distribution for the aggregate claims when the number of claims is large. This assumption simplifies the task of evaluating probabilities of ruin and expected annual claims, but it is unsuitable here. Often lodges experienced small numbers of claims (less than ten in a year). Also, the empirical distribution of aggregate claims from the twenty-seven lodges is skewed to the right. Consequently the assumption of a normal distribution would bias probabilities of ruin towards zero.

8 See Beard et al., 1984: 19; Mood, et al., 1974: 94. One can use any counting model to represent the claim-number process. For experimentation we estimated the compound process with a binomial model. The less restrictive Poisson distribution, however, produced a better fit between the expected and observed distributions.

9 Only total claim sizes are observed in the our data set. Thus the parameter of the exponential distribution, $\beta$, is estimated indirectly from the Gamma distribution representing the aggregate claim size. The recognition of the underlying exponential distribution for individual claim sizes is the consequence of representing the aggregate claim size with the Gamma distribu-

tion. The selection of the structure of the aggregate claim process imposes structure upon the individual claim size process.

10 Since the number of claims k is an integer, the Gamma function $\Gamma(k)=(k-1)!$.

11 This assumption admits common shocks such as an influenza epidemic that affects several lodge memberships in the same year.

12 Another issue is whether the imposed exponential functional form misses non-linear effects of membership size. The binomial counting method imposes a linear relationship. The expected number of claims is the number of members times the probability that an individual member makes a claim – which is independent of the number of members. In the Poisson case, the expected number of claims is a function of membership size.

13 British Columbia lodges averaged $5.27 in sick relief per member over the period 1891–1929. The comparable statistic for the study lodges was $3.13. The higher average for all lodges arose from the high weekly benefits paid in city lodges with large memberships. The lodges in Vancouver, Victoria, New Westminster, and Nanaimo had above-average assets (capacity to pay) and faced above-average competition for members (pressure to pay). The five study lodges in those cities closed by merging with other lodges.

14 Proportional risk loading (on the mean of the distribution) is convenient for the purpose here: to estimate a residual proportion of the insurance price. To estimate a prescribed but unknown parameter, one could define risk loading on higher moments of the claims distribution, such as the variance.

15 For convenience, operating costs are a residual category that includes all disbursements except those for sick claims.

16 Mood, et al., 1974: 114. For $\beta = 1$, $S^k(Z)$ is called the incomplete Gamma function. Thus the standardized Gamma distribution refers to the distribution of $X=Z\beta$ rather than Z.

# Bibliography


Achenbaum, W. Andrew. *Social Security: Visions and Revisions*. Cambridge: Cambridge University Press 1986.

Adams, William James, and Janet L. Yellen. "Commodity Bundling and the Burden of Monopoly." *Quarterly Journal of Economics* 90 (1976): 475–98.

Akerlof, George A. "Procrastination and Obedience." *American Economic Review* 81, 2 (1991): 1–19.

Allen, Robert C. "Real Incomes in the English-Speaking World, 1879–1913." In *Labour Market Evolution. The Economic History of Market Integration, Wage Flexibility and the Employment Relation*, ed. George Grantham and Mary MacKinnon. London: Routledge 1994, pp. 107–38.

Alter, George, and James C. Riley. "Frailty, Sickness, and Death: Models of Morbidity and Mortality in Historical Populations." *Population Studies* 43 (1989): 25–45.

Andrews, Margaret W. "Medical Attendance in Vancouver, 1886–1920." *BC Studies* 40 (1978): 32–56.

Applebaum, Leon. "The Development of Voluntary Health Insurance in the United States." *Journal of Insurance* 28 (1961): 25–33.

Armstrong, Barbara Nachtrieb. *Insuring the Essentials*. New York: Macmillan 1932.

Ayers, Edward L. *Southern Crossing, A History of the American South, 1877–1906*. New York: Oxford University Press 1995.

Beard, Robert Eric, T. Pentinkanen, and E. Pesonan. *Risk Theory: The Stochastic Basis of Insurance*. London: Chapman and Hall 1984.

Beharrell, Thomas G. *The Brotherhood, Being a Presentation of the Principles of Odd-Fellowship*. Indianapolis: Brotherhood Publishing Company 1875.

– *The Odd Fellows Monitor and Guide*. Indianapolis: Robert Douglass 1883.

Bell, D.K. "Health Insurance in British Columbia." MA thesis, University of British Columbia 1939.

Bennett, David H. *The Party of Fear, from Nativist Movements to the New Right in American History.* Chapel Hill: University of North Carolina Press 1988.

Bernstein, Irving. *The Lean Years: A History of the American Worker, 1920–1933.* Boston: Houghton Mifflin 1960.

Berkowitz, Edward D. "How to Think about the Welfare State." *Labor History* 32 (1991): 489–502.

– and Kim McQuaid. "Businessman and Bureaucrat: The Evolution of the American Welfare System, 1900–1940." *Journal of Economic History* 38 (1978): 120–41.

– and Kim McQuaid. *Creating the Welfare State: The Political Economy of Twentieth Century Reform.* New York: Praeger 1988.

– and Monroe Berkowitz. "Challenges to Workers' Compensation: An Historical Analysis." In *Workers' Compensation Benefits: Adequacy, Equity, and Efficiency*, ed. John D. Worrall and David Appel. New York: ILR Press 1985, pp. 158–80.

Beveridge, William. *Social Insurance and Allied Services Report.* New York: Macmillan 1942.

– *Voluntary Action, A Report on Methods of Social Advance.* London: George Allen & Unwin 1948.

Borch, Karl H. *The Economics of Insurance.* New York: North Holland 1990.

Bourbeau, Robert, et Jacques Légaré. *Evolution de la mortalité au Canada et au Québec 1831–1931.* Montréal: Les presses de l'université de Montréal 1982.

Boyer, George R. "What Did Unions Do in Nineteenth-Century Britain?" *Journal of Economic History* 48 (1988): 319–32.

Bradbury, Bettina. *Working Families, Age, Gender, and Daily Survival in Industrializing Montreal.* Toronto: McClelland and Stewart 1993.

Brandes, Stuart D. *American Welfare Capitalism 1880–1940.* Chicago: University of Chicago Press 1976.

Bristol, D. W. *The Odd Fellows' Amulet.* Auburn, NY: Derby Miller & Co. 1851.

Britton, Rollo H., Selwyn D. Collins, and James S. Fitzgerald. "Some General Findings as to Disease, Accidents, and Impairments in Urban Areas." *Public Health Reports* 55, 11 (March 1940): 444–70.

Brody, David. "The Rise and Fall of Welfare Capitalism." In *Workers in Industrial America: Essays on the Twentieth Century Struggle.* New York: Oxford University Press 1980, pp. 48–81.

Brooks, Charles H. *The Official History of the Grand United Order of Odd Fellows in America.* Philadelphia 1902.

Brumberg, Joan Jacobs, and Faye E. Dudden. "Masculinity and Mumbo Jumbo: Nineteenth-Century Fraternalism Revisited." *Reviews in American History* 18 (1990): 363–70.

Burley, David G. *A Particular Condition in Life, Self-Employment and Social Mobility in Mid-Victorian Brantford, Ontario*. Montreal and Kingston: McGill-Queen's University Press 1994.

Burrows, V.A. "On Friendly Societies since the Advent of National Health Insurance." *Journal of the Institute of Actuaries* 63 (1932): 307–401.

Campbell, James A. *The Story of the London Life Insurance Company*. London: London Life Co. 1965.

Carr, William H.A. *From Three Cents a Week, the Story of the Prudential Life Insurance Company of America*. Englewood Cliffs, NJ: Prentice-Hall 1975.

Carroll, Glenn R. "Concentration and Specialization: Dynamics of Niche Width in Populations of Organizations." *American Journal of Sociology* 90, 6 (1985): 1262–83.

Carnes, Mark C. *Secret Ritual and Manhood in Victorian America*. New Haven: Yale University Press 1989.

Charles, Jeffrey A. *Service Clubs in American Society: Rotary, Kiwanis, and Lions*. Urbana: University of Illinois Press 1993.

Clawson, Mary Ann. *Constructing Brotherhood, Class, Gender, and Fraternalism*. Princeton: Princeton University Press 1989.

Cordery, Simon. "Fraternal Orders in the United States: A Quest for Protection and Identity." In *Social Security Mutualism, the Comparative history of Mutual Benefit Societies*, ed. Marcel Van der Linden. Bern: Peter Lang 1996, pp. 83–110.

– "Friendly Societies and the Discourse of Respectability in Britain, 1825–1875." *Journal of British Studies* 34, 1 (January 1995): 35–58.

Costa, Dora. "The Political Economy of State Provided Health Insurance in the Progressive Era: Evidence from California." National Bureau of Economic Research Working Paper, no. 5328, 1995.

Cumbler, John T. *Working-Class Community in Industrial America: Work, Leisure, and Struggle in Two Industrial Cities, 1880–1930*. Westport: Greenwood Press 1979.

Davis, K. "National Health Insurance: A Proposal." AEA Papers and Proceedings, *American Economic Review* 79 (1989): 349–52.

Donaldson, Paschal. *The Odd-Fellows' Textbook*. Philadelphia: Moss and Brother 1851.

Derickson, Alan. *Workers' Health Workers' Democracy: The Western Miners' Struggle, 1891–1925*. Ithaca: Cornell University Press 1988.

Dublin, Louis I. *A Family of Thirty Million, The Story of the Metropolitan Life Insurance Company*. New York: Metropolitan Life 1943.

Dumenil, Lynn. *Freemasonry and American Culture 1880–1930*. Princeton: Princeton University Press 1984.

Ehrlich, Isaac, and Gary S. Becker. "Market Insurance, Self-Insurance, and Self-Protection." *Journal of Political Economy* 80, 4 (1972): 623–48.

Emery, George. *Facts of Life: The Social Construction of Vital Statistics, Ontario 1869–1952*. Montreal and Kingston: McGill-Queen's University Press 1993.

– and J.C. Herbert Emery. "The I.O.O.F. and Sickness Insurance in the United States and Canada, 1850–1929." Cliometric Society, annual meeting of the Allied Social Sciences Association, New Orleans, 4 January 1997.

Emery, J.C. Herbert. "Risky Business? Non-Actuarial Pricing Practices and the Financial Viability of Fraternal Sickness Insurers." *Explorations in Economic History* 33 (1996): 195–226.

Epstein, Abraham. *Insecurity: A Challenge to America*. New York: Random House 1933.

Falk, I.S. *Security against Sickness: A Study of Health Insurance*. New York: Doubleday 1936.

Faulkner, Edwin J. *Health Insurance*. New York: McGraw-Hill 1960.

Fischer, Stanley. "A Life Cycle Model of Life Insurance Purchases." *International Economic Review* 14, 1 (1973): 132–52.

Fishback, Price V., and Shawn Everett Kantor. "The Durable Experiment: State Insurance of Workers' Compensation Risk in the Early Twentieth Century." *Journal of Economic History* 65, 4 (1996): 809–36.

Follman, Dean A., Matthew S. Goldberg, and Laurie May. "Personal Characteristics, Unemployment Insurance, and the Duration of Unemployment." *Journal of Econometrics* 45 (1990): 351–66.

Follmann, J.F. "The Growth of Group Health Insurance." *Journal of Risk and Insurance* 32 (1965): 105–12.

Frager, Ruth A. *Sweatshop Strife, Class, Ethnicity, and Gender in the Jewish Labour Movement of Toronto 1900–1939*. Toronto: University of Toronto Press 1992.

Gagan, David. "'For Patients of Moderate Means': The Transformation of Ontario's Public General Hospitals, 1880–1950." *Canadian Historical Review* 70, 2 (1989): 151–79.

Galanter, Marc. *Cults, Faith, Healing and Coercion*. New York: Oxford University Press 1989.

Gilbert, Bentley B. "The Decay of Nineteenth-Century Provident Institutions and the Coming of Old Age Pensions in Great Britain." *Economic History Review* (1965, 2nd Series 17): 551–63.

– *The Evolution of National Health Insurance in Great Britain: The Origins of the Welfare State*. London: Michael Joseph 1966.

Gilkeson, John S. *Middle-Class Providence, 1820–1940*. Princeton: Princeton University Press 1986.

Gist, Noel P. "Secret Societies: A Cultural Study of Fraternalism in the United States." *University of Missouri Studies* 15, 4 (October 1940): 1–176.

Goldin, Claudia. *Understanding the Gender Gap: An Economic History of American Women*. New York: Oxford University Press 1990.

Goldsmith, Raymond William. *A Study of Saving in the United States*. Vols. 1–3. New York: Greenwood 1969.

Gosden, P.H.J.H. *The Friendly Societies in England 1815–1875*. Manchester: Manchester University Press 1961.

– *Self-Help, Voluntary Associations in the 19th Century*. London: B.T. Batsford 1973.

Graebner, William A. *History of Retirement: The Meaning and Function of an American Institution, 1885–1978*. New Haven: Yale University Press 1980.

Grantham, Dewey. *The Life & Death of the Solid South: A Political History*. Lexington: University Press of Kentucky 1988.

Grantham, George, and Mary MacKinnon, eds. *Labour Market Evolution: The Economic History of Market Integration, Wage Flexibility and the Employment Relation*. London: Routledge 1994.

Gratton, Brian. "The Poverty of Impoverishment Theory: The Economic Well-Being of the Elderly, 1890–1950." *Journal of Economic History* 56, 1 (March 1996): 39–61.

Green, David G., and Lawrence G. Cromwell. *Mutual Aid or Welfare State: Australia's Friendly Societies*. Sydney: Allen & Unwin 1984.

Greenberg, Brian. "Worker and Community: Fraternal Orders in Albany, New York, 1845–1885." *Maryland Historian* 8 (1977): 38–53.

Greene, B.M., ed. *Who's Who and Why 1919–20*. Toronto: International Press, n.d.

Greene, Mark Richard. *Risk and Insurance*. Cincinnati: South-Western Publishing Co. 1968.

Grosh, A.B. *The Odd Fellows Manual*. Philadelphia: Theodore Bliss & Co. 1871.

Guest, Dennis. *The Emergence of Social Security in Canada*. Vancouver: University of British Columbia Press 1980.

Hailman, David E. "The Prevalence of Disabling Illness among Male and Female Workers and Housewives." *Public Health Bulletin No. 260* (Washington 1941): 1–40.

Heckman, James J., and Burton Singer. "Econometric Duration Analysis." *Journal of Econometrics* 24 (1984): 63–132.

Hirschman, Albert O. *Exit, Voice, and Loyalty, Responses to Decline in Firms, Organizations, and States*. Cambridge, Mass.: Harvard University Press 1970.

*History of Odd-Fellowship in Canada under the Old Regime*. Brantford: Grand Lodge of Ontario 1879.

*History of the Maccabees, Ancient and Modern, 1881 to 1896*. Port Huron 1896.

Hogg, Robert V., and Stuart A. Klugman. *Loss Distributions*. New York: John Wiley & Sons 1984.

Hopkins, Eric. *Working-Class Self-Help in Nineteenth-Century England*. London: UCL Press 1995.

Houston, Cecil, and William J. Smyth. *The Sash Canada Wore: A Historical Geography of the Orange Order in Canada*. Toronto: University of Toronto Press 1980.

Ilse, Louise Wolters. *Group Insurance and Employee Retirement Plans*. New York: Prentice-Hall 1953.

Irving, Allan. "The Doctors versus the Expert: Harry Morris Cassidy and the British Columbia Health Insurance Dispute of the 1930's." *BC Studies* 78 (1988): 53–79.

Jacoby, Sanford M. *Employing Bureaucracy, Managers, Unions, and the Transformation of Work in American Industry, 1900–1945*. New York: Columbia University Press 1985.

James, John A. "Job Tenure in the Gilded Age." In *Labour Market Evolution. The Economic History of Market Integration, Wage Flexibility and the Employment Relation*, ed. George Grantham and Mary MacKinnon. London: Routledge 1994, pp. 185–204.

James, Marquis. *The Metropolitan Life: A Study in Business Growth*. New York: Viking Press 1947.

Johnson, Paul. "Credit and Thrift and the British Working class, 1870–1939." In *The Working Class in Modern British History*, ed. J. Winter. Cambridge: Cambridge University Press 1983, pp. 147–70.

– *Saving and Spending: The Working-class Economy in Britain, 1870–1939*. Oxford: Clarendon Press 1985.

– "Social Risk and Social Welfare in Britain, 1870–1939." L.S.E. Working Papers in Economic History, March 1992.

Kantor, Shawn Everett, and Price V. Fishback. "Precautionary Saving, Insurance, and the Origins of Workmen's Compensation." *Journal of Political Economy* 104, 2 (1996): 419–42.

Karlsson, T. "Silver Production in the Slocan Mining District." Mimeograph, University of British Columbia 1989.

Kiefer, Nicholas M. "Economic Duration Data and Hazard Functions." *Journal of Economic Literature* 26 (1988): 646–79.

King, John S. *Knights of Pythias*. Chatham, 1890.

– *The Early History of the Sons of England Benevolent Society*. Toronto 1891.

Kip, Richard de Raismes. *Fraternal Life Insurance in America*. Philadelphia: College Offset Press 1953.

Kotlikoff, Laurence J., and Avia Spivak. "The Family as an Incomplete Annuities Market." *Journal of Political Economy* 89, 2 (1981): 372–91.

Lancaster, Tony. *The Econometric Analysis of Transition Data*. Cambridge: Cambridge University Press 1990.

Laslett, Barbara. "Gender in/and Social Science History." *Social Science History* 16, 2 (1992): 177–95.

Leacy, F.H., M.C. Urquhart, and K.A.H. Buckley, eds. *Historical Statistics of Canada*. Ottawa: Statistics Canada 1983.

Lewis, Frank D. "Dependants and the Demand for Life Insurance." *American Economic Review* 79, 3 (1989): 452–67.

Lipset, Seymour Martin, ed. *Unions in Transition: Entering the Second Century.* San Francisco: ICS Press 1986.

Litchman, Charles H., ed. *Official History of the Improved Order of Red Men.* Boston: Fraternity Publishing Co. 1893.

Logan, H.A. *Trade Unions in Canada, their Development and Functioning.* Toronto: Macmillan 1948.

Lorwin, Lewis L. *The American Federation of Labor, History, Politics, Prospects.* Clifton: Augustus M. Kelly 1972.

Lubove, R. *The Struggle for Social Security: 1900–1935.* Cambridge: Harvard University Press 1968.

Lynd, Robert S., and Helen Merrell. *Middletown: A Study in Contemporary American Culture.* New York: Harcourt, Brace & World 1929.

MacDonald, Fergus. *The Catholic Church and Secret Societies in the United States.* New York: U.S. Catholic Historical Society 1946.

MacKinnon, Mary. "New Evidence on Canadian Wage Rates 1900–1930." *Canadian Journal of Economics* 19,1 (1996): 114–31.

Markey, Raymond. "The History of Mutual Benefit Societies in Australia, 1830–1991." In *Social Security Mutualism: The Comparative History of Mutual Benefit Societies*, ed. Marcel Van der Linden. Bern: Peter Lang 1996, pp. 147–76.

Marks, Lynne. *Revivals and Roller Rinks, Religion, Leisure, and Identity in Late-Nineteenth-Century Small Town Ontario.* Toronto: University of Toronto Press 1996.

Marland, Hilary. *Medicine and Society in Wakefield and Huddersfield 1780–1870.* Cambridge: Cambridge University Press 1987.

Marsh, L. *Report on Social Security for Canada.* Ottawa: King's Printer 1943.

Mayers, David, and Clifford W. Smith, Jr. "The Interdependence of Individual Portfolio Decisions and the Demand for Insurance." *Journal of Political Economy* 91, 2 (1983): 304–11.

McAfee, R. Preston, John McMillan, and Michael D. Whinston. "Multiproduct Monopoly, Commodity Bundling, and Correlation of Values." *Quarterly Journal of Economics* 114 (1989): 371–84.

McCallum, Margaret E. "Corporate Welfarism in Canada, 1919–39." *Canadian Historical Review* 71, 1 (1990): 49–79.

McIntyre, Duncan M. *Voluntary Health Insurance and Rate Making.* Ithaca: Cornell University Press 1962.

Millis, H.A. *Sickness Insurance.* Chicago: University of Chicago Press 1937.

Mitchell, B.R., and H.G. Jones. *Abstract of British Historical Statistics.* Cambridge: Cambridge University Press 1971.

Moffrey, R.W. *A Century of Odd Fellowship.* Manchester 1910.

Mood, A.M., F.A. Graybill, and D.C. Boes. *Introduction to the Theory of Statistics*. New York: McGraw-Hill 1974.

Naylor, C. David. *Private Practice, Public Payment, Canadian Medicine and the Politics of Health Insurance 1911–1966*. Montreal and Kingston: McGill-Queen's University Press 1986.

Neave, David. *Mutual Aid in the Victorian Countryside: Friendly Societies in the Rural East Riding 1830–1914*. Hull: Hull University Press 1991.

Nelson, Daniel. *Unemployment Insurance: The American Experience, 1915–1935*. Madison: University of Wisconsin Press 1969.

North, Douglass C. *Institutions, Institutional Change and Economic Performance*. Cambridge: Cambridge University Press 1990.

– "Transactions Costs, Institutions, and Economic Performance." Occasional Papers No. 30, International Center for Economic Growth, 1992.

Oi, Walter Y. "A Disneyland Dilemma: Two-Part Tariffs for a Mickey Mouse Monopoly." *Quarterly Journal of Economics* 85 (1971): 77–96.

Olssen, Erik. "Friendly Societies in New Zealand, 1840–1990." In *Social Security Mutualism, the Comparative history of Mutual Benefit Societies*, ed. Marcel Van der Linden. Bern: Peter Lang 1996, pp. 177–206.

Oronhyatekha, M.D. *History of the Independent Order of Foresters*. Toronto: Hunter, Rose & Co. 1895.

Orr, James R., and Scott G. McNall, "Fraternal Orders and Working-Class Formation in Nineteenth-Century Kansas." In *Bringing Class Back in Contemporary and Historical Perspectives*, ed. Scott G. McNall, et al. Boulder: Westview Press 1991, pp. 101–17.

Osborn, Grant M. *Compulsory Temporary Disability Insurance in the United States*. Homewood, Ill: Richard D. Irwin 1958.

Palmer, Bryan D. "Mutuality and the Masking/Making of Difference: The Making of Mutual Benefit Societies in Canada, 1850–1950." In *Social Security Mutualism, the Comparative history of Mutual Benefit Societies*, ed. Marcel Van der Linden. Bern: Peter Lang 1996, pp. 111–46.

Parr, Joy. *The Gender of Breadwinners, Women, Men, and Change in Two Industrial Towns, 1880–1950*. Toronto: University of Toronto Press 1990.

Pedoe, Arthur. *Life Insurance, Annuities, and Pensions*. Toronto: University of Toronto Press 1970.

Peebles, A. "The State and Medicine." *Canadian Journal of Economics and Political Studies* 2 (1936): 464–80.

Piva, M.J. "The Worker's Compensation Movement in Ontario." *Ontario History* 67 (1975): 39–56.

Preuss, Arthur. *Dictionary of Secret and Other Societies*. St Louis: B. Herder Co. 1924.

Quadagno, Jill. "Theories of the Welfare State." *Annual Reviews of Sociology* 13 (1987): 109–28.

– *The Transformation of Old Age Security, Class and Politics in the American Welfare State*. Chicago: University of Chicago Press 1988.

Riley, James C. "Ill Health during the English Mortality Decline: The Friendly Societies Experience." *Bulletin of the History of Medicine* 61 (1987): 563–88.

– *Sickness, Recovery and Death: A History and Forcast of Ill Health*. London: Macmillan 1989.

– "The Risk of Being Sick: Morbidity Trends in Four Countries." *Population and Development Review* 16, 3 (1990): 403–32.

– "Working Health Time: A Comparison of Preindustrial, Industrial, and Postindustrial Experience in Life and Health." *Explorations in Economic History* 28 (1991): 161–91.

– *Sick, Not Dead, the Health of British Working Men During the Mortality Decline*. Baltimore and London: Johns Hopkins University Press 1997.

Rosen, George. "Contract or Lodge Practice and its Influence on Medical Attitudes to Health Insurance." *American Journal of Public Health* 67 (1977): 374–78.

Rosenzweig, Roy. "Boston Masons, 1900–1935: The Lower Middle Class in a Divided Society." *Journal of Voluntary Action Research* 6 (July, 1977): 119–26.

Ross, Theo. A. *Odd Fellowship, Its History and Manual*. New York: M.W. Hazen, 1890.

Rotundo, E. Anthony. "Romantic Friendship: Male Intimacy and Middle-Class Youth in the Northern United States, 1800–1900." *Journal of Social History* 23, 1 (1989): 1–25.

Rubinow, I.M. *Social Insurance*. Henry Holt & Co. 1913; Arno & the New York Times 1969.

Salinger, Michael A. "A Graphical Analysis of Bundling." *Journal of Business* 68, 1 (1995): 85–98.

Schmidt, A.J. *Fraternal Organizations*. Westport: Greenwood Press 1980.

Senior, Hereward. *Orangeism: The Canadian Phase*. Toronto: McGraw-Hill Ryerson 1972.

Stalson, J.Owen. *Marketing Life Insurance: Its History in America*. Cambridge: Harvard University Press 1942; Homewood: R.D. Irwin 1969.

Starr, Paul. *The Social Transformation of American Medicine: The Rise of a Sovereign Profession and the Making of a Vast Industry*. New York: Basic Books 1982.

*Statistics Fraternal Societies, 1909*. Rochester: Fraternal Monitor 1909.

Storey, Robert. "Unionization versus Corporate Welfare: The 'Dofasco Way'." *Labour/Le Travailleur* 12 (1983): 7–42.

*Statistical History of the United States from Colonial Times to the Present*. Stanford: Farfield Publishers 1965.

Stevens, Albert C. *Cyclopaedia of Fraternities*. New York: E.B. Treat 1907.

Stillson, Henry L., ed. *History of Odd Fellowship, the Three-Link Fraternity.* Boston: Fraternity Publishing Co. 1897.

Struthers, James. *The Limits of Affluence, Welfare in Ontario, 1920–1970.* Toronto: University of Toronto 1994.

Taylor, Graham D., and Peter A. Baskerville. *A Concise History of Business in Canada.* Toronto: Oxford University Press 1994.

Taylor, Malcolm G. "The Canadian Health Care System 1974–1984." In *Medicare at Maturity: Achievements, Lessons and Challenges*, ed. R.G. Evans and G.L. Stoddart. Calgary: University of Calgary Press 1986.

– *Insuring National Health Care, the Canadian Experience.* Chapel Hill: University of North Carolina Press 1990.

Thelen, David. *Paths of Resistance: Tradition and Dignity in Industrializing Missouri.* New York: Oxford University Press 1986.

Tishler, Hace Sorel. *Self-Reliance and Social Security, 1870–1917.* Port Washington, NY: Kennikat 1971.

Tucker, Eric. *Administering Danger in the Workplace: The Law and Politics of Occupational Health and Safety Regulation in Ontario, 1850–1914.* Toronto: University of Toronto Press 1990.

United States. *Illness and Medical Care Among 2,500,000 Persons in 83 Cities With Special Reference to Socio-Economic Factors, 27 papers based on the National Health Survey of 1935–36.* Washington: U.S. Public Health Service 1945.

United States, National Industrial Conference Board. "Experience with Mutual Benefit Associations in the United States." *Research Report No. 65*, 1923.

Van der Linden, Marcel. "Introduction." In *Social Security Mutualism: The Comparative History of Mutual Benefit Societies*, ed. Marcel Van der Linden. Bern: Peter Lang 1996, pp. 11–38.

Vondracek, Felix John. "The Rise of Fraternal Organizations in the United States, 1868–1900." *Social Science* 47 (Winter 1972): 26–33.

Weaver, Carolyn L. *The Crisis in Social Security: Economic and Political Origins.* Durham: Duke University Press 1982.

– "On the Lack of a Political Market for Compulsory Old Age Insurance Prior to the Great Depression: Insights from Economic Theories of Government." *Explorations in Economic History* 20, 3 (1983): 294–328.

Weis, Harry, "Employers' Liability and Workmen's Compensation." In *History of Labor in the United States, 1896–1932*, Vol. III, ed. Don D. Lescohier and Elizabeth Brandeis. New York: Macmillan Co. 1935, pp. 564–610.

Whaples, Robert, and David Buffum. "Fraternalism, Paternalism, the Family, and the Market: Insurance a Century Ago." *Social Science History* 15, 1 (Spring 1991): 97–122.

Wilson, L.S. "The Socialization of Medical Insurance in Canada." *Canadian Journal of Economics* 18 (1985): 355–76.

Wolman, Leo. *Ebb and Flow in Trade Unionism.* New York: National Bureau of Economic Research 1936.

Young, Agnes Freda. *Industrial Injuries Insurance, An Examination of British Policy.* London: Routledge & Kegan Paul 1964.

Zahavi, Gerald. *Workers, Managers, and Welfare Capitalism, the Shoemakers and Tanners of Endicott Johnson, 1890–1950.* Urbana: University of Illinois Press 1988.

Zelizer, Viviana A. Rotman. *Morals and Markets: The Development of Life Insurance in the United States.* New York: Columbia University Press 1979.

# Index